PERFECTLY CONFIDENT

DON A. MOORE, PHD

PERFECTLY CONFIDENT

HOW TO CALIBRATE YOUR DECISIONS WISELY

HARPER
BUSINESS

An Imprint of HarperCollins*Publishers*

HarperCollins books may be purchased for educational, business, or sales promotional use. For information, please email the Special Markets Department at SPsales@harpercollins.com.

FIRST EDITION

Library of Congress Cataloging-in-Publication Data has been applied for.

ISBN 978-0-06-288775-7

20 21 22 23 24   LSC   10 9 8 7 6 5 4 3 2 1

For Sarah, Josh, and Andy, who help me calibrate my confidence,
sometimes boosting it and sometimes cutting it down to size

Contents

Introduction 1

PART I **OVER AND UNDER** 11

CHAPTER 1 What Is Confidence?. 15

CHAPTER 2 How Might I Be Wrong?. 41

CHAPTER 3 What Is Possible? 65

CHAPTER 4 How Bad Could It Be?. 89

PART II **JUST RIGHT** 113

CHAPTER 5 Clarify. 117

CHAPTER 6 Forecast. 139

CHAPTER 7 Consider Other Perspectives 165

CHAPTER 8 Find the Middle Way. 189

Acknowledgments. 213

Notes 217

Index. 249

PERFECTLY
CONFIDENT

Introduction

Before I accuse anyone of overconfidence, I have to admit my own complicated history. As a boy, I read about the power of positive thinking with wide-eyed enthusiasm. I was a connoisseur of self-help books with titles like *Grow Rich While You Sleep*, which promised boundless opportunity and broad vistas of wealth, success, and self-fulfillment. I spent altogether too much of my money on motivational cassette tapes that promised greater confidence. These tapes sounded like the ocean surf, but just below the audible level, there were spoken affirmations. The subliminal messages told me things like, "I am popular and well liked. I have many friends." These subconscious affirmations promised to circumvent the censors in my conscious mind and go straight to my deepest self-image to change how I viewed myself. They were part of my bold scheme to become the most popular kid in my high school in Pocatello, Idaho.

My scheme, needless to say, was not a success. Letting classmates copy off my physics homework didn't earn me real friends, and debate club did not turn out to be the royal road to glory. My marginalization in high school was marked by the reluctance of even my own little sister to acknowledge me, for fear some of my nerdiness would rub off on her. In fairness, it is impossible to know how much worse high school would have been for me without the assistance of those subliminal messages, yet it is hard to imagine falling further down the social hierarchy at Highland High School.

It was there, at the bottom of the heap, that I discovered the teachings of Tony Robbins. I was inspired by his ability to help me envision my best self and enact my greatest dreams. I read his books and tried to put their lessons into practice. It was partly due to inspiration from Robbins, and partly due to the economics class I took my junior year in college, that I took a job in business when I graduated. I turned out to be terrible at monitoring grommet inventories, which is what I was supposed to be doing, and more interested in the way the organization made decisions. I had the distinct sense that confidence played an oft-dysfunctional role in the process. For instance, managers routinely made hiring decisions with unwarranted certainty. They had excessive faith in their own judgment and too often promoted people whose confidence, like their own, outstripped their actual competence. I went back to graduate school in business, hoping to study the dynamics of decision making within organizations.

Years later, I got the opportunity to teach with Tony Robbins. He was hosting a course for his "platinum partners"—people who pay a great deal of money to receive invitations to special events and seminars—and I got to teach what I knew about negotiations and deal making. Sometime after that, I found myself at another Robbins event, his "Unleash the Power Within" weekend. Tens of thousands attended at the Los Angeles Convention Center. My wife and I sat up front, in the VIP section next to Oprah Winfrey, who happened to be filming a documentary about the event. The first day culminated in a dramatic fire walk.

Everyone there started out the day somewhere between apprehensive and terrified of the fire walk. In the hours leading up to the big event, Robbins worked the crowd into an enthusiastic frenzy, trying to convince our group of future firewalkers that we could conquer the world. He compared the fire walk to the obstacles we faced in life and invited us to confront the fears that prevented us from overcoming them. There was also some talk about the real dangers posed by walking barefoot over hot coals and what you needed to do to come through unharmed. Roll up your pants to prevent the fabric from catching fire. Walk briskly and do not dawdle. At the end, wipe off your feet and get them sprayed with water. Helpful members of the Los Angeles Fire Department were on hand with hoses to assist in this effort.

We carried the energetic fervor that Robbins had built in the convention hall with us as we all walked barefoot to the parking lot filled with bonfires. Seeing the fires glowing in the evening darkness brought home the reality of what we were about to do. The coals from those fires got shoveled onto a number of fiery walkways. As we waited for our turn to cross, we cheered and chanted, trying to keep our confidence and enthusiasm from flagging. When my turn came, I did not hesitate. The pain hardly pierced my armor of confidence. I celebrated my bravery on the other side, but in my euphoria, I neglected to wipe all the burning embers from my feet. Somehow that part of the instructions hadn't stuck in my mind— but the embers had stuck to the tender flesh on the soles of my feet.

Later in the evening, I felt blisters rising. On the walk back to the hotel, I realized that my feet were covered in burns. Carried away by my confidence, I had failed to take sufficient precautions. What had been pride quickly turned to humiliation. I was keenly aware that I had let myself get carried away. As I limped along in pain, I looked back to the confidence that had carried me across the fire walk and just felt stupid. What a fool I had been. For what? Was I trying to impress Oprah? She was too busy with her own fire walk to notice what I was up to. The other participants? I would never see these people again. Was I trying to impress myself? Whatever benefit I might have enjoyed from feeling that I could overcome scary obstacles had been quickly undone by the fact that I had tried walking through fire and had gotten burned.

My experience on the fire walk reveals one personal reason this optimist has become a skeptic on the subject of confidence: I know how easy it is to be overconfident. My experience has inspired research whose results have profoundly shaped how I see the world, documenting the risks, follies, and biases of miscalibrated confidence. I hope to impart these hard-won insights—without you having to suffer the painful consequences yourself.

A NEW VIEW OF CONFIDENCE

Chances are you are thinking about confidence wrong. If you have spent any time reading self-help books, you could be forgiven for coming away thinking that more confidence is better. There are books with titles like *Confidence: How to Overcome Your Limiting Beliefs and Achieve Your Goals* and *You Are a Badass: How to Stop Doubting Your Greatness and Start Living an Awesome Life*. They make greater confidence sound inviting. Such books tell you that you should grow your confidence. They imply that your challenge in life is to keep your confidence up, bolstering it against the haters who would tear you down or the misfortunes that would make you doubt yourself. Maybe you try to build your confidence through self-affirmations, or better eye contact, or a firmer handshake, or power posing.

The message that these books push is that you should maximize your confidence. They make me think of the terrible advice that "you can never be too rich or too thin." You do not need to suffer an eating disorder to know that it is possible to be too thin. But can you be too confident? Is it good for you to believe that the gods always smile on you, that good things come your way without your having to work for them, and that you are favored by fortune? Should you believe that everything in life goes right for you, that everybody loves you, and that you are invulnerable? Is it wise to believe that you, blessed among the many, will beat the odds and get lucky? Should you believe that you can drive at high speeds in heavy traffic while texting and eating? You do not need to suffer the disastrous consequences of these beliefs to know that there can indeed be confidence disorders.

I cannot blame you if you suspect that overestimating your potential, maybe just a little bit, could be good. Plenty of coaches and gurus advocate precisely this. But there are many problems with this approach in practice, not least of which is the problem of fooling yourself, and knowing precisely which parts of you are fooling which other parts. Moreover, it can be difficult to figure out exactly how much you ought to fool yourself. It is possible to go too far. Believing that you are the messiah can lead to some obviously dysfunctional behavior. But most of the problems associated with such grand delusions also hold, at a smaller scale, for believing that you are slightly taller, richer, better looking, or more virtuous than you actually are. As you read this book, there will be times when you will object to my encouragement to moderate your confidence. You will think of instances in which greater confidence might help you succeed. I am entirely sympathetic to that objection. We will explore when it is true, how it is true, and how you can benefit from that knowledge.

On the other hand, if you have read books on decision making, you might be aware of your vulnerability to overconfidence. Decades of research demonstrates how often people have an overinflated sense of their own wisdom. In fact, our beliefs are rarely as correct or as accurate as we think they are. If you suspect that you might be biased toward overconfidence, you might worry about how excessive faith in erroneous intuitive judgments can lead you to make mistakes. You might think you should bring your confidence down to earth, to reduce ego-gratifying self-enhancement and to become humbler.

But minimizing confidence is not the solution either. Underconfidence is an error all its own. Underestimating your potential deters you from undertaking challenges at which you would be successful, dissuades you from approaching others with whom you would get along, and leads you to forgo profitable opportunities. In the pages ahead, we will consider how underconfidence puts you at risk of shortchanging yourself. While overconfidence prompts errors of action, in which you do something you later regret, underconfidence is more likely to lead to errors of inaction, in which you decline an opportunity that would have turned out well. But both are errors.

I will encourage you to use facts and reality, not wishful thinking, to calibrate your confidence. That will require you to consider what it means to believe the truth about an uncertain future. What does it mean to hold accurate beliefs about outcomes, performances, and achievements that have not yet occurred? Calibrating your confidence will also force you to confront the fact that performance is often difficult to score or quantify. What benchmark is useful for assessing your own honesty, driving ability, or career potential? This book will provide answers.

This book offers a novel perspective on confidence that plots the middle way between having too much and having too little. Along the way, I will try to dispel some common misconceptions about what confidence is and how it operates. It is neither a personality trait nor a measure of self-worth. Rather, think of it as an assessment that takes into account both your beliefs and the facts. It is an appraisal of your abilities and what you can accomplish. It builds on a consideration of past performance and current potential. These, in turn, form the basis for predictions about the future and what one can realistically accomplish. For instance, well-calibrated confidence judgments can guide decisions about how much to bet and how to hedge those bets—whether you're betting on your poker hand, future product sales, or a stock's price.

MANIFESTATIONS OF CONFIDENCE

Throughout this book, we will look to the truth and seek to avoid the dangers of delusion or bias. I will invite you to let go of the woolly-headed thinking that characterizes so much of the advice on confidence. I will encourage you to be clear and specific in your assessments of yourself. I will strive to do the same. In the interests of clarity, I will distinguish three forms of confidence:

- Estimation quantifies how good you think you are, how likely you are to succeed, or how quickly you will get things done.
- Placement compares yourself with others.
- Precision assesses the accuracy of your beliefs, or how sure you are that you are right.

Overestimation occurs, for instance, when you overestimate how quickly you will get work done, committing yourself to more than you can humanly accomplish. One of the lures that can draw you into overestimation is wishful thinking. Its flip side is underestimation. You will be prone to underestimating yourself when you get stuck in worry and rumination, exaggerating risks and failing to appreciate your virtues, strengths, and potential.

Overplacement occurs when you exaggerate the degree to which you are better than others. All of us are prone to overplacement for easy tasks and for common events. Most of us believe we are better-than-average drivers. If you are usually kind, it is easy for you to believe you are kinder than others. If you usually behave ethically, you probably think you are more ethical than others, and you wind up feeling morally superior. On the other hand, for difficult tasks and rare events, it is easy to believe that you are worse than others. When performing a task that's hard for everyone, many people experience the impostor syndrome. Ignorance of others' struggles can leave even capable people afraid they cannot do a job as well as others.

Overprecision occurs when you are excessively sure that you know the truth. It leads you to be too confident that your interpretation of the facts is the right one. It leads investors to be excessively sure they know what an investment is worth. It leads you to be too quick to disparage those who disagree with you as either evil or stupid. Unlike estimation and placement, reversals of overprecision are vanishingly rare. That is, research has found little evidence of *under*precision, in which people report being *less* sure of themselves than they ought to be.

The chapters that follow will do more to distinguish these different forms of confidence and help you identify which are most likely to bias your judgments. Thinking about confidence the wrong way can leave you confused or even delusional. Delusion can come in the form of allowing yourself to be fooled by a smooth-talking salesperson or a charismatic candidate. It can also come in the form of self-delusion, such as believing you do not need to protect yourself from the risks of a fire walk. Or you might be tempted to delude yourself into thinking that if you somehow believe *hard* enough, good things will follow. After reading this book, you will understand why even smart people make this mistake.

CONFIDENCE CALIBRATION

You have choices about how confident to be. Your interpretations of past performance and current abilities affect what you believe about your future potential. But choosing to be overconfident is rarely in your interest. Choosing overconfidence involves self-delusion and all the follies that follow from it. On the other side, being underconfident causes other problems, including missed opportunities and the failure to appreciate your virtues and strengths. The middle way between these two is a narrow path and is not always easy to find. How optimistic should you be about an uncertain future? Again, this book provides answers.

The answers in this book come from decades of research. This research examines overconfidence and underconfidence, always holding accuracy as the benchmark. The comparison between people's confidence and their actual performance allows us to distinguish those who are accurate in their judgments from those who are either overconfident or underconfident. We will not content ourselves with an assessment of either confidence or competence but always a comparison between the two.

When my eight-year-old son said he thought he might be able to slam-dunk a basketball if he tried really hard, he was being over-confident. Overconfidence is not the same thing as confidence. The basketball star Shaquille O'Neal could be extremely confident about dunking without being overconfident. It is also possible to have low confidence but still be overconfident, such as when I look at the field of presidential primary contenders and think, "Maybe I could do that." Confidence is an estimate of one's potential, ability, or accuracy. The difference between this estimate and how one actually performs reveals overconfidence, underconfidence, or accuracy.

Confidence is about inner beliefs more than outward displays. I will not give you advice about your handshake, your posture, or your eye contact. I will not instruct you how to bamboozle investors, how to woo voters, or how to stare down a lion. These topics are for other books. Instead, I will provide you with tools to help you calibrate your own certitude. These tools will help you make better decisions about what paths to tread and which risks to take. They will help you decide how to invest your time, money, and love. And they may inform your voting and hiring decisions.

Confidence calibration is difficult. You won't always get it exactly right. It is nevertheless worth striving for good calibration. The Greek philosopher Aristotle praised those who "have neither that excess of confidence which amounts to rashness, nor too much timidity, but the right amount of each." Or in the words of US president Theodore Roosevelt: "I am just as little disposed to give way to undue pessimism as to undue and arrogant optimism. Both our virtues and defects should be taken into account." It is my hope that those who read this book will grow and profit from the insights offered herein, for understanding confidence—and, in turn, ourselves—can contribute to greater happiness and success.

PART I

—

OVER AND
UNDER

—

Chapter 1 introduces a new view of confidence—not as it exists in the popular imagination, but as it behaves in real life. Chapter 2 invites you to reconsider what you think you know and ponder the multitudinous and multifaceted ways in which you might be wrong. Chapter 3 gets serious about cataloging the many ways in which you might be wrong by helping you think about your uncertainty in distributions of possible outcomes and associating probabilities with each of them. Chapter 4 confronts the issue of wishful thinking and helps you consider how your preferences can bias your confidence and your forecasts for the future. Together, the first four chapters of this book illustrate how easy it is to wander off the middle way into over- or underconfidence. They identify the bad assumptions about confidence that may get in the way of finding the truth.

Part II is designed to help you find your way back to perfect confidence. Chapters 5, 6, and 7 identify reliable signposts to guide you toward the middle way, providing specific recommendations and useful strategies. Together, the book's two halves demonstrate how to manage and maintain well-calibrated confidence. Chapter 8 concludes with an ode to the middle way, rooted in well-calibrated wisdom. The middle way enables you to see the truth and understand all that you are capable of, and how to achieve it. It helps you steer clear of mistakes that can put you at risk for missed opportunities, embarrassment, and pain.

CHAPTER 1

What Is Confidence?

Confident people change the world. Consider Elon Musk, the South African immigrant to the United States who, as a young man, helped create PayPal, transforming the way people pay online. When Pay-Pal was acquired by eBay in 2002, Musk used the money to invest in Tesla, the electric car company that upended the automobile market. Tesla's market capitalization now makes it worth almost as much as General Motors. At the same time, Musk created SpaceX and revolutionized the business of launching satellites into space. He has announced plans for SpaceX to send humans to Mars in 2024 and, from there, to colonize other planets. Musk does not lack for ambition.

Musk's fascination with space exploration traces back to a youthful love of science fiction. His brother, Kimbal, remembers that, as a child, Elon would read for as many as ten hours a day. When he ran out of books to read in his school's library, he just started reading the encyclopedia. His sharp concentration and relentless work ethic were evident years later at Zip2, the company that Musk founded with Kimbal. Musk routinely worked late into the night. He would often wind up falling asleep in the beanbag chair next to his desk. "Almost every day, I'd come in at seven thirty or eight a.m., and he'd be asleep right there," recalled Jeff Heilman, one of Zip2's first employees. Musk would wake up and get right back to work. "Maybe he showered on the weekends," Heilman speculated.

As a child, Musk's bookishness did not always endear him to other children. "But Mom, he's not fun," his siblings objected when their mother implored them to include Elon in their play. Musk's social awkwardness continued into adulthood. Doris Downes, one of his colleagues at Zip2, recalls: "Someone complained about a technical change that we wanted being impossible. Elon turned and said, 'I don't really give a damn what you think,' and walked out of the meeting. For Elon, the word *no* does not exist, and he expects that attitude from everyone around him."

SpaceX has transformed the business of launching rockets by bringing the price down to a fraction of what it used to be. Musk achieved this, in part, through relentless innovation. He saw expensive waste built into the deals between the US government and the contractors who had been building its rockets for decades. Musk did better by pushing the company and his people to pursue ambitious goals for both production timetables and costs. He worked hard to accomplish these goals and had high expectations of those who worked with him. Kevin Brogan, employee number twenty-three at SpaceX, recounts, "He doesn't say, 'You have to do this.' He says, 'I need the impossible done by Friday at 2 p.m. Can you do it?'" And often Musk's employees do.

Musk's story is just one example of the close tie between confidence and success. More-confident entrepreneurs, like Musk, are often more successful. Confident applicants are more likely to get hired, and confident political candidates are more likely to get elected. All around us, we see confidence precede success, which makes it tempting to conclude that cultivating confidence increases the odds of success. But focusing on those who wound up as winners is problematic, because it ignores two problems.

The first problem is that it risks confusing cause and effect. Is confidence really the cause, or is it possible that it is merely a consequence of something deeper—actual talent, financial advantage, or strategic positioning? For instance, strong job applicants with great credentials and a proven record of success have good reasons to be confident. Elon Musk is an enormously intelligent and talented person with many impressive achievements to his credit. He has a lot of money, tremendous power, and good reason to be confident about his potential success. In many cases, both confidence and success may share the same underlying cause.

Sports is another domain in which confidence is closely associated with success. It is easy to think of confident and successful athletes, such as the talented LeBron James who, at the tender age of sixteen, had CHOSEN 1 tattooed on his back. Did the same confidence that led him to make such a bold claim at such a young age also contribute to his many subsequent successes? An answer to that question should consider other sixteen-year-olds and their own claims to greatness. In a sport like basketball, in which boasting has been elevated to an art form, plenty of big talkers have not experienced NBA success.

The second problem with focusing on confident winners is that it overlooks the instances in which confidence has preceded failure. Plenty of confident people fail. It is the same confident Elon Musk who has experienced great successes and great failures. In 1996, he was ousted as CEO of Zip2. Four years later, he was ousted from

PayPal. The first rockets launched by SpaceX blew up disastrously. The first Falcon 1 launch failed only twenty-five seconds after take-off. The second launch, a year later, flew for four minutes before breaking up. Tesla, too, has had more than its share of trouble. In May 2016, Musk announced plans to produce 200,000 Model 3 se-dans by the end of 2017. In fact, the company produced only a tenth of that number. Employees at Tesla were working overtime to ramp up production, but it just wasn't happening fast enough. "I'm back to sleeping at the factory," Musk tweeted in April 2018. "Car biz is hell."

CONFIDENCE INTERVALS

To help you calibrate your confidence, I would like to invite you to play a little game with me. The table that follows lists ten quantities of which you are uncertain. For each one, please identify your an-swer, with a 90 percent confidence interval. A confidence interval consists of two numbers, one below your best guess and one above your best guess. That range should be wide enough that you are 90 percent sure the right answer is somewhere between. Obviously, the surer you are, the narrower you can make the confidence inter-val. If the question was about the date of your own birth, you could make the confidence interval very precise indeed. The less certain you become, the wider you should make the confidence interval. Your challenge is to calibrate your intervals so that you are 90 per-cent sure the right answer is inside it.

One way to think about it is like this: Set the lower bound so low that there is only a 5 percent chance the truth is below it (and a 95 percent chance the truth is above it). Then set the upper bound so high that there is only a 5 percent chance the truth is above it (and a 95 percent chance the truth is below it). With only a 10 percent chance the truth is outside the range, you should have a 90 percent confidence interval.

Without consulting any reference materials or other people, please estimate 90 percent confidence intervals for the ten quantities in the table.

	Lower Bound	Upper Bound
1. World population, according to the US Census Bureau on July 17, 2019		
2. Year in which Orville Wright took the world's first powered heavier-than-air flight		
3. Hourly wage that Steve Jobs paid designer Dean Hovey for creating Apple's mouse		
4. Maximum depth (below sea level) of the Mariana Trench in the Pacific Ocean		
5. Total revenues of the Tesla corporation in 2018 (according to its annual report)		
6. Year in which Daniel Kahneman won the Nobel Prize in Economics		
7. Amount of money that Google paid to buy YouTube in 2007		
8. LeBron James's average points per game in his NBA career, as of July 2019		
9. Year in which William James first taught a psychology class at Harvard University		
10. Number of honorary degrees awarded to the author Maya Angelou		

Did you really take the time to answer the questions? Please do. It gives you some skin in this game. It improves your ability to apply the insights offered here to yourself and to your own decisions.

For how many of these questions should the right answer have landed between your lower and upper bounds? Well, if you have calibrated your confidence correctly, then each one should have a 90 percent chance of hitting. Out of ten items, nine should be inside the confidence interval. Read on to discover the right answers. How many did you get?

If you are like most people, your hit rate was substantially below 90 percent. In fact, hit rates inside 90 percent confidence intervals are closer to 50 percent. By drawing your confidence intervals too narrowly, you are acting as if you are surer than you deserve to be that your knowledge is correct. Your judgments reveal overprecision. This phenomenon also occurs for other ways people specify their confidence. It is not isolated to obscure trivia questions and 90 percent confidence intervals. In fact, overprecision emerges in nearly all the tests of it psychologists have devised. People usually act as if they are surer than they should be.

Research on "flashbulb memories" illustrates the *illusion of knowing*. These are memories that feel as accurate and faithful as a photograph. Many people, for example, recall with vivid clarity the moment they first learned of the terrorist attacks of September 11, 2001. If your flashbulb memories are as accurate as you think they are, then the same incident should be remembered the same way by others who shared that moment. But they are not. When researchers cross-checked people's recollections, they discovered that those who were present in one another's flashbulb memories often had inconsistent recollections of what happened—but they were nevertheless absolutely convinced that their own memories were correct.

When the question is not "What is the world's population?" but "How much steel reinforcement is needed to prevent my bridge from collapsing?" then calibrating confidence judgments may be a matter of life and death. An architect who is too confident in a bridge's design could skimp on structural supports. You probably

	Correct answer
1. World population, according to the US Census Bureau on September 12, 2019	7.598 billion
2. Year in which Orville Wright took the world's first powered heavier-than-air flight	1903
3. Hourly wage that Steve Jobs paid designer Dean Hovey for creating Apple's mouse	$35
4. Maximum depth (below sea level) of the Mariana Trench in the Pacific Ocean	36,070 ft.
5. Total revenues of the Tesla corporation in 2018 (according to its annual report)	$21.46 billion
6. Year in which Daniel Kahneman won the Nobel Prize in Economics	2002
7. Amount that Google paid to buy YouTube in 2007	$1.65 billion
8. LeBron James's average points per game in his NBA career, as of July 2019	27.2
9. Year in which William James first taught a psychology class at Harvard University	1873
10. Year in which Maya Angelou was awarded the Presidential Medal of Freedom	2010

also don't want the underconfident architect who doubles the cost of the building, adding expensive earthquake reinforcements to your office building in Minneapolis, where earthquakes are unheard of. What you want in an architect, what you want in an employee, what you want in a life partner, and what you want in yourself is good calibration: the wisdom to see the truth, and to be as confident as evidence justifies.

OVERCONFIDENCE

Overconfidence sits at the center of decision biases that lead to error and irrationality. Scott Plous wrote that "no problem in judgment and decision making is more prevalent and more potentially catastrophic than overconfidence." Daniel Kahneman, who won a 2002 Nobel Prize in Economics for his research on cognitive biases, wrote that overconfidence is "the most significant of the cognitive biases." These claims are built on a strong consensus among those who have studied overconfidence, underscoring the importance and pervasiveness of overconfidence in human judgment. It would not be an exaggeration to say that overconfidence is the mother of all psychological biases. I mean this in two ways.

First, overconfidence is one of the largest and most ubiquitous of the many biases to which human judgment is vulnerable. "Perhaps the most robust finding in the psychology of judgment is that people are overconfident," write Werner De Bondt and Richard Thaler. Overconfidence has been blamed for the sinking of the *Titanic*, the nuclear accident at Chernobyl, the loss of the space shuttles *Challenger* and *Columbia*, the subprime mortgage crisis of 2008 and the Great Recession that followed, the *Deepwater Horizon* oil spill in the Gulf of Mexico, and more. Overconfidence may contribute to excessive stock market trading, high rates of entrepreneurial failure, legal disputes, political partisanship, and even war.

Overconfidence further earns its title as the mother of all biases by giving the other decision-making biases teeth. It is, if you will, a gateway bias. These other decision-making biases arise from the many simplifying heuristics that we use to navigate our complex physical, intellectual, social, and informational worlds. These biases are the focus of several other books on the psychology of decision making, including Daniel Kahneman's *Thinking, Fast and Slow*, Dan Ariely's *Predictably Irrational*, and my book with Max Bazerman, *Judgment in Managerial Decision Making*.

If you were appropriately humble about your judgment, you would be better able to protect yourself from the errors to which everyone is prone. Intuitive human judgment is vulnerable to many such biases and errors. The problem with intuition is that because it results from unconscious processes, you cannot audit it. It arrives, fully formed, in our conscious minds, and it just "feels right." Some possibilities feel more likely, some people feel more charismatic, and some risks just give you a bad feeling. Your confidence in these intuitions means that you too often accept them and forget that intuitive judgment is not perfect.

I ask my students to rate themselves relative to others in their class using a percentile scale. This scale quantifies the percentage of others to whom they are superior. The very worst in the class should get a zero on the percentile scale. The very best in the class should get one hundred. The median person, right in the middle of the pack, gets a fifty. Half the class is better than that person; the other half is worse. If all the students knew exactly where they stood, agreed on how to measure it, and answered honestly, the average for the class would have to come out to fifty. Those who rate themselves as better than others when they're not are demonstrating overplacement: the exaggerated belief that they place above others in the rankings. When I ask my students to rate their honesty, their answers average to around seventy-five.

I wouldn't want to accuse my students of dishonesty for making this glowing assessment of their own honesty, but I might accuse them of being vulnerable to bias. To get their views on this issue, I also include the following item on the questionnaire:

Research has led psychologists to conclude that when people rate themselves in terms of socially desirable qualities or performance, they tend to see themselves as being better than average when they are really not. This tendency is often referred to as a "self-serving bias" in judgment. To what extent do you believe that you avoid this bias relative to other members of the class? Again, give yourself a percentile rank that rates your objectivity, relative to the other members of the class. A score of 100 would indicate that you are less vulnerable to self-serving biases than all the other members of the class. A score of 0 would indicate that you are more vulnerable to self-serving biases than all the other members of the class.

Average responses to this one are consistently above fifty.

When you, as an individual, make biased decisions, it can lead to costly mistakes. But when we, collectively, are biased, the consequences can be momentous. Many have noted the role of collective overconfidence in the lead-up to the 2008 financial crisis. The 2008 subprime mortgage collapse and the Great Recession that followed were caused by a unique set of circumstances, many of which are closely tied to overconfidence. I begin with the investors, banks, and sovereign wealth funds that were buying up mortgage-backed securities. Their willingness to buy these securities was based on their belief that they knew what they were worth. Their confidence appears, in retrospect, to have been excessive. Had it not been for these investors' overprecision, they would have been less interested in investing in subprime loans.

As it was, the investing market was so eager for mortgage-backed securities that normal mortgages to worthy borrowers were not enough. Zealous brokers resolved to give the investors what they wanted and developed what have been euphemistically called "innovations" in the mortgage market: NINA loans, appropriate for people with no income and no assets. Then NINJA loans for people with no income and no job or assets. Next came "liar loans," in which borrowers were invited to lie about jobs, income, and assets that could justify the loan. Mortgage brokers advertised that their loan approval process omitted the onerous step of verifying the borrower's income. *You're an intermittently employed actor making half a million dollars a year? Right. We have just the mortgage for you.*

How did intermittently employed actors afford payments on million-dollar mortgage loans? Many of these loans were structured so that the payments started out small but ballooned over time. That wouldn't be a problem if (1) your income was going to go up dramatically in the future, or if (2) the property value kept going up and you could refinance with another liar loan in a year or two. But in 2007 it became apparent that borrowers had been overestimating the prospects of at least one of these. The number of people who were not even making the first payment on their brand-new mortgages climbed steadily that year. Only then did investors start to suspect that the risk models they had been relying on to estimate default rates might not be doing a perfect job of forecasting the risk of default in mortgage portfolios full of NINJA loans.

Investors all over the world had been buying up mortgage-backed securities as if they knew the risk of default by borrowers. Default is the great risk with any loan or bond. It is why the interest rates are so much higher on credit cards issued to people with question-able credit than they are on US government bonds. For the banks to make money on those credit cards, they need to charge enough interest to the people who pay that it can cover those who default.

Had it not been for the overconfident buyers of mortgage-backed securities, there would have been no incentive to create NINA, NINJA, and liar loans. There would have been no balloon payment plans. And all those mortgage brokers could have kept their more honest jobs as bartenders, construction workers, and exotic danc-ers. There would have been no boom in housing prices that drew otherwise sensible people into the business of "house flipping," in which a house is purchased and then resold after being spruced up with a new coat of paint and fresh layer of sod that, with luck, will survive the escrow period until closing. There would have been no cottage industry of books, TV shows, and infomercials touting opportunities for those who wanted to make a quick buck selling real estate, flipping houses, or originating mortgages. Without the massive global market for mortgage-backed securities, there would have been no global housing bubble.

So what fed the demand for mortgage-backed securities? At the very bottom was overprecise beliefs in bad risk models. The banks acted as if they were certain that the rates of default on the mort-gages in their portfolios would be below 5 percent, consistent with historical trends and data covering decades of mortgage lending and borrower default. And in their defense, I must enthusiastically agree with the absolutely fundamental importance of making such estimates based on good data. Investors placed enormous bets—totaling trillions of dollars—on banks' risk models being right. But their estimates were overprecise because they failed to consider the important fact that the historical data on which so much rested did not include NINJA loans and their ilk. When some "low-risk" mortgage portfolios saw default rates exceeding 50 percent, it's easy to see why the investments in these securities turned out to be worth less than everyone thought.

When the crucial characteristics of the underlying loans started to change, no one updated the risk models—until it was too late. So why didn't the alarm bells sound sooner? There were certainly people on the ground who knew that the liar loans they were selling weren't all going to get paid back. These mortgage brokers kept getting paid as long as the big investors kept buying the mortgages. Most of the brokers knew that at some point the music would stop and there wouldn't be enough seats for everyone to sit down and get out of the maelstrom. "But as long as the music is playing, you've got to get up and dance," said Citibank's CEO Chuck Prince in July 2007. Many justified their continued involvement with the belief that they were smarter than the suckers who would get stuck holding the bag. "I'll be gone, you'll be gone" was what they told each other. Maybe some of them did manage to get out. For the rest, this belief represented overplacement: they thought they were cleverer than others, but they weren't.

UNDERCONFIDENCE

Given the risks of overconfidence, you might think that it would be wise to reduce your confidence. But by how much? Too little confidence is a recipe for self-doubt, inaction, and (as the self-help books will tell you) missing out on an awesome life. Every day, you decline to strike up conversation with others, go rock climbing, or start a new company. Some of your failures to act are attributable to underconfidence, especially when taking a risk would actually pay off. These failures qualify as mistakes.

Underconfidence is rife, and in many cases it is the mirror image of overconfidence. The same students in my classes who claim to be more honest than their classmates and more immune to self-serving bias are perfectly willing to rate themselves as below average. On average, my students think they are worse at juggling than their classmates. They also underplace their knowledge of Latin, their ability to ride a unicycle, the number of companies they will found, and the number of lives they will save.

The psychologist Justin Kruger deserves the credit for identifying the fact that people tend to believe that they are worse than others at difficult tasks for which success is rare. In his dissertation research at Cornell University, Kruger showed how easy it is for people to underplace themselves. Ask them about some difficult task, a task on which most people perform poorly or fall short of some salient standard, and they will tell you that they are worse than average. Most of the students in my class cannot juggle very well. They think, "I know I'm no good at juggling, but maybe someone in here can juggle. If so, then I'm definitely worse than they are."

This line of reasoning highlights precisely the situation in which people are most prone to underplace themselves: when they know about their own ineptitude but aren't so sure about the abilities of others. Justin Kruger and his colleague Ken Savitsky noted that people display such underconfidence when considering their success not only at difficult tasks, but also rare behaviors. People think they use their shoehorns and waffle irons less than other people use theirs. If I hardly ever use my shoehorn, the reasoning goes, I am likely to be using it less than average. But when nobody uses a shoehorn very often, that can lead people to mistakenly infer they use theirs less than others.

The impostor syndrome leads competent people to fear that they are not good enough—that they are impostors. Thomas Jefferson,

founding father of the United States, principal author of the Declaration of Independence, crafter of the US Constitution, the nation's
first secretary of state, ambassador to France, third president, pro-
lific writer, speaker of many languages, and polymath, insisted that
"more confidence is placed in me than my qualifications merit."
John Steinbeck, winner of both the Nobel and Pulitzer Prizes for
literature, insisted, "I am not a writer. I've been fooling myself and
other people." Maya Angelou, celebrated author, winner of the National Medal of Arts, the Presidential Medal of Freedom, Grammy
and Tony Awards, and twenty-two honorary degrees from presti-
gious institutions of higher education, confessed, "I have written
eleven books, but each time I think, 'Uh oh, they're going to find
out now. I've run a game on everybody, and they're going to find me
out.'" And the actress Jodie Foster worried about both her Academy
Award and her admission to college: "I thought it was a big fluke.
The same way when I walked on the campus at Yale, I thought
everybody would find out, and then they'd take the Oscar back."

The impostor syndrome was first named in a 1978 article that examined the degree to which the syndrome afflicts high-achieving
women. *The Confidence Code* by Katty Kay and Claire Shipman reprised the theme, bemoaning female underconfidence and encouraging women to be more confident. The book features interviews
with impressive women, such as Christine Lagarde (the former
head of the International Monetary Fund), the US senator Kirsten
Gillibrand, and the basketball star Monique Currie. When asked
whether they ever experienced self-doubt, these capable and successful women confessed that they did. Did the men with whom
they competed experience self-doubt? "For guys," Currie offered,
"all the way down to the last player on the bench, who doesn't get
to play a single minute, I feel like his confidence and his ego is just
as big as the player who is the superstar of the team."

Others' inner doubts are invisible, making it easy to imagine that others are less afflicted by self-doubt than you are. Kay and Shipman did not ask men about their self-doubts for their book, and it is entirely possible that that last player on the bench is just putting a brave face on his feelings of inadequacy. In my research, I rarely find gender differences in confidence, nonverbal confidence expression, or interpretation of others' confidence. I do find plenty of evidence that both women and men worry about their credibility, that they both experience self-doubt, and they are sometimes sure that they are worse than others, even when they are not. Research also establishes that those who feel the impostor syndrome most keenly are rarely those who ought to. Frauds, posers, and con men often get away with arrogant displays of enormous confidence, without possessing true competence. Instead, it is the most hardworking and conscientious in any organization who worry most about their ability to deliver what others expect of them.

You are most prone to feel like an impostor when others' flaws and self-doubts are hidden. To pick one example: You have privileged information about how you look naked. It is tempting to believe that your naked body has more moles, stretch marks, and inconvenient sproutings of hair than do others'. The naked truth is that every body is imperfect, but you are simply more familiar with your own naked body than with others'. It doesn't help that most published photos of naked bodies are those of young, beautiful, fit people with perfectly coiffed pubic hair and whose imperfections have been meticulously photoshopped out.

Interestingly, the very same psychological mechanisms that lead to underplacement can also lead to overplacement. My students think they are more honest than their peers because they know more about themselves than they do about others. They know they are honest and cannot know for certain how honest others are.

Assessing honesty, after all, depends on confirming that a person says what he or she believes; for others, you can only speculate about what they truly believe. If my students reason, "If I know I'm honest ninety-seven percent of the time, there is more room for others to be less honest than I am, so I am probably more honest than average," then they will exaggerate the degree to which they are more honest than others, and in turn overplace their honesty. Knowing that they brush their teeth regularly can likewise lead to the mistaken inference that they brush their teeth more often than others.

There exists another example with profounder consequences than underconfidence about one's naked body or use of toothbrushes, and that is the enrollment of qualified students from low-income households into higher education. Only a third of the most talented high school graduates from the bottom quartile of the income distribution attend the United States' top universities, compared with 78 percent from the top quartile of the income distribution. The single biggest reason for this difference is that the lower-income students just don't apply. In part, they don't know about the opportunities and financial aid available to them. But they are also overly pessimistic about their chances for admission.

Part of their pessimism could be caused by their not knowing others who have attended such institutions. They infer that it is unlikely to happen. But in truth, talented kids from poor families are very much in demand at elite universities. Most universities are eager to increase their student diversity in matters of race, gender, culture, geographic representation, and socioeconomic background. The most selective private universities help poor families afford their high price tags. That often means they will provide generous financial aid packages that make tuition free for families who cannot afford it. The eligible students who fail to apply could clearly benefit from a bit more confidence.

Another task at which many people feel inadequate is writing. Writing is devilishly difficult, and even accomplished writers frequently feel incompetent. Take, for example, Hugh Howey's blog confession, "I suck at writing." Howey, a bestselling author of eleven published books, wrote: "I assure you that my writing skills are well below par. Watching a rough draft emerge from my fingertips in real time would induce nausea. It's a haphazard, drunken affair." Writers are keenly aware of their own difficulties, but it is rare to obtain insight into others' writing challenges. Instead, you see the completed text, bound handsomely and displayed in the bookstore. It all looks so beautiful and orderly and competent.

The brilliant writer David Rakoff knew better. He described sitting down at the computer to start writing just as toddlers were being dropped off at their day care next door. Despite earlier frustrations, the new day afforded optimism:

> *Today will be good, you think. Not like the previous day's lack of industry, a shameful waste of phone calls, e-mail, snacking, and onanism. Yes, it is all about today. But first, the crossword. And what does Paul Krugman have to say? Oh, that Gail Collins. Love her. E-mail, has it been checked in the last forty seconds? And now a snack. Friend Patty calls . . . Midday already? The toddlers, now screaming, are picked up from next door. Sit down and write a sentence for God's sake. One fucking sentence, it won't kill you. It almost kills you.*

Even when it doesn't almost kill you, writing is hard for just about everyone. You probably deserve to be a little more confident about your writing abilities, compared with those of others, and a little less confident about your honesty. For confidence to be well calibrated, it must be matched by underlying facts, evidence, and competence. It means actually understanding how you place relative to others. It means separating your beliefs from assumptions, fantasy, or delusion. But delusion can be awfully inviting, as William James reminds us.

BELIEVING IN YOURSELF

William James, widely regarded as the father of modern psychology, was a brilliant intellect and a visionary scholar. James's book *The Principles of Psychology* is a classic that garnered high praise from the most eminent psychologists of his day, including Carl Jung and Sigmund Freud. The book's wide-ranging exploration of what psychology is and what it could be anticipated many of the most important topics that have engrossed the field to this day. His ideas and his theories have endured remarkably well, especially when compared with those of other, more famous psychologists (including Jung and Freud).

But James had a difficult start in life. As a boy, he suffered ailments of the body and the mind, from back problems to depression severe enough that it brought him close to suicide more than once. He wanted to be an artist but studied medicine out of practical necessity. He hated it. Of his time in medical school, he wrote, "I was, body and soul, in a more indescribably hopeless, homeless, and friendless state than I ever want to be in again." He completed his degree in 1869 but never practiced medicine. Instead, James met the anguish of his debilitating depression with a search for meaning. "I drifted into psychology and philosophy from a sort of fatality," he reported. His search revealed a fascination with the connections between the mind and the body. This led him to a faculty position at Harvard University in 1873, where he developed one of the very first psychology courses the university ever offered, entitled The Relations between Physiology and Psychology. "I never had any philosophic instruction," James confessed, "the first lecture on psychology I ever heard being the first I ever gave."

In 1878, James wrote about the power of positive visualization. He imagined himself climbing in the mountains and getting stuck at a spot from which he needed to take a "bold dangerous leap." He wrote, "I may wish to make the leap, but I am ignorant from lack of experience whether I have the strength for it." James describes two possible outcomes. In the first, he believes what he desires. He imagines that his confidence gives him the strength to make the leap successfully. The confident James believes in himself, he jumps, and he makes it.

The second outcome imagines self-doubt. This doubting James hesitates, wavers, and then, "weakened and trembling, compelled to take the leap by sheer despair, I miss my aim and fall into the crevasse." James concludes that in a situation like this, "I should be a fool if I did not believe what I wished, as my belief happens to be a preliminary condition which is essential to the accomplishment of the end which it affirms." In other words, James imagines a situation in which his beliefs make themselves come true. As such, a wise person would have faith, and that faith would bring success.

When I first read James's account, I took it as a persuasive argument for the benefits of optimism. There are undeniably situations in which the belief in a positive outcome increases the chances that one will choose to go for it, and thereby increases the opportunity for the positive outcome one expects. If believing you can leap the crevasse increases the chance that you jump, it must also increase the chance that you make it. On the other hand, the fear of failure can easily scare you off from the attempt.

All parents have observed their children talking themselves into failing. Children are routinely reluctant to try new things: a new class, a new sport, a new food. "Try it, you might like it," you encourage gently. The child insists that she can't: "What if I mess up? What if I hate it?" Her imagined failure keeps her from trying, making her fear a self-fulfilling prophecy. Yet at other times, parents get to witness the thrill of a child jumping enthusiastically into a new project with both feet. When she does, her enthusiasm begets a persistence that increases her chances of success. Once again, her belief is borne out by reality.

One implication you might be tempted to take away is that positive visualization leads to good outcomes in life. You would not be the first to think so. However, you would also be right to be skeptical of this. While there is some evidence for the benefits of visualization, that evidence suggests that its value is limited. While simply imagining your company's rocket successfully making it into orbit may be pleasurable, it will not directly increase the odds for a successful launch any more than visualizing yourself as the pope will transport you to Rome.

In one study of the effectiveness of visualization, psychologists instructed college students to visualize getting good grades on a midterm examination. When that instruction included visualizing the process of studying and preparing for the exam, it led to longer hours of actual study and to better exam performance. By contrast, when the visualization centered exclusively on the positive outcome—that is, the exam result—the researchers did not find that it increased either the hours spent studying or the student's performance on the exam. For visualization to be effective, it has to influence the actual behavior that affects the fantasized outcome, such as studying, practicing, or working out. In case you're wondering whether those subliminal audio tapes to which I listened as a teenager might have helped, they probably didn't do anything for me or any of the other people who paid good money for them.

Further reflection on William James's story of his alpine adventure raised additional concerns that I had failed to consider the first time. If the doubting James really expected to fall into the crevasse, then making the jump seems like a bad call. If it were me, I'd like to think I would explore other ways out of the predicament that were less likely to end in my death. But more important than that, if the moral of his story is that it's always better to believe that you can jump the crevasse, that seems wrong. Sometimes you can't jump the crevasse. Sometimes it is just too wide.

Perhaps the doubting James could jump a five-foot crevasse. Let's say that believing in himself could get him a foot farther. Then if the crevasse were less than six feet across, James should repeat some empowering self-affirmations and go for it. But if the chasm were twenty feet wide, no amount of positive self-talk would get him across. Believing in yourself, if it prompts you to jump to your death, would qualify as a mistake—however much it displays an admirable confidence in your capabilities. It is an error that could be avoided with better-calibrated confidence. There are many domains in life in which confidence can help you perform, but its benefits will be limited. Believing in myself did not prevent my feet from getting burned on the fire walk. Setting impossible goals can be like leaping into a twenty-foot chasm: inspiringly ambitious but doomed to end badly.

THE RISKS OF OVERCONFIDENCE

"Pride goeth before destruction, and an haughty spirit before a fall," predicts the book of Proverbs. There are many situations in which being too sure of yourself can indeed undermine the very success you envision, as the work of the psychologist Jeffrey Vancouver shows. He has examined circumstances in which an increased sense of personal self-efficacy impairs future performance. Such experiments require manipulations of self-efficacy. If researchers had simply measured self-efficacy and performance, they would find many reasons why the two correlate that had nothing to do with any causal effect of confidence. For instance, those who were capable at a given task because they had prior success would be both confident and successful.

Experimental evidence is required in order to answer the question of whether one should choose to be confident, since the question is about the *causal* effect of confidence. This is exactly what Vancouver and his colleagues did. In one study, research volunteers played the game Mastermind, which involves guessing the color and order of hidden pegs. Vancouver's devious computer program rearranged the hidden pegs to make it easier or harder for participants to win the game. Those who easily won then became more confident in their own abilities, and they reported significantly higher feelings of self-efficacy. How did they do in subsequent rounds of play without the computer helping them out? They did worse than those who had lower feelings of self-efficacy. When performance depends on effort, being too sure of yourself can reduce your effort and undermine success.

The students in my class who are most confident that they will ace the exam, and who therefore do not study, are not those who get the best grades. The skydivers, mountain climbers, and bungee jumpers who are most convinced of their invulnerability are not those with the longest life expectancies. The psychologist Gabriele Oettingen has spent her career identifying the many ways in which imagining success can increase failure. She has examined people who want to lose weight, students who want to perform well on exams, and the lovelorn who want to find romance. She finds that those who fantasize most about a positive future do not actually obtain what they desire; on the contrary, they tend to obtain worse outcomes.

Michael Raynor writes about the threats overconfidence poses to businesses in *The Strategy Paradox: Why Committing to Success Leads to Failure*. The problem he points out is that prior success breeds complacency, and this complacency undermines an organization's ability to respond to new market challenges. Some of this is due to the inertia that afflicts organizations as they grow and age. Successful companies are built on successful people, products, and processes. These people, products, and processes naturally resist change if they fear that doing so could undermine their future success, prestige, or influence. But success can also breed confidence and persistence, especially for those at the top of an organization. All of this makes it difficult for businesses to adapt to changing market conditions.

For a time, parents were encouraged to build their children's confidence by telling them they could do anything. Now many developmental psychologists worry about the unintentional harm we may have done to our children by trying to pump up their confidence and increase self-esteem. In her book *The Self-Esteem Trap*, Polly Young-Eisendrath argues that affirming our kids with positive and empowering messages can lead to greater disappointment and disengagement. This message echoes that of the psychologist Carol Dweck, who maintains that by telling our children that they are smart, talented, and capable, we make them afraid to take chances that come with some risk of failure. Kids are aware of their own limitations and worry that by failing they might expose our confidence-boosting affirmations as false.

And what would Elon Musk the businessman have to say to William James the scholar? To what degree were Musk's audacious goals a key to success at Tesla and SpaceX? Did Musk successfully make so many bold, dangerous leaps simply because he believed he could do it? When asked, Musk has insisted that goals work best when they are realistic and achievable: "I certainly don't try to set impossible goals. I think impossible goals are demotivating." He has also seen the chaos created by excessively optimistic goals, and he has resolved to do better: "I'm trying to recalibrate to be a little more realistic."

CHAPTER 2

How Might I Be Wrong?

Harold Camping foretold that the world would end on May 21, 2011. Camping was the president of the Christian Family Radio network, and his reading of the Bible had convinced him that the end times were at hand. The Rapture and Judgment Day would take place as prophesied in the book of Thessalonians: "For the Lord himself shall descend from heaven with a shout . . . then we which are alive shall be caught up together with them in the clouds, to meet the Lord in the air." Camping explained the numerical basis for his prediction by saying, "I was an engineer, I was very interested in the numbers." The numbers he found in the Bible, leavened with a little of his own interpretation, led Camping to conclude that Judgment Day would come seven thousand years from Noah's Great Flood. Why seven thousand? Well, there are seven days in the week, and "one day is with the Lord as a thousand years, and a thousand years as one day" (2 Peter 3:8). By Camping's figuring, that pointed to May 21, 2011.

Camping used Family Radio to publicize the coming apocalypse. Many who were convinced by Camping's prophecy donated their money—indeed, all their worldly goods—to fund the publicity campaign. Their sacrifices helped pay for more than three thousand "Judgment Day" billboards around the world, in locations as far-flung as the Dominican Republic, Indonesia, Jordan, and Tanzania. Family Radio spent over $100 million spreading the news, including the purchase of five specially painted recreational vehicles that fanned out across the United States.

Some of the believers quit their jobs, sold their homes, and liquidated their savings. Many dedicated themselves to spreading the word, driving around RVs and handing out pamphlets. As for Camping himself, he professed absolute conviction. He had learned from his previous experience predicting the end times, he said. This would be different from 1994, when Camping had also predicted the apocalypse. This time he really meant it. When asked what he would do if Judgment Day did not arrive as promised, Camping responded emphatically, "I don't even think about those questions, because I won't be here. It's going to happen." He repeated even more vehemently, pausing after each word: "It is going to happen!"

Four economists—Ned Augenblick, Jesse Cunha, Ernesto Dal Bó, and Justin Rao—set out to test confidence in Camping's prophecy by offering his followers bets with payouts arriving after May 21. On May 8 and 15, 2011, the researchers set up tables outside gatherings of the faithful and offered a choice to those who were willing to talk to them: they could have $5 immediately or a larger amount in four weeks. How much larger would that amount have to be for them to forgo the $5 on the spot? Would they wait for $50? For $500? Refusing every postapocalyptic payment, no matter how high, would indicate a sincere belief in the prophecy. The result? No amount of money could convince Camping's followers to take a later payment. They preferred $5 immediately to any amount after May 21, insisting that nothing could entice them to bet against the imminent May 21 apocalypse. The one respondent who was willing to take a larger (postapocalyptic) payment confessed that he didn't really believe in the prophecy, but that a friend had dragged him to the meeting.

Camping's followers, no doubt, had the best intentions. They were good people, many of whom sacrificed a great deal to warn the world of the apocalypse they believed was coming. But it also seems likely that their evaluation of the evidence and the logical basis for their beliefs was less rigorous than you might hope. How high a standard of rigor and logic do you hold yourself to? How can you avoid falling for false or misleading claims? By way of trying to assess the calibration of your own beliefs, I would like to ask you for a forecast about the end of the world, or at least some people's part of it. Of all those who died last year, what percentage of global deaths were due to each of the following causes? Please make

Cause of Death	Percent of All Deaths
Road injuries, including vehicular collisions	
Accidental falls	
All other unintentional injuries (drowning, fire, poisoning, etc.)	
Self-harm, including suicide	
Interpersonal violence, including murders	
All other intentional injuries, including genocides and wars	

these estimates without consulting any reference materials or other people.

I will provide the answers in short order. But first, let's think about another way to help you calibrate confidence in your beliefs. Chapter 1 asked you to assess your confidence in your beliefs by specifying 90 percent confidence intervals for your estimates of uncertain quantities. Now we're going to use another measure. Without consulting any reference materials or other people, please make your best guess for each of the ten quantities in the following chart.

	Best Guess	Confidence
1. Number of (full-powered) radio stations in the Christian Family Radio network as of July 2018		
2. Number of deaths worldwide due to motor vehicle accidents (in millions)		
3. Net worth of Jeff Bezos, as of July 2019, according to *Forbes* magazine		
4. Year in which the English king Charles I was beheaded		
5. Number of deaths in the September 11 attacks		
6. Total revenues of Amazon corporation in 2018		
7. Age at which Oliver Cromwell, Lord Protector of England, died		
8. Number of Jewish Zealots who died on Masada		
9. Assets under management by the hedge fund Bridgewater Associates		
10. Number of new saints canonized by Pope John Paul II		

Then indicate how confident you are in your answer by estimating the likelihood (0 to 100 percent) that your answer is close to (within 5 percent of) the right answer.

Did you really take the time to answer the questions above? Do it. C'mon! It'll be fun.

HYPOTHESIS TESTING

The way in which you test hypotheses directly influences your confidence in them. When you tried to assess your confidence in your responses to the ten questions above, you probably reflected on how sure you felt that you were right. In so doing, you asked your mind for supportive data. That is, you searched your memory for information on whether your estimates were correct. That turns out to be how people test most questions they consider. Asking my students, "Was today's reading assignment interesting?" produces a different train of thought and more positive responses than the question "Was today's reading assignment boring?" Your default is to consider data, evidence, and memories that allow you to say yes to the question at hand. This is in part because it is easier to identify the presence than the absence of something. But it is also just a natural function of the way human minds search for evidence.

In one classic psychology study, Mark Snyder and William B. Swann Jr. asked the volunteers in their experiment to prepare to interview another person to find out where he or she belonged on the continuum of extroversion to introversion. The researchers asked half the volunteers to find out whether the interviewee was an extrovert. They asked the other half to find out whether the interviewee was an introvert. Volunteers chose their interview questions from a list that included some questions designed to elicit extroverted answers, such as "What would you do if you wanted to liven things up at a party?" Other questions, like "What factors make it hard for you to really open up to people?" were more likely to prompt introverted responses. All volunteers chose from the same list of possible questions, but those intending to test extroversion chose twice as many extroversion as introversion questions. Obviously, the questions you ask influence the answers you get, and even the shyest introvert can have ideas for how to liven up a party.

When you go into the world asking, "Is this hypothesis true?" you may be tempted to believe you are taking a neutral approach, but you are not. Simply the way you pose the question can influence the answer in subtle and surprising ways. It will be easier for you to think of evidence that allows you to answer yes. You will formulate questions that are more likely to generate affirmative answers. When you ask other people these questions, they will be more likely to respond in the affirmative or to provide you with evidence that supports your hypothesis. The question "Is this hypothesis false?" generates a different approach, a different line of thinking, different responses, and different conclusions. Ignorance of the way you bias your search for information leads you to be too confident in the biased conclusions that result.

Now let's compare how confident you said you were with your hit rate. How often were your guesses actually within 5 percent of the right answers?

To test your calibration, compare your average confidence across all ten questions with the frequency that your answers were actually within 5 percent of the truth. How did you do? If you're like

	5% Below	Right Answer	5% Above
1. Number of (full-powered) radio stations in the Christian Family Radio network as of July 2019	47	49	51
2. Number of deaths worldwide due to motor vehicle accidents (in millions)	1.28	1.35	1.42
3. Net worth of Jeff Bezos, as of July 2019, according to *Forbes* magazine	$155 billion	$163 billion	$171 billion
4. Year in which the English king Charles I was beheaded	1566	1648	1730
5. Number of deaths in the September 11 attacks	2,846	2,996	3,146
6. Total revenue of Amazon corporation in 2018	$221 billion	$232.9 billion	$245 billion
7. Age at which Oliver Cromwell, Lord Protector of England, died	56	59	62
8. Number of Jewish Zealots who died on Masada	912	960	1,008
9. Assets under management by the hedge fund Bridgewater Associates	$152 billion	$160 billion	$168 billion
10. Number of new saints canonized by Pope John Paul II	459	483	507

most people, your confidence exceeded your accuracy. But you probably also did better than you did on the confidence interval task from chapter 1. As a rule, people show better calibration for probability estimates than for confidence intervals. There are a couple of reasons for that. First, understanding the logic of confidence intervals depends on thinking about uncertainty as a probability distribution, which few people do naturally. Second, everyday life rarely requires us to specify confidence intervals, and so we get little practice or feedback using them.

Let me ask you for one more probability estimate, this one for your forecast of the percentage of all deaths this year worldwide that will be caused by injuries (as opposed to disease and starvation). Please do not look back at your previous answers, but just estimate this one on its own:

Cause of Death	Percent of All Deaths
Injuries, both intentional and unintentional	

Probability estimates, while better than confidence intervals, also show predictable biases. We tend to inflate the probability of the focal hypothesis. That is, we overestimate the probability that the hypothesis we are considering is actually true. In one study, Craig Fox and Amos Tversky asked basketball fans to predict the probability that each of the eight teams headed to the NCAA quarterfinals would win the tournament. When fans considered each team one at a time, they asked themselves, "Could this team win it?" Each team, of course, had its strengths. That made each team's winning, when considered in isolation, plausible. On average, these eight probabilities added up to 240 percent, even though logically the actual probabilities needed to sum to 100 percent. Focusing on any one hypothesis tends to inflate the subjective sense of its plausibility or truth. Sometimes you can help yourself correct this error by just adjusting each probability estimate down proportionately, forcing the total to sum to 100 percent.

Maybe this pattern was evident in your estimates of the prevalence of causes of death. Please look back now and add up the probabilities you assigned to the different risks of death by injury. How does that compare with the probability you assigned to the overall category? If you are like most people, you wound up with a higher total probability when you rated each of the component parts separately than when you just estimated the overall category. According to the World Health Organization, the risk of death due to all injuries in all age groups is about 11.1 percent. That total comes from these components: road injuries and vehicle accidents, 3.1 percent; falls, 1.4 percent; other unintentional injuries, 3.5 percent; self-harm, 1.4 percent; interpersonal violence, 1.2 percent; all other intentional injuries, 0.5 percent. If you, like most people, overestimated the prevalence of each of these causes of death, then you recognize how focusing on a particular hypothesis inflates our sense of its likelihood. It's just too easy to neglect the cancer, heart disease, infections, and malnutrition that cause so many more deaths.

It is obviously a problem that our minds search memory in a way that disproportionately produces hypothesis-consistent information. This problem is exacerbated by a world that can also help us confirm our beliefs. For instance, the hypotheses you bring to your internet searches drive the results that you get. Searching Google for "God exists" produces 123 million results, most of which enthusiastically support God's existence. That enthusiasm is contradicted by many of the 86 million websites turned up by the search "God doesn't exist."

You can be sure that the questions coming from the adherents of Harold Camping's Family Radio prophecy were different from the questions asked by the four economists who studied them. When the economists asked the faithful how their beliefs might be affected if Camping's prophecy proved to be wrong, many refused to answer the question, denying even the possibility. In contrast to religious faith, scientific research is designed, first and foremost, to seek the truth. So scientists worry about the degree to which their expectations and hypotheses influence the results they get.

Researchers' expectations may have tainted a famous study by John Bargh, Mark Chen, and Lara Burrows. I was among those impressed by the results when I encountered their paper in graduate school. The study was the most well known in a literature on "social priming." Bargh, Chen, and Burrows primed some of the volunteers in their study with words related to stereotypes of the elderly by having them complete a word-search puzzle in which they looked for words like *wrinkled, ancient, Bingo,* and *Florida.* Those in the control condition searched for neutral words like *thirsty* and *clean.* The researchers then measured how quickly volunteers walked down the hall to submit their completed puzzles. The researchers reported that those primed with the elderly stereotype walked more slowly. They then argued that the automatic activation of concepts related to stereotypes of the elderly had led to slower walking by those primed with the word *wrinkled.*

"Isn't that unbelievable?" I bragged to my friends after I read it. It turns out I wasn't the only one who thought so. Stéphane Doyen and his colleagues later published their attempts to replicate Bargh's finding. A direct replication using the same experimental procedures and a substantially larger sample size failed to obtain the effect—that is, until Doyen turned his attention to the research assistant with the stopwatch whose job it was to time how long research volunteers took to walk down the hallway. When that research assistant knew the hypothesis and the experimental condition of the person being timed, the results successfully replicated Bargh's result. Even a small, unintentional influence on pressing the stopwatch was enough to get the difference between conditions. This story serves as a reminder of why it is useful to keep those collecting and analyzing data blind to the research's hypotheses.

Karl Popper wrote, "If we are uncritical we shall always find what we want: we shall look for, and find, confirmations, and we shall look away from, and not see, whatever might be dangerous to our pet theories. In this way it is only too easy to obtain what appears to be overwhelming evidence in favor of a theory which, if approached critically, would have been refuted." Popper, widely regarded as the twentieth century's greatest philosopher of science, stressed the foundational importance of theory falsification in the conduct of science. That is, he argued that testing your beliefs requires you to ask, "Is my hypothesis false?" or, more specifically, "What evidence is there that could disprove my hypothesis?"

Taking Popper's advice to heart leads to a straightforward solution to the problem of confirmatory hypothesis testing: test the alternative hypothesis. In other words, *ask yourself why you might be wrong.* This is the simplest, most all-purpose debiasing strategy identified by decision researchers. In 1984, it was dubbed "consider the opposite" by Charles G. Lord, Mark R. Lepper, and Elizabeth Preston. They demonstrated its effectiveness for debiasing both the way people test their hypotheses and the way they interpret new evidence. Since then, the same debiasing strategy has been successfully deployed to correct a number of the biases to which human judgment is vulnerable.

Lord, Lepper, and Preston noted that they were not the first to recommend the wisdom of asking yourself why you might be wrong. Indeed, the approach they advocate comes from a proud intellectual lineage. It was memorably articulated by Oliver Cromwell when he found himself fighting against the Royalists in the English Civil War. Following the public beheading of King Charles I on a balcony at Whitehall Palace in London in 1649, rival forces battled to determine who would succeed him. When the Church of Scotland decided to support the royal lineage and accept Charles II as heir to the throne, Cromwell begged the church leaders to reconsider: "I beseech you, in the bowels of Christ, think it possible you may be mistaken."

Regardless of whether Christ's bowels are relevant, those who want to avoid having confirmation bias impair their decisions have to actively push themselves to consider the opposite. That's because considering the opposite is the opposite of what most of us do naturally. On the contrary, human minds are better at positive hypothesis testing. Our automatic impulse is to search for consistent or supportive information. Thirty years before Cromwell's plea, the English philosopher Sir Francis Bacon put it this way: "The human understanding when it has once adopted an opinion (either as being the received opinion or as being agreeable to itself) draws all things else to support and agree with it."

To illustrate his point, Bacon recalled the widespread belief that praying to God for protection from storms at sea helped sailors return safely home. This belief was supported by the many sailors who had prayed and survived. What evidence would disprove this hypothesis? Well, what about those sailors who had prayed just as fervently but hadn't made it back? Bacon bemoans the failure to ask this latter question: "It is the peculiar and perpetual error of human intellect to be more moved and excited by affirmatives than by negatives; whereas it ought properly to hold itself indifferently disposed towards both alike. Indeed in the establishment of any true axiom, the negative instance is the more forcible of the two." Popper would concur that hypothesis disconfirmation is essential for getting closer to the truth. In our reluctance to ask ourselves why we might be wrong, all of us behave like zealots reluctant to question their beliefs.

SOME RISKS OF BEING WRONG

The original Zealots were an orthodox Jewish sect around the first century CE. The Zealots believed they should be obedient to no master but God. They rebelled against the Roman occupation of Jewish lands, inflicting ruthless punishments on both Romans and on Jews they believed to be insufficiently religious or Roman collaborators. Rome generally tolerated a fair amount of religious freedom in its occupied territories, but the Zealots' brutality made Judea difficult to govern. The Zealots were successful in provoking a Jewish-Roman conflict. However, what they did not anticipate was its consequence—the destruction of the Jewish Temple in Jerusalem and the scattering of the Jewish diaspora out of Judea and around the world. After the fall of Jerusalem, the hardest core of the Zealots fled to the mountain fortress of Masada, where they managed to hold off the Roman armies for several months. When the Romans finally breached the fortress, the Zealots chose to die rather than be taken prisoner. Since Jewish law forbade suicide, they killed each other.

These days, zealots come from many religious traditions, but what they have in common is their conviction that they alone possess the truth. The zealots who believed in Camping's 2011 apocalypse made some tragically misguided decisions for themselves. But the zealots from al-Qaeda who crashed airplanes into the Twin Towers in New York on September 11, 2001, provoked a more dramatic consequence. Thousands of innocents lost their lives that day, but hundreds of thousands more died in the wars in Iraq and Afghanistan that followed. Those wars have resulted in enormous death and destruction, including the hobbling of al-Qaeda and the death of most of its leadership, most notably the high-profile assassination of Osama Bin Laden. The conflicts have inflamed tensions between many Muslim and non-Muslim communities around the world.

"The fundamental cause of the trouble is that in the modern world the stupid are cocksure while the intelligent are full of doubt," wrote the philosopher Bertrand Russell in 1933. Religious zealots may be an extreme example, but each of us prefers to believe that he or she is right. In truth, even the wisest among us is vulnerable to overprecision. Admitting our vulnerability to error is rarely easy. Even when we are willing to acknowledge, in the abstract, that our beliefs and opinions could be wrong, it can be difficult to calibrate our confidence in our current beliefs, let alone identify any particular belief that we currently hold as being incorrect.

This is a problem that Kathryn Schulz wrote about in her wonderful book *Being Wrong*. When she told people what her book would be about, they replied: "You should write about me! I'm wrong all the time."

"That's interesting," Schulz would respond. "What are you wrong about right now?" They could only stare blankly in response. They had no idea. Clearly, they knew that they had been wrong in the past. But were their current beliefs wrong? This is a devilishly difficult question. After all, we believe the things we believe because we believe them to be true. If we knew they were false, we wouldn't believe them.

What happens when we find out that one of our beliefs is false? We stop believing it. In that moment, it's natural to look back and think, "Silly me—I used to believe that wrong thing. I know better now." In this way, realizing you were wrong can feel like being right, allowing you to savor the sweet sanctimony of rectitude both when you were right and when you were wrong. And so it is that you can get used to feeling like you are right about everything all the time.

In *The Narcissism Epidemic*, the psychologists Jean Twenge and Keith Campbell wonder whether overconfidence may be getting worse. They worry that rather than living in an age of enlightenment, we're living instead in an age of entitlement. They trace a history in which mental health professionals encouraged parents to help develop their children's self-esteem with messages of positive encouragement. The well-intentioned proponents of self-esteem stressed its many potential benefits, including greater confidence, greater persistence, greater risk tolerance, and greater self-reliance. They were less inclined to consider the potential for overconfidence, conflict, arrogance, and entitlement that is evident in our leaders, celebrities, and politicians. There are indeed benefits of higher self-esteem, but, like confidence, more is not always better. Twenge, for instance, worries about young people entering the workforce with unrealistic expectations: "They don't set the right goals for themselves, because they are overconfident—and that's when it blows up in their face." Setting the right goals is facilitated by well-calibrated and honest self-assessment.

BEING LESS WRONG

There are two ways to defuse overprecision in the accuracy of your beliefs. The first is to bring your confidence down. For instance, you probably ought to have been less confident in your estimate of the number of new saints canonized by John Paul II. The second is to bring your accuracy up. Gathering more information can often help inform your answers to trivia questions, your estimates of others' abilities, or your forecasts of the future. Ask yourself what information would help you form more accurate judgments, and then search out that information.

Considering the opposite is useful for both reducing your confidence and raising your accuracy. In my research, I find that when people force themselves to explicitly consider and estimate the probability that they might be wrong, it brings down the confidence they attach to being right and simultaneously brings their beliefs closer to the truth. If I just ask, "How likely is it that you are right?" my research volunteers express more overconfidence than if I ask them to specify both the probability that they are right and the probability that they are wrong. Explicitly considering how you might be wrong and exploring its likelihood can help.

As of this writing, Jeff Bezos qualifies as the wealthiest person in the world. Wealth is a poor measure of wisdom, but it is hard to deny that Bezos has been a shrewd leader. Amazon's fourteen leadership principles articulate the key components of his management philosophy. One of them is: "Good managers are right a lot." Bezos explained it this way: "People who are right a lot change their minds a lot." Being right requires you to change your mind, he elaborated, because the world is complicated enough that we constantly have to adjust to its realities. This requires considering the opposite: "People who are right a lot seek to disconfirm their most profoundly held convictions, which is very unnatural for humans."

You can help those around you calibrate their confidence by inviting them to disconfirm their beliefs and assumptions. There are many ways to do it. Another one of Amazon's leadership principles states, "Have backbone; disagree and commit: Leaders are obligated to respectfully challenge decisions when they disagree, even when doing so is uncomfortable or exhausting." It can be uncomfortable when disagreement manifests itself as conflict. Sometimes, disagreement may put colleagues at odds with one another. However, the differing beliefs that underlie disagreement also often create opportunities for each side to benefit.

One obvious benefit is the chance to learn from the other side. Most of us feel the natural inclination to defend ourselves and our beliefs against those who disagree. However, considering the possibility that you could be wrong will enhance your ability to listen to those who disagree with you, gaining from them information that you lack, and then considering how you should modify your beliefs to account for that information. In so doing, your beliefs are likely to become more accurate, and you may find that you no longer disagree. If disagreement persists, it opens the opportunity for you to bet on what you believe.

When they invited Harold Camping's faithful followers to bet on their belief in the apocalypse, my economist colleagues were challenging them to quantify how certain they were in their beliefs. The economists professed the belief that they would be around after the anticipated apocalypse to pay up. The presence of other people ready to bet on an outcome you think is unlikely ought to be instructive. What do they know that you don't? After having considered their perspective and the evidence supporting it, do you want to modify your own beliefs?

Constructive disagreement has an important, even sacred place in academic institutions. It is part of one of the most important personnel decisions an academic institution makes: the decision to grant a professor tenure. Tenure gives faculty job security; it creates some perverse incentives and has real problems, but universities seem unlikely to abolish it. Given this, we try to take the decision seriously. Here at the Haas School of Business at UC Berkeley, every tenure case must come before the faculty for consideration. At that meeting, the discussion begins with two people familiar with the candidate's work. One speaks in favor, presenting all the reasons why the person deserves tenure. The second speaks against the case, questioning its merits and highlighting its weaknesses.

Getting tenure is a big deal, but all sorts of sinners have been granted tenure. A higher hurdle is being elevated to sainthood. The Catholic church makes a momentous decision when it canonizes a new saint. In the interests of avoiding errors, Pope Sixtus V established the role of the Advocatus Diaboli, the devil's advocate, in 1587. The devil's advocate had the job of speaking against candidates for sainthood: "To prevent any rash decisions. . . . It is his duty to suggest natural explanations for alleged miracles, and even to bring forward human and selfish motives for deeds that have been accounted heroic virtues." In the next 396 years, the Catholic church canonized 330 new saints, less than one each year, on average.

In 1983, Pope John Paul II reduced the power of the devil's advocate. His pontificate saw the canonization of 483 new saints, more than one each month. The impressive pace of canonizations has continued, unimpeded by the skepticism of the devil's advocate. This has included the speedy (if controversial) canonization of

John Paul II himself, now the patron saint of families. Recently, Pope Francis was going for a saintly record when he canonized 813 people in a single day. I wouldn't want to question the holiness of any of them, but I would just note that having an effective devil's advocate does seem to have been associated with a more deliberate pace of canonization.

You can learn from the devil and use constructive disagreement to improve the quality of the decisions you make by ensuring there is a devil's advocate who is ready to speak against important decisions before you make them. You may have some people in your organization who voluntarily play the role of devil's advocate. They are your critics, rivals, and complainers. They may not make you feel better about yourself, but these malcontents offer a gift of inestimable value if they help you consider the opposite. If listening to their criticisms can help you shore up your weaknesses before they are exposed by a newspaper or a court of law, then the damage they may inflict on your self-esteem will have been well worth it.

QUESTIONS, NOT ANSWERS

Those who disagree with us are useful in a direct and practical way: they provide a diversity of viewpoints. Often disagreement is taken as a negative within an organization because it is evidence of conflicting views, not all of which can be right. But it is better for some to be right than everyone agree and be wrong. It would be nice to have everyone agree on the right course of action all the time, but if you can't have that, at least you can have some of the people who are closer to being right. The diversity of viewpoints then allows you to capitalize on the wisdom of the crowd. Research attests to the enormous value of being able to average across diverse viewpoints to help get closer to the truth.

Consider two friends coming out of a Harold Camping sermon on May 8, 2011. The friends happen to wander over to a table where an earnest doctoral student from Berkeley offers them a choice. They can have $5 immediately or $500 in four weeks, on June 5. One, the true believer, insists he will not be around to collect the $500, so he would prefer the $5 now. The second friend, whom the first had dragged along to the meeting, protests: "We should definitely go for the five hundred dollars! I think there is only a one percent chance of a May twenty-first apocalypse."

"I'm convinced of the prophecy," says the true believer. "Ninety-nine percent sure." The two of them could argue a long time, the believer reiterating the logic of Camping's prophecy. The skeptic might point out the low accuracy of earlier apocalyptic prophesies, including Harold Camping's own, or even the dubious evidence for an almighty bent on destroying His creation.

Fortunately, there is a more constructive alternative to fighting over a forecast: average the discrepant opinions. The wisdom of this small crowd of two people advises that they should average the differing estimates. The friends disagree about the probability of a May 21 apocalypse. Averaging their probability estimates yields a 50 percent probability. A 50 percent chance at $500 in four weeks is worth more than $5 for sure, and so they would likely choose to wait for the larger payout.

It is possible both are wrong and that the true probability is below either forecast. In that case, the average will be as far off as each forecast was, on average. But if the truth is between the two estimates, as it often is, the average will be more accurate than either of the individual forecasts. The evidence shows that averaging opinions usually winds up being more accurate than relying on the most knowledgeable person or forcing everyone to discuss until they arrive at consensus around a single number. In this way, disagreement with others can directly help generate more accurate judgments.

Respectful disagreement is so useful that some successful organizations have built it into their DNA. Inviting people to consider why a decision could be wrong might not make life easy for managers, but doing so is essential to helping organizations make better decisions. Amazon's leadership principles enshrine an obligation to dissent. This holds even when dissent exposes problems, flaws, or errors. Another principle holds that leaders should be "vocally self-critical. Leaders come forward with problems or information, even when doing so is awkward or embarrassing." Organizations that want to empower people to behave in this way have to back it up by rewarding those who have the courage to step forward and dissent.

Similarly, one of the defining principles of my own institution, the Haas School of Business, is "Question the status quo." We aspire to educate the business leaders of tomorrow, and we figure that innovative leadership is more likely to break with the status quo than bolster it. Plus, questioning conventional wisdom is compatible with the rebellious spirit of Berkeley, California, where we are located. The place has a well-earned reputation for deviance and protest.

Encouraging people to question the way things are done is useful because organizational hierarchies so often reward compliance and obedience. Organizations, like people, often wind up affirming established ways of doing things and channeling support for preferred conclusions. In addition to the psychological processes that occur at the individual level, top managers are often insulated from criticism by the people who depend on them. Rich Lyons, a former dean of the Haas School, put it this way: "The higher people get in organizations, often the harder it is to accept honest feedback. It's also true that increasingly feedback doesn't get to them due to people strategically censoring what they say. . . . Honest, constructive feedback is so valuable that there's only one way to respond: 'thank you.'"

The former Minnesota senator Al Franken proudly tells the story of a congressional hearing at which he was skewering a witness by poking holes in his testimony. As Franken was going in for the kill, a staffer slid him a note that read simply, "You're being an asshole." After the hearing, Franken hastened back to his office and called an all-staff meeting, at which he recounted what had just happened. "Hannah did me an enormous favor," he told his staff. "I don't want anyone in this office ever to be afraid of calling me an asshole. Okay, meeting over." Few leaders have the courage to confront their errors so directly. It was courage that Franken again displayed when he resigned from the Senate following accusations of inappropriate behavior by several women. And it also seems appropriate to note that his resignation might have been avoided if, earlier, he had considered more critical interpretations of his questionable behavior.

The role of critic is a sacred one. You can save yourself heartache and embarrassment if you serve as your own critic by considering the opposite of your pet theories and asking yourself why you might be wrong. Doing so could save you from believing erroneously in the impending apocalypse, jumping into a crevasse, or being an asshole. Questioning the status quo and being willing to criticize comfortable assumptions can also help your organization avoid errors and identify opportunities. Having a devil's advocate can be very useful. But in the interests of full disclosure, I should note that the job's official title was not actually the "Devil's Advocate." The post's official name? That person was the Promotor Fidei, the "Promoter of the Faith"—a sacred trust indeed.

CHAPTER 3

What Is Possible?

Confident people aren't the only ones who change the world. Many know that the Wright brothers took the world's first heavier-than-air powered flight over the dunes of Kitty Hawk, North Carolina, in 1903, but few know the story of frustration and despair that preceded that flight. Two years earlier, in 1901, the Wrights went to Kitty Hawk and set up camp among the dunes with the intention to build and fly a glider. The entire experience was more or less miserable from start to finish. The list of annoyances and frustrations included the stifling heat and ferocious mosquitoes that "seemed giant in size and still they passed through the finest mesh." More life-threatening dangers came when they tried flying their glider, which had a tendency to nose-dive into the ground. It nearly killed Orville. They couldn't get its balance right, and its wings just failed to generate as much lift as they should have. "When we left Kitty Hawk, at the end of 1901, we doubted that we would ever resume our experiments," Wilbur reported. "We considered our experiments a failure." Wilbur told his brother that "man won't be flying for a thousand years."

Fortunately for frequent fliers everywhere, the Wright brothers were persuaded to try again. In 1903, they went back to Kitty Hawk. On December 17 of that year, Orville took to the air in a contraption that weighed as much as a piano and was powered by a crude twelve-horsepower engine. He managed to fly just over one hundred feet and spent only three and a half seconds aloft. That flight proved that it was possible for heavier-than-air craft to fly. Their success came despite Wilbur's earlier pessimism. "Ever since," he noted ruefully, "I have distrusted myself and avoided all predictions."

While humility in the face of the challenges of prediction is warranted, none of us has the luxury of avoiding all predictions. Every decision we make depends, in part, on a prediction. Deciding to climb into an airplane depends on whether I believe I will arrive safely at my destination. Deciding where to invest my money depends on which investments I think will increase in value the most. Deciding what to order for dinner depends on which dish I expect to enjoy the most. Today I chose to bike to my office rather than drive because I expected the weather to be pleasant and expected it to be easier to find a parking space for my bike than for a car. Each of these decisions depends on a forecast of its consequences. Chapter 2 encouraged you to sharpen your forecast by asking why it might be wrong. This chapter invites you to think about your forecast as a probability distribution.

FORECASTING

Because it is so essential for good decisions, every organization engages in some form of forecasting. The Wright brothers, for their part, attempted to anticipate how each glider they built would fly and how much lift its wings would generate. Most companies have to plan productive capacity in order to satisfy customer demand. The German multinational corporation BASF has to do this a lot. It is the largest chemical producer in the world, with over $70 billion in annual revenues. Some years ago, BASF came to me to ask for help forecasting. They confessed to me that, too often, the demand for their products was different from what they expected. By the time they figured it out and responded, they had either built stockpiles of excess inventory or had frustrated customers who couldn't get their orders filled.

The way BASF forecasted product sales was the way most companies do it: they asked the product manager most familiar with each product to make a "best guess" of what sales would be in the coming quarter, and they based their production quantities on these point predictions. As it turns out, there are at least three problems with forecasting using point prediction.

First, the number is wrong. If you forecast that customers will buy 100,000 kilograms of ibuprofen pills next quarter, there is just about no chance that orders will total precisely 100,000. BASF cannot anticipate the precise quantity of next quarter's sales any more than the Census Bureau can forecast precisely, down to the person, what the population will be in ten years. It's silly to pretend you can forecast the future with certainty, when in fact you face a distribution of possible outcomes.

Second, a single best-guess point prediction neglects the full range of possibilities. Focusing on a best guess when you face a probability distribution is like averaging all the numbers on the roulette wheel and then betting all your money on 18. While 18 may be the number in the middle, it makes more sense to think about a distribution of possible outcomes. It is easy to see the sense in this approach for purely random events, like spins of the roulette wheel or the flip of a coin. The best prediction for a coin flip is 50 percent heads and 50 percent tails, not halfway between heads and tails. Just so, there is a whole range of possible outcomes for ibuprofen sales—a probability distribution. There is a chance that ibuprofen demand will be in the range from 90,000 to 110,000. But demand could also be much lower—say, below 30,000—or much higher: for instance, over 170,000 kilograms.

Third, focusing on a single point prediction exacerbates overprecision in judgment, for many of the same reasons that focusing on a single hypothesis inflates our confidence in its accuracy. We are already prone to being too sure of our forecasts. But asking people to focus on a single best guess makes it worse. In my research I often ask people to estimate something uncertain. For instance, sometimes I show my research volunteers a picture of someone, like the one below, and ask them to estimate how much the person in the picture weighs. If I ask them for a "best guess" estimate and follow that up by asking how confident they are that the right answer is within ten pounds of their best guess, they will tell me they are 60 percent or 70 percent confident. In reality, their best guesses are within ten pounds of the truth only about 30 percent of the time.

The superior alternative is asking about a probability distribution rather than a single point. In the case of weight guessing, that might look like this:

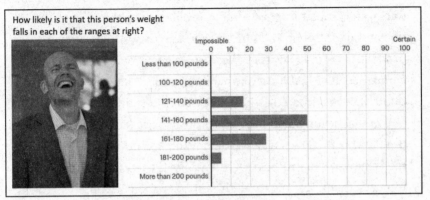

Histogram response scale

Asking people to complete a histogram like this forces them to broaden their thinking and consider the possibility that their best guess is wrong. When I ask the question this way, the one twenty-pound bin rated "most likely" to contain the right answer drops from 60 percent to 40 percent. In other words, when I ask them which twenty-pound bin is most likely, people tell me that, on average, they are 60 percent sure they picked the right one. But when I ask them to rate all the bins' probability of containing the right answer, no bin gets higher than 40 percent. Forty percent is still higher than it should be if hit rates average only 30 percent, but it's a whole lot closer to good calibration. Moreover, it produces a useful distribution that can help make decisions. For instance, if the question was about ibuprofen sales rather than body weight, knowing the distribution of possible sales figures would be quite helpful.

Even the most basic forecasting and production models assume that customer demand is drawn from a probability distribution. If you have a sense of the distribution, you can use it to figure in the relative costs of over- versus underproduction and use that to make your decision about production quantities. If ibuprofen has a long shelf life and you have plenty of space in your warehouse, then producing too much might not be a problem. On the other hand, if your product has no shelf life, like a daily newspaper, then excess production is pure waste. These sorts of computations can help companies like BASF use probability distributions to think about optimal production quantities given an uncertain future.

The classic formulation of this problem is called the news vendor problem. It imagines a newspaper vendor who must decide how many newspapers to buy each day, given the uncertainty in customer demand. In this case, any unsold papers become worthless tomorrow, when today's news gets old. The solution depends critically on what the distribution of demand looks like. A uniform distribution, in which all quantities (within some range) are equally likely, produces different results than does a normal distribution, with a single peak and few extreme outliers.

One difficulty generating a histogram forecast, however, is that some people are not used to thinking about their uncertainty in those terms. Because it is unfamiliar, they have difficulty filling out a probability distribution. If you are among those for whom this approach is unfamiliar, do not despair. There is hope for you.

THINKING ABOUT UNCERTAINTY

When we attempt to forecast an uncertain future, many of us simplify the subtle shadings of a probability scale into three categories:

- "It's going to happen," treated as 100 percent likely;
- "It's not going to happen," treated as 0 percent likely; and

- "Who knows?"—a broad middle range often described vaguely as a 50/50 chance.

When young people estimate the risk of contracting AIDS from sexual partners, their answers reveal this simplified perception of probability. In one study, researchers at Carnegie Mellon University asked college students to estimate the probability of their becoming infected with the HIV virus (which causes AIDS) following a single unprotected sexual encounter with an HIV-positive partner. About 15 percent of participants estimated the risk at 50 percent. My initial reaction to this result was astonishment. This is an important probability for people to know. AIDS has the potential to turn a roll in the hay with an attractive stranger into a slow and painful death.

Most people will, at some time, consider the possibility of sex with someone when they do not have protection such as a condom. Anyone in such a situation should consider, among other things: (1) "What is the probability my partner has HIV?"; and (2) "If my partner has HIV, what is the probability I'll get infected?" It is easy to underestimate the first probability, and most people assure themselves that if their partner had HIV, he or she would have said so. In fact, evidence suggests that as many as a quarter to half of those with HIV have not informed their sex partners.

Epidemiological data can help estimate the second probability, but the heat of the romantic moment might not be the best time to go do some background research. It is the rare teen who says, "Hold on a minute," when someone is trying to unzip his or her pants. "If you don't have a condom I need to go consult the medical literature for data on the risks of HIV transmission."

According to the US Centers for Disease Control and Prevention, the actual risk of infection from a single act of unprotected sex is below 1 in 1,000, or 0.1 percent. That's pretty far from 50 percent.

The same people who reported their risk of HIV infection were also asked about other probabilities, including the risk that they would fall ill with cancer at some point in their lifetimes. The actual lifetime risk is about 40 percent, but the percentage of respondents who estimated the risk as 50 percent was roughly the same as those estimating a 50 percent risk of HIV transmission—16 percent. These responses reveal the simplification of the probability scale into "yes," "no," and "maybe."

These responses reveal that the psychological weight accorded to a possible outcome is not the same as its objective probability. The relationship between the two is usefully illustrated in this subjective probability weighting function. In this graph, the x-axis shows true probability and the y-axis shows subjective psychologically weighted probability. The dotted line shows how a perfectly rational person would weight the probabilities. The solid curve illustrates the psychological reality:

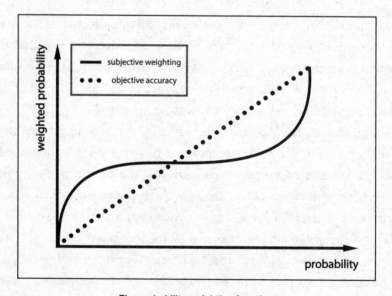

The probability weighting function

The subjective probability weighting function was originally published in a 1979 paper by Amos Tversky and Daniel Kahneman that has become one of the most cited and influential papers in all of social science. The figure above shows that when actual probability is in the wide "maybe" range, even large differences fail to register as psychologically distinct in their subjective weighting. The solid line is fairly flat in the middle of the range, where an awful lot of substantial changes in probability produce a "meh" response of indifference. But the distance between the dotted diagonal line in the middle and the solid line is greatest near the ends. At the low end, this means that small probabilities loom large, such as when people are beset by fears of terrorist attacks. At the high end, highly likely events are often neglected if their probability is less than 100 percent. Tobacco companies, for instance, exploited the lack of perfect scientific consensus around the risks of smoking to avoid regulation for years. Today, fossil fuel companies are making the most of what little scientific controversy remains around the human causes of global climate change to lobby against their taxation and regulation.

Among its many other important contributions, Tversky and Kahneman's theory helps explain the popularity of both insurance and gambling. The simultaneous success of these two industries would seem to represent a bit of a puzzle. People who buy insurance are behaving in a risk-averse way by choosing to pay a sure premium in order to avoid a possible loss. When those same people go gambling, they pay to play a risk-seeking game in which they pay a sure cost for the chance of a possible win. So is the person who buys travel insurance on her trip to Las Vegas risk seeking or risk averse?

Buying insurance and gambling are both negative expected-value bets. That is, you can expect to pay more in insurance premiums than you will collect from the insurance company. If that weren't the case, then the insurance company would have trouble staying in business. You can also expect to pay more to gamble than you will win. If that weren't the case, then casinos and lotteries would have trouble staying in business. The reason why these bets have a negative expected value for the consumer but work out just fine for insurance companies and casinos is that the actual probability of their having to pay out is so low. But regardless of whether they are generally risk seeking or risk averse, people who overestimate these small probabilities will be more interested both in buying insurance and in gambling than they should be.

When consumers make the mistake of lumping a very low probability of winning the lottery in with the broad middle range of vague uncertainty, they will overestimate their chances of winning. For instance, when I asked Carnegie Mellon undergraduates to estimate their chances of winning over $10 million in the lottery, the average probability they told me was 14 percent. Call me a killjoy, but that is almost certainly an overestimate of the probability of winning, given that the chance of winning with a ticket they could have purchased in the Pennsylvania lottery was closer to 0.0000008 percent.

Corporate leaders face innumerable important decisions that depend on forecasts of the future. For instance, the decision to sell a company depends crucially on whether the acquirer is offering more than the company would earn on its own. Steve Chen, one of the cofounders of YouTube, faced that decision when Google offered to buy his little startup.

YouTube began offering videos online in February 2005 and grew rapidly. By July 2006, YouTube was delivering one hundred million videos per day. Would the company's spectacular growth continue? YouTube was making about $15 million a month from advertising but was not yet profitable. Whether its stream of ad revenue would someday be sufficient to exceed the company's costs of delivering online videos depended crucially on its trajectory for growth. Steve

Chen was skeptical: "There's just not that many videos I want to watch," he groused memorably. Chen and his partners decided to sell YouTube to Google for $1.65 billion. Since then, YouTube has grown spectacularly. By 2019, YouTube was delivering billions of videos each day. Could Steve Chen have made a better decision about YouTube if he had thought probabilistically about its prospects for continued growth? Probably.

GOOD JUDGMENT AND BETTER FORECASTING

My approach to thinking probabilistically has been profoundly influenced by my work with Phil Tetlock, Barbara Mellers, and a big team of collaborators on what we modestly called the "Good Judgment Project." GJP was part of a four-year forecasting tournament sponsored by the Intelligence Advanced Research Projects Activity (IARPA), which serves as the research arm of the US federal government's intelligence community. IARPA was keenly aware of the challenges associated with forecasting geopolitical events like the rise of China on the world stage and the future of the European Union. Will the tensions between China and the Philippines in the South China Sea lead to military conflict? Will any more member countries exit the European Union?

Getting even a little better at predicting events like these would offer enormous potential benefits to the US intelligence community and the United States' ability to plan its foreign policy. And so, in an attempt to make better probabilistic forecasts of consequential geopolitical events, IARPA sponsored a forecasting tournament. GJP was one of five teams competing to make the most accurate forecasts. Our team was also the most academic of the bunch. Head-in-the-clouds professors are not renowned for their ability to manage large projects, and I started out quite pessimistic about our chances against the other four teams, especially since my institution was the prime contractor, and that meant that the rest of the team was relying on me to keep the administrative trains running on time.

There was an enormous amount of work to do recruiting, training, and motivating forecasters. Our team was determined to employ the wisdom of the crowd. Even if we could get the top scholars of Chinese and European politics to participate, we were skeptical, based on existing research, that they would provide more accurate forecasts than well-informed and motivated laypeople. One of the big problems with experts, as Tetlock has documented, is that they so often come to new forecasting problems with preformed views and an ideological orientation. Their strongly held philosophy helps organize their thinking and provides them with a sense of confidence; unfortunately, that does not translate into greater accuracy.

We knew that more important than getting the worlds' experts on our team was getting our forecasters to think probabilistically. The probability training that Mellers designed led our forecasters through the basics of probability and tested them on the calibration of their subjective probabilities. It taught them to recognize and calibrate uncertainties, both the uncertainty created by their own lack of knowledge on some topic and the inherent uncertainty in predicting complex social phenomena like political uprisings and military conflicts. And this training turned out to be successful for improving the accuracy and calibration of the probabilities the experts reported for the events we asked them to predict. It was also useful in addressing the objections of those who are skeptical of using probabilities in the first place.

When considering a question like "What is the probability that Bashar al-Assad will vacate the office of president of Syria in the next year?" some people deny the premise. "It's going to happen or it's not," they protest. "Probabilities aren't useful." In their defense, looking back at history we cannot see probabilities, only what happened or didn't.

On the other hand, most people are comfortable thinking about the probabilities associated with the flip of a coin or the roll of dice. It's easy to flip a coin lots of times and observe a distribution in outcomes and the probabilities associated with different outcomes. But it is difficult to draw a large sample of Syrian presidents and measure the rate at which they leave office during civil wars. However, this does not mean that one cannot think of unique historical events in probabilistic terms. Indeed, it is possible to offer the same objection to a single coin flip. There is only one actual outcome for a given coin flip—why muddy the clarity of a given prediction by attaching a probability?

In 1825, the French scholar Pierre-Simon de Laplace noted that as we gain in knowledge, our uncertainties about the world shrink. Laplace argued that, if only we knew enough, we would be able to wring the uncertainty out of life entirely. He imagined a being so omniscient that it knew the location and trajectory of every particle in the universe. Such a being could anticipate even the outcome of the coin flip because it could predict exactly how it would flip and how it would land.

However, it is doubtful whether any intelligence, either natural or artificial, could possibly predict everything in the world with such accuracy. On a grand scale, our finite universe has trouble accommodating the colossal computational demands such an intelligence would require. And on a small scale, subatomic particles do not behave in deterministically predictable ways. There, too, the best we can do is to specify the associated probabilities. Even if you are Laplace's omniscient demon, a probability distribution is the most we can hope for when forecasting the future of coin flips, ibuprofen sales, civil wars, and airplane flights.

PROBABILITY THEORY

Antoine Gombaud was a French gambler who, in 1654, earned himself a place in history by asking a good question. It was a question that spawned the field of probability theory. Gombaud had been playing a game in which he bet on rolling a pair of sixes at least once in twenty-four rolls of a pair of six-sided dice. What determined whether a given throw of the dice would come up boxcars? In 1654, many would have answered that question the way they answered the questions about the great uncertainties of life: "How good will my harvest be? How long will I live? God will decide."

After losing money on the game, Gombaud was not content with the explanation that divine providence had interceded to redistribute his money to his gambling partners. So Gombaud asked his friend Blaise Pascal why. Pascal was a gifted mathematician who, in working out an answer to Gombaud's question, laid the foundation for probability theory. Pascal calculated that the probability of Gombaud's getting his pair of sixes was only 49.14 percent. So when Gombaud was betting even odds on an event that occurred less than 50 percent of the time, he was bound to lose money in the long run. If people have trouble distinguishing a 0.0000008 percent chance from a 14 percent chance of winning the lottery, how can we expect them to tell the difference between a 49 percent bet and a 51 percent bet? The answer is that we shouldn't, at least not using an untrained intuitive sense of probability.

But all of us can cultivate our skill at probabilistic thinking. Annie

Duke, a professional poker player, says that the difference between poker-playing heavyweights and amateurs is that the heavyweights know the difference between a 60/40 bet and a 40/60 bet. Poker pros are not born with a finely tuned sense of probability, but they work hard to train themselves to get a better sense of it. How do they do it? They get lots of practice making clear predictions (in the form of poker bets) and then getting prompt, unambiguous feedback on whether they were right. And although poker players are generally comfortable with the notion that it is useful to calculate probabilities of certain cards being dealt from the deck, many are reluctant to live with uncertainty in other domains. One interesting instance comes from personnel selection.

After college, I worked for a few years at an industrial supply company, where I was puzzled by how the firm selected employees. The CEO liked to interview rookies. Company lore told of one such interview in which he kicked off his shoes, put his feet up on the table, and groaned, "You don't want to work here. It's so boring!" His approach could be called "stress interviewing." The idea is that the candidate's "true self" comes out in that stressful and unscripted situation. Mostly, however, it perplexed job candidates and gave the CEO a false sense of insight.

I quit that job and went back to graduate school determined to study the uses and abuses of the employment interview. I was sure that corporations could benefit from better understanding how to use interviews. I was right about that, but I found out very quickly that it was a terrible research topic. The problem is that interviews have been studied to death and the answers are already in: interviews, as they are commonly used, are rotten at predicting future job performance. Scholars have understood this basic fact for some time. The shocking part is how little influence this research insight has had in the corporate world. Why?

Part of the answer is that there is no perfect selection method. Better assessment methods can improve the correlation between interviewees' scores and actual job performance a bit, but that takes the correlation between interviews and subsequent work performance from 0.38 to 0.53. That represents an improvement, but it is far from perfect. In truth, no selection method can precisely forecast how a new hire will perform on the job. There will always be both false positives (people you hire who turn out to be bad at the job) and false negatives (people you reject who would have been successful). Going from one imperfect tool to another is hardly satisfying.

Too often we seek certainty when it is not possible. We act as if improving our hitting percentage from 38 percent to 53 percent doesn't matter much. It's still in the gray area of "maybe" and cannot provide guarantees. The truth is that a change of that size can make a colossal difference. In baseball, one measure of a player's performance is the batting average. It measures how often players get a hit, as a percentage of their times at bat. In the autumn of 2019, the player with the best batting average in Major League Baseball was Tim Anderson. His average was .333, meaning he successfully got a hit 33.3 percent of the time. The worst batting average in the league was .207. The difference between these percentages is a superstar and a dud. Analyses suggest that an increase in batting average from .200 to .300 will earn a player about $5 million per year, all else being equal. Small probabilities in the middle of the range can make an enormous difference.

CALIBRATING YOUR CONFIDENCE

On May 25, 2017, the probability gods smiled on a young man named Ryan Belz when he played Plinko. Plinko is a part of the game show

The Price Is Right in which contestants drop a plastic game chip into a grid full of offset pegs. At the bottom are nine bins, labeled with numbers ranging from $0 to $10,000, indicating how much the contestant will win. As the chip descends, it bumps over the pegs, bouncing either to the left or to the right at each peg. Ryan Belz set a Plinko record when he won $31,500. He then did what winning contestants are supposed to do on the show, and indulged in an ecstatic display of joy so ostentatious that he appeared to be having some sort of breakdown.

Plinko is a version of the Quincunx, a device useful for generating random distributions. The Quincunx, also known as the Galton Board, is a device invented by Sir Francis Galton to demonstrate the normal distribution generated by chance. Here is what it looks like:

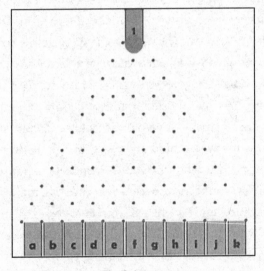

The Quincunx

The ball, when released from the slot on top, bounces over a series of pegs and lands in one of the bins at the bottom. The lesson I take away from the Plinko game is that thinking about probability distributions can be more exciting than most people assume. I have run something like twenty experiments in which I show people the Quincunx and ask them to predict which bin the ball will land in. And although they rarely display the sort of ecstasy that Ryan Belz showed when he won, my research volunteers do behave in some pretty interesting ways.

Many look at the mechanism and, realizing that chance determines where the ball lands, tell me they think all bins are equally likely. That's a bit like saying because you don't know whether you'll get AIDS, the chance is 50/50. Just because chance is involved, that does not mean all outcomes are equally likely. For the ball to land in bin A it has to bounce to the left over each of ten pegs. That's as likely as ten coins all coming up heads. That probability is 0.5^{10}, or less than a tenth of one percent—roughly one out of every one thousand tries.

Sometimes you need a precise estimate of something uncertain. In 1999, I needed to know how many people were going to come to my wedding in Chicago. My college sweetheart, Sarah, and I were trying to figure out how many people we could invite. Our venue could accommodate 125, but our list of friends and family members was far larger. If we knew which ones would accept our invitations, we could figure out how many we could invite without going over our limit.

Of course, each invitation would include a response card. But those responses would come back weeks after we mailed the invitations. If we waited until we heard from everyone and only then invited more, we would be letting all those additional invitees know they were not on the "A-list" and leaving them less time to make their travel arrangements. This was a particular concern because we wanted to invite many friends and family members scattered all over the world. What we wanted to do was just send out one wave of invitations, but that depended on a risky bet predicting who would accept and who would decline.

Our solution? We went through every name on the list and esti-mated the probability that each person would come. We based these estimates on what we knew about our friends. Kelly had just moved to London to start a stressful new job; she got a 40 percent chance. Max had moved to Boston, but he would probably be glad for a reason to visit Chicago; 80 percent chance. His wife, Marla? Seventy-five percent chance. If Max and Marla came, that increased the chance that Keith and Beth would come; they each got 65 percent. Lane and his wife, Valerie? I had stood at Lane's side at his wedding in Minnesota in Feb-ruary the year prior; 94 percent chance the two of them would come.

After adding up the estimated probability for each of the 223 people on our list, we wound up with an expected attendance of 127.7. All 223 people got invitations. How many came? 126. Sarah and I have been happily married ever since, and most of the time we even agree when computing expected values.

Thinking in expected values can be useful in all sorts of other ar-eas of life. Consider, for example, when you will complete a major project that you are working on right now. It could be the length of time it will take to finish an important report, finish a new build-ing, or complete a new software product, or maybe the length of time until you get a major promotion. Really take a moment to identify a particular project. You may have already forecast when you will be done, and maybe you have told your forecast to other people, such as your boss or a customer. Now consider the possibil-ity that it will take twice as long as you expect. How likely is that? It is also possible it will take half as long as you expect. If you estimate the probability of each of these possible completion times, you have just completed a histogram distribution. This simple process has created a histogram with four bins to which you can assign proba-bilities, as illustrated in the following table. *The very act of thinking through these possibilities will help you make a more accurate forecast.*

If, on January 1, you guessed that your project would probably be done in six months, then the procedure above would produce this binning arrangement:

Bin	Probability
Before April 1	
April 1 to June 30	
July 1 to December 31	
After December 31	

A histogram for forecasting the completion of a hypothetical major project.

However, there are probably more useful binning arrangements to consider than the one I threw out. Take some time and think through the possibilities. Maybe it makes more sense to have the bins represent months, or perhaps weeks. If the range of possibilities is narrow, then there may be few bins. Or maybe you want to consider as many as twenty or thirty bins. Once you have your bins, go through and specify the probabilities on each one. At first, don't worry if the probabilities don't sum exactly to 100 percent, just try to get them proportionately right. After you have that, you can go back and correct them so they sum to 100 percent. You may want to share your histogram distribution with others if it will help calibrate their expectations of you, providing them with more accurate and useful information. Naturally, you may want to share selectively. For instance, to an audience expecting a point prediction, you may want to share a later time point by which you are more than 90 percent confident you will be able to deliver.

But even more important than that is to share your forecast with your future self so that you can follow up and learn from it. Save your forecast in a place where you will be able to find it later. Then plan to hold yourself accountable for your forecast. Put a note on your calendar to review its accuracy down the line. Maybe you want to do that at the time of the first milestone, or maybe at the time of your best-guess forecast.

When my friend and colleague Julia Minson recently asked me to read and comment on a paper of hers, I told her that I would love to help but was unsure when I would be able to make the time. I could make a point prediction of a single date, but there were so many uncertainties about how long it would take that pretending to know with certainty was foolhardy. Instead, I gave her the following probability distribution:

Bin	Bin Probability	End Date	Cumulative Probability
1 day	0%	Within 1 day	0%
2–7 days	15%	Within 1 week	15%
8–14 days	25%	Within 2 weeks	40%
15–21 days	30%	Within 3 weeks	70%
22–28 days	20%	Within 4 weeks	90%
28–35 days	8%	Within 5 weeks	98%
Later	2%	Later	100%

A histogram for my forecast of when I would read my colleague's paper. The bin probability specifies the probability the outcome will land in that bin. The cumulative probability indicates the probability that it will happen before the end date.

By liberating myself from the false certainty of the point prediction, I enabled a more honest elaboration of the possibilities
and became better able to communicate it to others, including my
friend. That same information illustrated as a cumulative probability distribution looks like this:

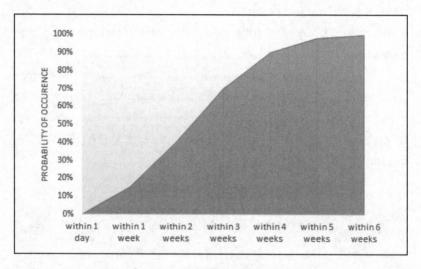

Cumulative probability distribution

Thinking about uncertainty in terms of probability distributions can help you become better calibrated in your confidence. It
demands that you think about the full range of possibilities and
their likelihoods. And so, it places your confidence in the probability distribution, as opposed to a far more fallible best guess. If you
had neglected to consider the chance that your invention would
sell millions per year, pausing to reflect on that *possibility* would
be worthwhile. Thinking about the future in terms of a probability distribution may not come naturally at first, but the effort pays

off. When you grow more comfortable thinking this way, you can more clearly see the potential before you, improve your forecasts, and make better decisions. This provides a stronger foundation for well-founded expectations, whether you are trying to fly a plane, get your business off the ground, or play Plinko.

CHAPTER 4

How Bad Could It Be?

When I was finishing my PhD, I had to wonder whether the five years of hard work for pauper's wages were worth it. Was I employable? "You'll get a job," my mentor and doctoral advisor, Max Bazerman, assured me.

"What if I don't?" I pressed anxiously.

Max's response was to offer me an insurance policy. "Listen," he said, "if you don't get a job, I promise to pay you, from my own pocket, next year's prevailing starting salary for assistant professors: $90,000." But this insurance would come at a price. I would have to pay Max $5,000. Was it a good deal?

Let's assume for the moment that Max had the money and that

I wouldn't feel bad taking it from him. Assume further that taking Max up on his offer would not affect my subsequent employability. That is, my salary and career prospects would be the same after a year on Max's gravy train as they would after a year of employment as an assistant professor.

If I bought Max's insurance, I could count on $90,000 minus the $5,000 insurance premium, so $85,000. On the other hand, if I declined Max's insurance policy and didn't get a job, I'd be out of luck: $0. If, however, I did get a job, I'd get to keep the full $90,000. So how much was Max's insurance policy worth? That depended on the probability that I would get a job. If I stood only a 50 percent chance of getting a job, then multiplying the $90,000 salary by 50 percent yielded an expected value of $45,000. The $85,000 I could get with Max's insurance would be much better than that.

How bad would my chances have to get to make Max's insurance policy a good deal? To estimate the probability at which the cost of Max's insurance exceeded its value, I divided $5,000 by $90,000. That's 5.6 percent. If my chance of being unemployed was greater than 5.6 percent, I reasoned that I would be better off buying Max's insurance.

This is the logic of expected value. To assess the present value of an uncertain prospect (like an insurance policy), multiply its probability by its value. When I teach this lesson in class, I do not offer my students employment guarantees. Instead, I offer them a chance to bid on a coin flip: If they correctly anticipate how the flip will come out, I pay $20. Otherwise, they get nothing. One person in class gets to play. When I open up the bidding, it quickly goes to $10 and then stops. That makes perfect sense because a 50 percent chance at $20 has an expected value of $10.

Using the logic of expected value, the insurance policy Max offered was a good deal only if the probability of my getting a job that paid $90,000 was less than 94.4 percent. I thought about it seriously and decided to say no to his insurance policy. "See?" Max responded with satisfaction. "You also think you're going to get a job."

WISHFUL THINKING

In hindsight, I believe I was right to reject Max's insurance. But it is easy to make mistakes calculating expected value. One of the most common is to let desirability influence your assessment of probability. This can sometimes happen as a matter of wishful thinking: the fact that you want something to happen affects your estimate of its likelihood. Sports fans, for example, routinely overestimate the chances that their favorite team will win. Partisan political pollsters routinely overestimate their favored candidates' chances. And corporate leaders sometimes let wishful thinking bias their beliefs, as happened to Jerry Yang in 2008.

Jerry Yang's family had emigrated from Taiwan to California when Yang was ten years old. At the time, he knew only one word of English: *shoe*. It was not particularly useful. "We got made fun of a lot at first," Yang recalls. He quickly overcame this early handicap. Yang graduated first in his class in high school in San Jose while also playing on the tennis team and serving as student body president. He completed his bachelor's and master's degrees in electrical engineering at Stanford in four short years, while working part time.

In 1995, Yang was pursuing a PhD when he and his classmate David Filo grew frustrated that the massive amounts of information becoming available online lacked any useful organization. In response, they created "Jerry and David's Guide to the World Wide Web." Their service was so popular that Yang dropped out of the

PhD program to run the company that he and Filo created. Fortunately, they realized the company needed a shorter name, and
they dubbed it Yahoo! From the start, Yang was one of the company's most enthusiastic champions. In the words of Stanford president John Hennessey, an adviser to Yang, "He's everything from
technical visionary to chief strategist to corporate spokesman and
cheerleader to Washington lobbyist to the company's conscience."
Yang took the title "Chief Yahoo" and told employees, "All of you
know that I have always, and will always bleed purple" (Yahoo!'s
signature color).

It was Yang who decided to reject an offer from Microsoft to buy
Yahoo! for $44.6 billion in 2008. At the time, it was already clear to
many that Google spelled the end for Yahoo!'s internet search business. But Yang insisted, "Yahoo is positioned for accelerated financial growth. We have a powerful consumer brand, a huge global
audience, and a highly profitable operating model." In retrospect, it
seems possible that Yang's rosy assessment might have been biased
by wishful thinking. Yahoo!'s stock fell after it rejected Microsoft's
offer, and Yang was ousted as CEO by Yahoo!'s board later that year.
In 2016, Verizon bought Yahoo!'s core businesses for $4.83 billion,
roughly one-tenth of what Microsoft had offered eight years earlier.

Sometimes people intentionally overestimate the probability of
positive outcomes. This overestimation often reflects an attempt to
be optimistic. For a research paper entitled "Prescribed Optimism:
Is It Right to Be Wrong about the Future?" David Armor, Cade
Massey, and Aaron Sackett asked research volunteers if they prefer
to be accurate in their beliefs about the future or whether it is instead
better to be optimistic, even when optimism means exaggerating
the probability of positive outcomes. Optimism won in a landslide.
One reason is the faith that optimism increases the chances of positive outcomes. For example, volunteers recommended that a pa-

tient undergoing physical therapy should be confident about her ultimate prospects for recovery because it would make that recovery more likely.

The book *The Secret* takes this view to an extreme verging on the ridiculous. The author, Rhonda Byrne, advises readers to believe they already have the things they desire: "Your belief that you have it, that undying faith, is your greatest power. When you believe you are receiving, get ready, and watch the magic begin!" She tells the story of her mother and a house she wanted: "My mother decided to use *The Secret* to make that house hers. She sat down and wrote her name and the new address of the house over and over. She continued doing this until it felt as though it was her address. She then imagined placing all of her furniture in that new house. Within hours of doing these things, she received a phone call saying her offer had been accepted."

Before we dismiss Byrne's "secret" as delusional fantasy, it is worth appreciating the evidentiary basis on which these beliefs may be built. All around us, we see that confidence precedes success. Confident political candidates are more likely to win. Cancer patients who are most confident and optimistic about their survival chances actually live longer. Confident entrepreneurs are more likely to secure backing from investors. Confident athletes are more likely to prevail. In these instances, as in innumerable others, the belief that you will succeed is inextricably tied to success. It is a durable correlation that we observe again and again.

But correlation is not causation. Just because two things are associated with one another does not mean one causes the other. The world is full of correlations that are not causal. Spring's flowers reliably predict summer's heat, but they do not cause it. Young people have more acne than do old people, but acne is not a cause of youth. Wealthy companies find themselves as defendants in more lawsuits, but those suits are not a cause of their profitability. And just because confidence is correlated with success does not mean that confidence causes success. It is entirely possible, even likely, that there is a third variable that accounts for the relationship. In the case of confidence and success, the oft-neglected third variable is competence.

Of course, truly competent people will usually be more confident. They have good reason to be. If you know that you can win the game, leap the chasm, or fly the plane, then you may proceed with confidence. You can do it. You have nothing to fear. Someone observing you in that moment may be tempted to conclude that your confidence has led to your success. Your confidence is evident for all to see. Invisible are the many hours you have invested in training and practice. If you have never before flown a plane, then you ought to lack the confidence to take the controls. It is when you lack competence that your confidence will be shakiest.

That is not to say that confidence and competence always move together. Sometimes they do, and then the combination of competence and confidence implies well-calibrated excellence. In the words of the boxer Muhammad Ali: "It's not bragging if you can back it up." Competence without confidence can also lead to success, provided one has the gumption to step up and make the effort despite uncertainty. But confidence without competence puts you in the danger zone, on the high wire without a net. Confidence invites you to dare and to take risks that, without underlying skill, are unlikely to work out well. Con men will attempt to impersonate trained professionals, but their indomitable confidence does not make them expert pilots or surgeons. While the notorious con man Frank Abagnale was impersonating a doctor, his confidence nearly proved fatal to a baby who was handed to him for treatment.

Is it possible for our beliefs about the future to be both accurate and optimistic? Many people believe that it is. In a study I conducted with Elizabeth Tenney and Jennifer Logg, we replicated the results obtained by David Armor and his colleagues: more than 80 percent of our research volunteers told us they believe that it is possible to be both optimistic and accurate. When we asked why, they told us that optimism causes success.

We attempted to test their optimistic beliefs. We wanted to give optimism its best chance, so we asked people what sorts of tasks they thought would most benefit from optimism. They told us that optimism is important on tests that require effort, including math tests. So we asked a different group of volunteers, whom we called the "predictors," exactly how much they thought optimism would affect the performance of another group, the "test takers," on a ten-question math test. We showed them all ten questions on the test so they knew exactly what was on it. We then led about half of those in the test-taker group to be optimistic, telling them they should expect that they would get 70 percent of the questions right. We told the other half of participants to expect they would get only 30 percent of questions right.

We invited the predictors to bet on the outcome and told them we would pay them more if their predictions were accurate. The predictors bet that the group led to feel optimistic would outscore the pessimists. They were wrong. In fact, there was no significant difference between the scores of test takers with optimistic and pessimistic expectations. In our study, optimism about the potential benefits of optimism was unwarranted.

We worried that the math test might not have given optimists the best opportunity to shine, despite the fact that people had told us they expected optimism to matter there. So we did the study again using another task. Optimism did not turn out to affect performance on a trivia test either. Likewise, it did not affect performance in tasks requiring physical persistence, athletic effort, or mental vigilance. It did not even help people find Waldo in a Where's Waldo? challenge, but it did lead them to persist a little longer in looking for him. Volunteers in our studies were always eager to bet on the optimists. Yet none of the studies was able to document an effect of optimism on actual performance.

These results may come as a surprise to you, as they did to the predictors in our study. Maybe you feel skeptical, because you are thinking of all the times that optimism seemed to go along with better performance, and pessimism with poor performance. Again, the two are strongly correlated. But correlation does not mean that confidence causes better performance. Our studies were designed to understand the *causal* role of optimistic beliefs; that is, to answer the question, "How does optimism affect performance, separate from actual ability?" Answering this question requires experiments that manipulate optimism and observe its effect (or lack thereof).

What was crucial about my research with Tenney and Logg was that we randomly assigned some people to be optimistic and some people to be pessimistic. Life seldom provides the sort of well-controlled experimental evidence necessary to systematically test the effectiveness of optimism, as we did in our study. Consequently, common sense and daily experience are of limited value for assessing this relationship. Instead, we usually find ourselves in just one state: optimistic or pessimistic. Lacking the data we would need to accurately assess the effects of our optimistic expectations on performance, we are left to imagine how much worse things would have been if we had been less optimistic, without actually knowing how much of a difference it would have made. The evidence from our research suggests that it often makes little difference for performance; it certainly makes less difference than most of us think it does.

WHAT DO YOU HAVE TO FEAR?

This chapter explores the logic of expected value and the benefits of well-calibrated numbers to feed into those calculations. Thus far, I have dwelt on biases due to wishful thinking. But people are not always overly optimistic. The opposite of wishful thinking occurs when our fears exaggerate the subjective probability of some undesirable possibility. I, like many of my classmates in the PhD program, was terrified of being unemployed after graduation. That fear led me to obsess about what would happen, and to dwell on the humiliation of being ignored or neglected by institutions I so fervently wished would hire me. The bet Max offered invited me to put my money where my mouth was and forced me to think through my honest assessment of the probabilities.

Another example of exaggerated pessimism is stoked by terrorism. After the September 11 terrorist attacks, Americans estimated their chances of being injured or killed in a terrorist attack at 20 percent. Another poll found, shortly after 9/11, that fully 58 percent of Americans feared that they or their families would become victims of terrorism. These fears are outrageously exaggerated; even in 2001, the year of the attacks, less than 0.0001 percent of Americans could be counted as victims of terrorism. However, the inflated fear of terrorism persists, in part thanks to radical groups like ISIS that do what they can to publicize their appalling acts of violence. Even now, the number of people who fear for themselves and their families remains around 45 percent.

But the threat represented by ISIS was always far smaller than the danger posed by an overreaction to ISIS by the United States. Terrorists armed with knives, guns, trucks, bombs, or planes can inflict loss of life, but these tragedies do not come close to representing any sort of existential threat to the United States. Their

risks are minuscule compared with the consequences of our nation's actions. The American invasion of Iraq following the September 11 attacks, for example, has resulted in greater loss of life than
the original attacks, including the deaths of over four thousand
US military personnel and hundreds of thousands of Iraqis. Over
thirty thousand Americans have suffered grievous battle injuries
in Iraq, and the military operation has cost more than $2 trillion.

US president Franklin Roosevelt was thinking of another threat
when he warned the nation, "The only thing we have to fear is fear
itself—nameless, unreasoning, unjustified terror." But his admonition still holds today. Our fear of terrorism has driven us to exaggerate its risks. This fear has led us to overreact, with grave costs
to our nation and the world. This is not to belittle the potential
risks of terrorist attacks. They are real. But the probabilities of any
one person becoming a victim of terrorism are also minuscule, and
those probabilities ought to figure in to how we react to the risk.

Likewise, it would be terrible to be infected with the Ebola virus, but I do not spend much time worrying about it, because the
chance is so small. I worry more about cancer, heart disease, and
diabetes, since their probabilities are far higher. On average, something like 60 percent of men will develop heart disease late in life;
a healthy lifestyle can cut that risk by as much as half. Because of
the higher probabilities associated with these risks, investments in
doing something about them have a higher expected return.

When I was three years old, I asked my father to open the win-
dow so that the birdies could come in and sing to me. He refused:
"No, no. They're going to come in and poo-poo on you." He lived his
whole life beset by fears about what would get him in the end. We
had a defibrillator in the house, and the trunk of our car was so full
of disaster-preparedness equipment that we could not fit anything
else in it. Indeed, as my sister noted in her eulogy at his memorial

service, my father met his cancer diagnosis with a measure of relief. Finally, he knew what was going to get him. My father's penchant for pessimistic rumination rivaled that of people who make their living doing much more dangerous work than he did.

Firefighters, soldiers, and police officers have more reason to cultivate pessimism. Their very survival depends on well-calibrated confidence. They know the risk that overconfidence poses for their lives and livelihoods. So they scrupulously practice the safety procedures with the equipment that protects them. In their own attempt to resist complacency, those who do dangerous work like coal mining or flying airplanes tend to cultivate a pessimistic sense of what could go wrong, understanding that optimism can put them at risk. It is easy to imagine that people who do dangerous things like big-wave surfing or rock climbing must be overconfident thrill seekers. But those who succeed in these endeavors have a keen sense of their vulnerabilities and their limitations. They worry about overconfidence. In the words of the big-wave surfer Brett Lickle, "As soon as you think, *I've got this place wired. I'm the man!* you're about thirty minutes away from being pinned on the bottom for the beating of your life."

When is it wise for people to cultivate a sense of foreboding? When they face real risk. People who live in Northern California should do more to protect themselves from earthquakes than people in Illinois. When their lives are at stake, it makes sense for people to take risks seriously. Where should we land between underconfidence and overconfidence? The best advice is to make realistic estimates of the probability and the consequence of potential disasters. When I was on the academic job market, I spent a lot of time thinking about how things could go wrong. That motivated me to plan ahead and do what I could to reduce the chances of these risks. But I also chose to decline Max's insurance when he offered it, because I thought its price was too high relative to its expected value.

THE ENTREPRENEUR'S DILEMMA

My recommendation to hold rational and well-calibrated beliefs meets what might be its stiffest challenge from entrepreneurs. The San Francisco Bay Area in which I live is a hotbed of entrepreneurial activity, and many of my students at UC Berkeley have ideas for starting new businesses. Some seem to believe the advice offered in a 2014 article in *Entrepreneur* magazine: "If you want to be a successful entrepreneur, you have to bleed confidence." This admonition fits comfortably with the mountains of advice encouraging would-be entrepreneurs to bolster their confidence.

It is true that entrepreneurs are an exceedingly confident lot. One study of nearly three thousand entrepreneurs found that 81 percent of them rated their chances of success at least 7 out of 10, and fully one-third of them rated their chances at 10 out of 10. Some of this is attributable to self-selection: only those most confident about their prospects choose to found new businesses. But there may also be another reason why entrepreneurs want to display confidence about the future of their business. As the journalist James Surowiecki put it, "Successful entrepreneurship involves hucksterism, the ability to convince investors and employees that they should risk their money, their time, and their effort on you. Like a con artist, you're peddling optimism. . . . Of course the fundamental difference between entrepreneurs and con artists is that con artists ultimately know that the fantasies they're selling are lies."

Is delusion any better for you when it's self-delusion? There are good reasons to think it's likely to be worse. Fooling yourself about the chances that your startup will succeed poses real risks. If you have convinced yourself that your chances of success are 10 out of 10, then it might make sense to invest everything you can in giving your venture its best shot. In addition to toiling long hours at the expense of your family and your health, you should cash out your retirement plan, max out your credit cards, and take out a second mortgage on your house. Moreover, you should convince your friends and family members to do the same and loan you the money because it will prove such a lucrative investment.

This sort of optimism has got to qualify as overconfidence much of the time, given the high rates of entrepreneurial failure. Studies suggest that nearly 80 percent of new businesses are out of business within five years. Even so, the risks of entrepreneurship can still be worth it if the potential upside is big enough. In other words, life is so great if you turn out to be Jeff Bezos or Bill Gates that it's worth the high probability of failure. However, this claim is undermined by analyses that suggest, even taking all this into account, that the average entrepreneurial venture has a negative expected value. The probability of hitting it big is just so small. Most potential entrepreneurs would be better off keeping their steady jobs and investing their money in index funds.

This is not to say that I think there should be less entrepreneurship. On the contrary, the dynamism of American entrepreneurship contributes to the vibrancy and growth of our economy. My home state owes much of its prosperity to the courage of entrepreneurs through history, from gold to technology. Yet although it is great for our country and our economy that there are so many eager entrepreneurs, it does not follow that founding your own company is a good career move. To draw an analogy, starting a new company in the hopes that you might become wealthy is a bit like buying a lottery ticket. Lotteries, like entrepreneurship, can have positive economic side effects. In some places, revenues from state lottery programs fund schools or other worthy programs. But that does not mean I recommend to my students that they should buy lottery tickets because it's good for the elementary schools. Lottery tickets are still bad bets.

Imagine a set of one hundred potential entrepreneurs. Each one has to choose between keeping a steady job and entering a new market. Potential entrepreneurs should enter only when the expected value of entry is higher than the wages paid by their steady jobs. Let's say that only one will strike it rich and will earn ten times what the steady job would have paid. If potential entrants cannot tell which among them will be more likely to strike it rich, then ten should enter. One will earn the big prize and the other nine will rue their bad luck. These nine may feel sorry for their misfortune, but their decisions to enter were justified by their expected value.

This analysis changes if some of the potential entrepreneurs delude themselves into thinking that their chances of victory are higher. Suppose if instead of thinking they possess an equal chance to win the big prize, they all fool themselves into thinking that their chance to win the big prize is twice as good as the other entrants'. Then twice as many of these optimistic strivers will enter, and the expected value of entry will fall to half the value of keeping the steady job. So fooling yourself doesn't sound like such a great strategy. What should you do if you know that the other potential entrants are overconfident? You should probably stay out of the competition. Matching their level of delusion would be a mistake.

If there is natural variation in people's optimism regarding their entrepreneurial prospects, then those who are most optimistic will be those most likely to enter. They will enter at higher rates than the realists, and they will drive down the expected value of entry.

And just because the successful entrepreneur is one of the optimistic strivers, it does not follow that being more confident is a wise strategy for promoting your own success. Yes, your probability of striking it rich might go up, but the expected value will go down. It's a bit like buying lottery tickets: buying more lottery tickets does increase your chance to win the lottery, but each ticket costs you more than its expected value. The more lottery tickets you buy, the poorer you should expect to be.

REALISTIC GOALS

One instance in which I have often seen people's poorly calibrated confidence judgments get them into trouble is in the context of negotiation. I have taught negotiation classes to business students and working executives around the world, including Tony Robbins and his platinum partners. The single most important concept I teach in my negotiation classes is the BATNA: Best Alternative To a Negotiated Agreement. Your BATNA is what you get if you walk away from the negotiating table. Your BATNA defines how demanding you can be and when you should walk away. If you have a great alternative to this deal, you can hold out for a lot, knowing that if your negotiating counterparts don't give you what you want, you can walk away. If your BATNA is terrible, then you have much less leverage.

Understanding this concept is crucial for negotiation planning. Before you walk into the meeting room, you should have a sense of how good your BATNA is and therefore when you might choose not to make a deal. As a part of my classes on the topic, I ask my students to prepare for negotiation by writing down what they think their BATNA is and what that implies about an offer so bad it would make them walk away. What I see over and over is students planning a walk-away price based on wishful thinking. It is common, for instance, for students to insist that they will hold out for what they believe is fair or what they deserve, even when that is far better than their BATNA.

Graduating MBA students, for example, have a strong sense of what a fair salary is, given what their classmates are getting. I encourage them to make these arguments forcefully at the bargaining table, explaining why their skills are at least as valuable as those of classmates who are getting paid more. However, when deciding whether to accept a particular job offer, the decision should depend not so much on what they think they deserve but on what other job offers they have (or are likely to get). Having the confidence to hold out for a $160,000 starting salary is just stupid if there are no such offers coming along. Appropriately calibrating your confidence in negotiation depends on having a sense of what you're worth to the other side. What value do you offer to potential employers, and what sorts of salary offers can you expect? What does that mean for your BATNA?

I see a related error in the way organizations set goals and targets. Knowing that goals can focus attention, increase effort, and produce results, most companies set regular performance targets and provide rewards for their attainment. Insufficiently ambitious goals can depress performance, so managers instead err on the side of setting "stretch" goals. How far should they stretch? Well, if performance is correlated with the ambitiousness of the goal (the logic goes), then more ambitious goals are better. Taking this reasoning to its logical conclusion implies infinitely ambitious goals, with the obvious problem that unattainable goals undermine motivation. Workers who know they will earn a bonus only if they pick a thousand bushels of strawberries in a day or sell a hundred cars in a month are unlikely to be motivated by these goals. They are simply unattainable. Even Elon Musk avoids setting unattainable goals.

Unattainable goals undermine the motivation to actually achieve them, but they may motivate other, less desirable actions. For example, in an effort to address the growing problem of air pollution, the Chinese government set pollution-reduction targets and rewarded their attainment. Attainable goals led to measurable reductions in air pollution, with commensurate benefits for air quality and health. But in regions with more ambitious "stretch" goals for pollution reduction, official reports deviated from the objectively measured reality. In other words, local officials started lying about their pollution measurements. This highlights one of the ethical risks of overconfident ambition: it increases the temptation to engage in cheating and deception.

TAKING THE RIGHT RISKS

In 1963, the Nobel Prize–winning economist Paul Samuelson was at lunch with a colleague when he offered the following bet: If the colleague won a coin toss, Samuelson would pay him $200. If not, the colleague had to pay Samuelson $100. Would he take the bet? It is easy to see that this bet has positive expected value, since $50\% \times \$200 - 50\% \times \$100 = \$50$. Nevertheless, the colleague declined. He explained that he would feel the pain of the $100 loss more keenly than the pleasure of the $200 gain, giving the bet a negative expected utility. He was distinguishing between the expected value in monetary terms and expected utility. Utility enhances the computation of value by including subjective feelings.

The logic behind the sentiment of Samuelson's colleague was formalized by Kahneman and Tversky's prospect theory, mentioned in chapter 3. One tenet of prospect theory is that losses loom larger than gains. In other words, a loss of a given size is more painful—something like twice as painful—as a gain of the same size is pleasurable. Finding $20 on the street is delightful, but it does not affect your well-being as much as losing $20 undermines your happiness. There are many important implications of this asymmetry, but one of them is that we are often reluctant to take risks that entail a possibility of loss, even if they have a positive expected value.

Maybe you can relate to Samuelson's colleague and agree that you would decline the bet. But this decision has a problematic implication. If you react this way to every risky opportunity that comes your way, you will wind up behaving in exceedingly risk-averse ways. Every day, you face versions of Samuelson's bet. When you buy an apple, it could turn out to have a worm in it. Trying a new restaurant might be great, but there is also the risk of a disappointing meal. Taking a new colleague to lunch could be enjoyable but could get weird if he starts offering you bets on coin flips. Avoiding all apples, new restaurants, and lunches with new colleagues because they entail the possibility of loss will leave you worse off.

After declining the bet, Paul Samuelson's colleague made a curious counteroffer. He said that although he would not take Samuelson's bet, he would gladly take one hundred such bets. Averaged across a hundred repetitions, the probability of a loss is vanishingly small—less than 1 percent. And after you consider them as a bundle like this, what seemed like a risky prospect seems almost like a sure thing. Offered a gamble with a 99 percent probability of winning, most people would be inclined to take it. The problem is that life presents us with risky prospects one at a time. Each day we face a hundred separate small gambles, on everything from choosing restaurants to apples.

Here it is worth thinking of our behavior as implying a policy about how to behave in such situations. If you had lunch with Paul Samuelson every day and every day he offered you his bet, you should make a policy of accepting it. If you check your investment accounts every day, there will be many days on which the value of your portfolio has dropped. Those losses will hurt, and you might be tempted to sell. But you also know that there will be market fluctuations, that it is difficult to identify peaks and troughs that allow you to time the market, and that market returns are likely to be positive over the long term. The rational response to this series of risky daily bets with positive expected value is to make a policy of taking them. That is, let your money ride so that you can be sure you are fully invested on the days when the market goes up.

It is often tempting to violate your own policies. Even though you usually hold yourself to one dessert, the options on this particular dessert buffet look exceptionally enticing. Even though you usually have no more than two drinks at a sitting, you may be tempted to have more when the atmosphere is particularly convivial and the cocktails especially tasty. Even though you plan to go to bed by eleven, the show you are watching is especially engrossing. In such circumstances, it is worth considering what you would want yourself to do, faced with a hundred such choices. It's okay to decide that this really isn't like other desserts, and this time it really is worth indulging. But don't fool yourself into thinking "this time is different" if it isn't. Don't pretend "I'll be virtuous from now on" if you will succumb to the same temptation again tomorrow.

Here I must warn you of one of the most dangerous pitfalls when computing expected values: confusing utility for probability. It happens sometimes that consequential outcomes loom larger than they should. Because aviation accidents seem so scary, they loom large enough to induce real terror. By one estimate, a pathological fear of flying afflicts as much as 6 percent of all people. While going down in a fiery plane crash would be unfortunate, it is also fantastically unlikely. Airplane travel is, per mile traveled, among the safest modes of transportation. It is a mistake to inflate the risk of being in an airplane accident just because the prospect is scary. To pick a more positive example, your probability of winning the lottery does not go up just because the prize gets more alluring. Indeed, as the Powerball jackpot goes up, your probability of winning might go down if the prize money entices more people to buy lottery tickets. You do a better job computing expected value when you clearly distinguish probability from utility, making the most accurate estimates of each independently and using them to compute accurate expected values.

KEEPING SCORE

Applying the logic of expected value requires that you specify both the value of an outcome and its probability. When Max invited me to bet on my job prospects, he specified the dollar outcomes and challenged me to reflect on my subjective probabilities to determine the bet's expected value. This turns out to be a worthy endeavor. Keeping track and writing down expected value calculations for your important decisions offers three clear benefits.

First, writing down your expected value calculations helps you learn over time. You might be concerned that your expected value calculations are imperfect. That's okay; most are. But imperfect estimates are better than nothing. Having committed yourself to a specific prediction allows you to go back and score yourself. Get better at keeping track and keeping score. Forcing forecasters in the Good Judgment Project to commit to specific probability forecasts and then providing them with feedback on their accuracy was one of the most important things we did to help them get better. If you don't write down your probability estimates ahead of time, it is too easy to fall victim to the hindsight bias and believe afterward that the outcome was inevitable. The hindsight bias fools the Monday-morning quarterback—the football fan who, on Monday after having watched his team lose Sunday's big game, grouses, "How could they have run that dumb play? I knew it was going to turn out that way."

Now, the problem that you will notice right away with tracking probabilities and outcomes is that while probability forecasts are continuous (ranging from 0 percent to 100 percent), the actual outcomes are much lumpier; things happen or they don't. The meteorologist forecasts a probability of rain, but either it rains or it doesn't. Nevertheless, it is possible to score probability estimates in such a way as to reward good calibration. Moreover, when you have a lot of data, you can average across outcomes to compare average hit rates with average predicted probabilities. The very exercise of looking for comparable events helpfully forces you to think about analogies between your situation and others like it. This gives you a better sense of the underlying probabilities, what could happen, and what you should expect.

The second benefit of documenting your expected value calculations is that it helps protect you from the capricious winds of chance. Sometimes you will make a good bet that turns out unlucky. This is always a risk with innovative products. Consider, for example, Apple's bet on the Newton. Newton was a personal digital assistant—a handheld computer—that Apple released in 1993. Apple had invested about six years and $100 million developing the Newton ahead of its release. Let's just say it was not a commercial success. After being widely lampooned as an overpriced digital notepad, the Newton was discontinued in 1997.

The Newton was ahead of its time. It was a risky bet, but one that could have paid off. Indeed, a few years later Apple released the iPhone, which was based on some of the innovations found in the Newton. The iPhone wound up succeeding where the Newton had failed. As of 2018, Apple had sold something like 1.4 billion iPhones. If each one produced $150 in profit for Apple, that's over $200 billion in profits. If we imagine that, at the time of its release, the Newton had even a 5 percent chance of making the company $200 billion, then its $100 million price tag would have been well worth it.

Companies pursuing real innovation try to encourage risk taking by celebrating failure. Amazon and 3M are two examples of companies that have managed to innovate successfully over time thanks to their courage in rewarding employees who pursue bold and promising ideas even when they wind up failing. Both companies give their people the freedom to take costly risks and reward well-intentioned failure. What does it mean for failure to be well-intentioned? It means it has a positive expected value. After your innovation fails, how can you show it had a positive expected value? That is easier if you document its expected value before you take the plunge.

Document your reasoning for making a decision, based on its expected value. It can help you persuade your superiors or your bankers why they should bet on your risky idea. It can help you, as a boss or as an investor, figure out which risks are worth taking. Yes, people might be biased in the assessment of their ideas, but an explicit expected value calculation can help you unpack a rosy forecast into testable claims about potential revenues and probabilities of success. Moreover, this sort of documentation can be enormously useful after an outcome is known. This is the third benefit of writing down your expected value calculations.

Documenting your thinking at the time of a decision—when you make the bet—is also essential for helping you avoid the hindsight bias. I have reason to suspect that my PhD adviser, Max, did not take good notes of his reasoning at the time he offered me the insurance policy on my income. To my surprise, when I brought it up recently, he did not remember the conversation. "What insurance premium did I ask for?" he inquired.

"Five thousand dollars," I told him. Having seen that I managed to get a job and even remain employed, it was tempting for Max to think that that outcome was more likely than it actually was.

"Boy, it sounds like I was ripping you off." Max smiled.

PART II

—

JUST RIGHT

—

If the first four chapters have left you feeling bad about your vulnerability to bias, take heart. You're not perfect—you're human. Understanding the role that confidence plays in your judgment can help you improve. Part II goes deeper into the causes and consequences of the errors, biases, and follies documented in part I. It then builds on these insights to offer advice on how to get better at calibrating your confidence.

Chapter 5 encourages you to get serious about how you measure, assess, and quantify your confidence. It delves into the messy gray areas of subjective assessment and considers how to turn vague evaluations into numerical scores. To avoid overconfidence, learn to define performance, forecast outcomes, and calculate expected values.

Chapter 6 helps you think about forecasting and optimism by taking you along for some mental time travel. It begins by looking back at prior failures and then learning from them using postmortem analysis. It next applies that logic to forward-looking and premortem analyses and disaster preparedness to help you temper your expectations and prepare for likely futures. Backcast from a desirable future to determine what you need to do now to make that future likely. Looking forward and looking backward highlight the risks of temporal inconsistency and irrationality created by false optimism. Well-calibrated confidence can help you avoid this irrationality.

Chapter 7 invites you to calibrate your confidence by seeing it from different perspectives. Instead of assessing yourself and your prospects from your own familiar vantage point, consider the views of others, including rivals who might be willing to bet against you or enemies who disagree with you.

Chapter 8 maps signposts to help you find the middle way between overconfidence and underconfidence. It summarizes when you are most vulnerable to each. The chapter reminds you of tools, strategies, and ideas from prior chapters and notes when they are most likely to be useful.

CHAPTER 5

Clarify

In March 2018, Kathleen Colby Dunn performed on the show *American Idol* under her stage name, Koby. She delivered what is remembered as one of the "longest, loudest, and oddest vocal runs in 'Idol' history." When she began belting out her song, the singer Katy Perry, one of the competition's judges, covered an ear. As Koby continued, the judges cringed. When Koby was eliminated from contention, her reaction was, "I thought I sang really, really fucking well. I'm sorry. I'm really good—I don't know what happened." Her assessment of her own performance was not diminished by the judges' reactions: "I'm pretty sure I just nailed it. I don't know . . . I guess they wanted mediocre singers?" Koby looked into the camera and offered an explanation: "I think Katy's just a little jealous. She can't hit those notes."

Believing that you are better than others has powerful implications. On the plus side, it can help you feel good about yourself and give you the courage to enter competitions. But believing that you are a "really good" singer when you're not can lead to public embarrassment on *American Idol*. Believing that your jokes are funnier than they are can make you annoying. Faith in your superior virtue can prompt sanctimonious stances that are more costly than vindicating. Instead, I want to help inoculate you against errors of self-aggrandizement in which you make an ass out of yourself. I also want to help protect you from errors of self-criticism in which you are too critical of your shortcomings, or errors of underconfidence that discourage you from opportunities that would have been successful.

DRIVERS OF OVERCONFIDENCE

A large literature documents the many circumstances under which the average person thinks that she is better than average. The most frequently cited result comes from a 1981 paper published by the Swedish psychologist Ola Svenson. Svenson asked American drivers to compare their skills with those of other drivers. Svenson found that 93 percent of them claimed their skill put them in the top half of all drivers. This result features as exhibit A in a lineup of evidence showing that people exaggerate the degree to which they are better than others. But let's consider what exactly Svenson's respondents were telling him. I see at least three possibilities.

The first possibility is that they knew they were exaggerating, but were nevertheless trying to impress. Their claims of superiority may have been like telling the person interviewing you that you think you have what it takes to do the job. You're not actually completely sure, but in an interview you know you're supposed to put your best foot forward. Maybe Svenson's respondents weren't convinced they were actually great drivers, but they were trying to give him a positive impression nonetheless. If this explains their overplacement, then clarifying for them that accuracy is the goal ought to reduce overconfidence. One way to clarify this is to pay people for being accurate. However, when other researchers have paid monetary incentives for accuracy, it did not do much to reduce inaccurate claims of superiority.

A second possible explanation is that instead of trying to fool others, drivers are simply fooling themselves about how skilled they are. For example, people might claim to be better drivers than others because they choose to forget the traffic tickets they get, or they convince themselves that they didn't really deserve that ticket for going 83 on a residential street with a speed limit of 30. If such self-delusion is at work, then clarifying the standards shouldn't matter. Delusional drivers will still be overconfident even if we explain how they ought to evaluate their own driving skill. In truth, however, clarifying the standards makes an enormous difference.

One study explored the consequences of clarifying the standards. In the general category of "driving skill," participants claimed to be well above average. However, their overplacement reduced substantially when they rated themselves on specific driving skills such as alertness, patience, checking for blind spots, using car mirrors, braking, speeding, and signaling. My colleagues and I have found, in related work, that although people will claim to be more intelligent than others, inaccurate claims of superiority disappear if the question is clearer: "How did you do, relative to the other participants in this study, on that intelligence test you all just took?" As the standards become clearer, people are less likely to believe that they are better than others. This result highlights the third explanation for Svenson's overconfident drivers: different drivers have different definitions of skill.

If every person had his or her own idiosyncratic definition of what it means to be a good driver, then all drivers could rate themselves as the best, and all of them could be right. And it makes sense that different people have different perspectives on what makes for good driving. Just as people have different opinions on what it means to be funny or smart or a good singer, different opinions about what constitutes good driving lead people to behave differently when they are behind the wheel. My father regarded caution as the paramount skill of a good driver, and he employed it in abundance. My son regards quick reaction times as a sign of good driving, and so he brakes later than would have pleased my father. Each would regard himself as a better driver than the other, according to his own definition.

Ambiguity about how to measure performance accounts for a good deal of "better than average" effects like Svenson's. Clarifying what it means to be smart, or honest, or a good driver substantially reduces overplacement, and people's self-assessments become better calibrated. This implies a simple remedy for overplacement: clear definitions. Clarify what it takes to qualify as a safe driver, and fewer people will think they are better than everyone else. Clear definitions can help in situations as diverse as work performance and grade grubbing.

One domain rife with overplacement is assessments of professional work performance. People often believe that they are better at their jobs than their coworkers. If your employees grouse about being passed over for raises or promotions, you might consider clarifying the performance standards. Explaining exactly what behavior earns promotions will have the dual effect of helping people understand who got promoted and also clarify what they will have to do to earn promotions themselves. This works in the classroom as well as in the office. I used to get complaints from students who thought they all deserved A's. I started sharing copies of excellent work and, when I send out grades, provide detailed explanations of how I computed them. Now I hardly ever get those complaints.

A DOSE OF REALITY

This chapter encourages you to define and measure performance for yourself and your colleagues, the better to make accurate assessments. You might be thinking that one of the implications of my advice is that you should be more results oriented. Indeed, many managers and organizations proudly describe themselves as results oriented. Online resources offer advice to job seekers on how to demonstrate to potential employers that they are results oriented or advice to managers on how to make their organization's culture more results oriented. What is the alternative to being results oriented? Some see a choice between being results oriented or being people oriented. If results-oriented leaders are stern taskmasters who care only about performance and profits, then maybe the antidote to being a demanding jerk is to be more people oriented. People-oriented leaders are more considerate, sensitive, and personable.

As for me, I think it is a mistake to be results oriented. That's not because I think leaders should necessarily spend more time going drinking and singing karaoke with their employees. I am convinced that leaders can get better results by being less results oriented. If being results oriented means you reward successful results and punish failures, you will wind up rewarding luck, incentivizing caution, penalizing the unlucky, and discouraging well-intentioned risk taking. The reason is that when luck plays a role—as it does in the success or failure of any organization, project, or product— then the best people and best ideas are not necessarily always successful. Sometimes people succeed or fail due to circumstances beyond their control.

You want the people in your company to be making bets with positive expected values, even when they are risky. Consider a new product that will cost you $100 million to develop but stands only a 5 percent chance of succeeding. Despite the long odds, if success means making $200 billion in profits, that's a good bet. It has an expected value of $99.5 billion ($200 × 5% − $0.1). But a savvy engineer who understands the opportunity and is working for a results-oriented boss would be wise to turn down the chance. Why? There is a 95 percent chance that it will end in failure. A $100 million failure is a big deal and the engineer has only one career. Being out of a job might be unpleasant enough that the safe alternative seems better. It would be safer to work on the next little thing, a modest incremental improvement on an existing product that stands a high probability of success, even if the expected value is lower.

The people at Apple decided to take a big risk when they developed the Newton. And it failed spectacularly, as you remember from chapter 4. But there is good reason to believe Apple's risky bet on the Newton had a positive expected value. How can you encourage the people with whom you work to pursue risky projects with positive expected values? Reward well-intentioned failure. You would be right to object that expected value is often uncertain. Yet given its essential importance to any decision, it makes sense to get good at computing expected values. Indeed, expected value is what any sensible decision must be based on. Doing so depends on thinking through both of its components: value and probability.

Value is usually the easier variable to pin down. What is the range of possible outcomes, and how valuable is each? In earlier chapters, I offered guidance on how to think about these questions of estimating value and utility.

The more difficult component to quantify is the probabilities associated with each of the various outcomes. How likely is it that the product hits big? How likely is it that it flops? How likely is the entire range of possible sales? Answering these questions requires a probability distribution, as chapter 3 discussed. When it comes to something like rolling dice or flipping coins, most of us are comfortable thinking about outcomes as probability distributions. But for single instances, such as the fall of Syrian dictators or an individual's job performance, we like to think of the unique causal forces at work in determining that particular outcome. However, such thinking often fails to appreciate the complexity of those causal forces and the degree to which that generates a set of possible outcomes best thought of as a probability distribution.

Chapter 4 recommended that you keep track of your expected value calculations and keep score of their accuracy. There, I noted the value in communicating those calculations with others. Here I extend that advice to suggesting that you encourage others to compute expected values and share them with you. If your work requires you to assess the claims of others, you can invite them to report their expected values. Venture capitalists, for instance, must assess entrepreneurs' forecasts of future success. Managers at Apple had to assess the expected value of investing in creating the Newton. Koby had to assess the expected value of competing on *American Idol*. Ask for help from your colleagues and subordinates to calculate expected value. What is the probability that a given project will be an abject failure, losing all the money invested? What is the probability that the project will pay back double the amount invested within five years? Later on, go back and see how those forecasts have held up. You might also consider reminding others of how their forecasts did. Scoring these forecasts and providing feedback to the forecasters will help them improve with experience.

Here I must insert another caveat. By encouraging you to compute expected value and make choices based on rigorous analysis, I am not suggesting that money is the right benchmark for measuring success or that you should neglect your feelings. Good decisions must reflect the interests, utilities, and feelings of the decision maker. Just because subjective experience may be difficult to measure does not make it any less important. Your rational head should not get to overrule your emotional heart just because emotions are harder to quantify. Good decisions take subjective utilities into account. What you want is not to let either your head or your heart rule, but instead put them in dialogue with each other. If your heart rebels against the counsel of your expected value calculations, consider what information your heart has that is not included in the numbers. Then try to update the numbers to reflect this information.

THE NEWS FROM LAKE WOBEGON

The "Lake Wobegon effect" was named by John Jacob Cannell for the fictional little town in Minnesota where, according to Garrison Keillor, "all the women are strong, all the men are good-looking, and all the children are above average." As with the children in Lake Wobegon, Cannell noted that most states claimed that their children scored above average on nationally normed tests of school achievement. These are the sorts of high-stakes tests tied to federal education funding by the law known as No Child Left Behind.

NCLB had the laudable goal of establishing material incentives for teachers and schools to contribute to the real and verifiable skills of their students. In particular, NCLB relied on standardized testing to gather objective data on how students, teachers, and schools were performing.

Test takers had every reason to care about test results, and no one likes to hear that he or she is below average. Competition among testing companies means that they have incentives to make school districts happy. Might that motivation lead them to sugarcoat test results, telling districts that their students place better, relative to national norms, than they do? Cannell estimated that more than 70 percent of the children taking standardized tests received the feedback that their test performances were above average. Cannell tried to investigate the evidence for this feedback, but his investigation ended in frustration: "None of these companies would supply the data necessary for a proper statistical analysis of their test scores." Cannell makes his accusation clear: "Publishers are more interested in sales than accurate achievement tests."

This problem extends beyond standardized tests. All of us find it easier to hear flattering news. Peter Ditto has made a career out of studying the ways that our preferences for good news affect how we scrutinize information. One study examined people's responses to a health diagnosis that they liked or disliked. Volunteers in Ditto's study learned that they would be taking the "TAA saliva reaction test." This (fictitious) test purported to diagnose a condition called "TAA-negativity" characterized by the absence of the (fictional) enzyme thioamine acetylase. Volunteers spit on a "TAA-reactive strip" that they were told would change from its normal yellow to green when exposed to saliva containing TAA, but that the color change could take some time. In reality, there is no such thing as "TAA-negativity," and the strip never turned color. The implication of this negative signal was that volunteers were indeed TAA-negative.

The researchers measured how long volunteers waited before deciding that they had their answer. The result depended on what they thought the consequences were. Some volunteers learned that people who are TAA-negative are ten times more likely to develop pancreatic disease. These people waited two and a half minutes before reluctantly concluding that the strip wasn't changing color and they were probably TAA-negative. On the other hand, volunteers happily concluded in just a minute and a half that they must be TAA-negative when they were told that being TAA-negative was a good thing because it came with one-tenth the risk of pancreatic disease.

Ditto's result is consistent with evidence suggesting that people naturally apply different standards of scrutiny to evidence depending on whether it is consistent with their preferences and beliefs. That does not mean you ignore bad news. Indeed, you often ruminate on bad news. After all, volunteers in Ditto's study gave extra attention to the bad news, scrutinizing their TAA-reactive strip for an additional minute before concluding they had no choice but to accept its unfortunate verdict.

The inclination to happily accept good news and skeptically resist bad news can blind us to risks. Leaders who isolate themselves from news that they don't want to hear may be ignoring potential crises. Since 1961, American presidents have received a daily briefing from the director of national intelligence. John F. Kennedy introduced the President's Daily Brief in the wake of the Bay of Pigs debacle. The failure of US intelligence at the attempted invasion of Cuba was so catastrophic that Kennedy never wanted anything like it to happen again. He instituted a daily intelligence briefing designed to update the president on current issues and looming threats. Getting coverage in the PDB was, for insiders at the CIA, the equivalent of a reporter getting her story on the front page.

Reports are, however, that Donald Trump found the PDB too dense and boring. Instead, he asked for a "clip book" that showed how the press was reporting on him. Many politicians ask for a sample of news clippings that provide a sense of how the press is covering them. But what Trump wanted was not a representative set of stories from the nationwide press. Instead, word is that Trump asked for a daily briefing of positive press reports praising him and featuring photos of him looking powerful. It might be good for Trump's ego to be able to enjoy press reports praising his talent and showing off his unreal mane of blond hair. However, there is reason to worry that Trump's ego-gratification might come at the cost of an accurate understanding of the real risks confronting his presidency and the nation.

Presidents are not the only ones tempted to believe the adulation that comes their way. Celebrity CEOs are often lionized as geniuses. The CEOs who receive disproportionate credit for their company's success are often tempted to believe it. Evidence suggests that idolizing corporate leaders has a real downside when it comes to a company's performance. Celebrity CEOs, on average, perform worse than their humbler counterparts. Elon Musk, for example, has seen more worshipful praise than most modern CEOs. While he has undoubtedly accomplished a great deal, he has also done some remarkably stupid things. Many Tesla shareholders shuddered in September 2018 when they saw him smoking marijuana during a live interview broadcast on YouTube. But even more unfortunate was his claim, broadcast over Twitter, that he was trying to take control of Tesla by buying back all of its publicly traded stock and making it a private company: "Am considering taking Tesla private at $420. Funding secured." The credibility of

Musk's momentous message was not increased by reports that he might have been on LSD at the time. His ill-advised tweet, with powerful implications for the value of Tesla stock, prompted the US Securities and Exchange Commission to investigate whether it constituted securities fraud. The result was a $20 million fine for Musk and requirement that he step down as chairman of Tesla.

CEOs who exaggerate their own superiority will pursue corporate acquisitions believing that their superior skills will allow them to more effectively manage the target companies. The most over-confident of them will also bid most aggressively, making their bids most likely to be accepted. But the high proportion of failed acquisitions attests to the fact that these beliefs are often erroneous. On average, corporate acquisitions lose money for the acquirer. To pick one example, GE's long decline has been marked by a series of unfortunate acquisitions. Indeed, some have called GE "the poster child for bad acquisitions." One was the company's ill-fated acquisition of the investment bank Kidder Peabody in the 1980s. Describing how his own overconfidence led him to overestimate his understanding of Kidder Peabody and its business, Jack Welch, GE's bald, five-foot, seven-inch CEO, remarked, "I didn't know a diddly about it. I was on a roll . . . I thought I was six-foot-four with hair." Such delusion is facilitated by the failure to clarify and quantify.

THE SMARTEST GUYS IN THE ROOM

Like most people, Joe Cassano preferred praise to criticism. As head of AIG's financial products division (AIG-FP) from 2001 until 2008, he got plenty of praise. During much of that time, AIG-FP delivered impressive profits to its parent, the American insurance giant AIG. AIG-FP was a small part of the larger company, but by 2005 it was generating a substantial portion of the company's $10 billion in annual profits. That success afforded Cassano the freedom to run the division as his personal fiefdom. "This is my company," Cassano would tell his employees. According to one former employee: "Under Joe the debate and discussion that was common under Tom [Savage, Cassano's predecessor,] ceased." Said another, "The way you dealt with Joe was to start everything by saying, 'You're right, Joe.'"

Cassano demanded results, and his people produced them. In particular, they sold lots of credit default swaps (CDSs): insurance policies against mortgage default. In the early part of the first decade of the twenty-first century, the sale of CDSs appeared to be wonderfully profitable. While the housing bubble was inflating and home values increased, AIG-FP could collect buyers' money and had to pay out next to nothing in claims. But when employees at AIG-FP tried to sound the alarm about the potential risks, Cassano would hear none of it. He took such criticism as a personal insult. Eventually, of course, when the bubble burst and subprime mortgage holders defaulted in large numbers, AIG-FP became liable for something like $25 billion in losses. Cassano lost his job and AIG survived bankruptcy thanks only to a bailout from the US government.

Like AIG, Enron was a company that, for quite some time, appeared to be spectacularly profitable. Like AIG, its success fed the egos of those at its helm. Enron became famous for the way it lavished generous pay and benefits on those deemed the most talented. Those who succeeded at Enron's high-stakes game often wound up feeling superior to others inside and outside the company. Indeed, that sentiment gave Bethany McLean the title for her book about Enron, *The Smartest Guys in the Room*. McLean's insightful investigation revealed the financial shell game that Enron played with its accounting. Like AIG-FP, the confidence of those at Enron did not protect them from failure. Unlike AIG, Enron did not get bailed out by American taxpayers. Enron became the largest corporate bankruptcy in American history at the time.

In contrast to organizational cultures that place their leaders on pedestals that isolate them from criticism, some companies do try to practice critical inquiry. Ray Dalio attempted to make his company an idea meritocracy. He wanted Bridgewater Associates to be a place where honest criticism and rigorous analysis would allow the best ideas to rise to the top, whether they were proposed by a senior executive or a lowly intern. He admonishes his employees to seek out the truth because it will prove the best basis for informing wise decisions. Amazon similarly professes a commitment to constructive criticism and respectful disagreement. Jeff Bezos tells Amazon employees, "When you're criticized, first look in a mirror and decide, are your critics right? If they're right, change. Don't resist."

Although it can be painful to admit that your critics are right, confronting our imperfections opens the way to improvement. In her book, *The Person You Mean to Be*, Dolly Chugh observes that clinging to the belief that you are a good person can sometimes get in the way of actually getting better. When you react defensively to the possibility that you could be biased, you deny that you might have room for improvement. When you insist that you are good, or honest, or moral, you reject the possibility of getting better. In truth, no one is perfect, and seeking to improve is the best way to manifest your good intentions. That is, you should accept the fact that perfection is an unattainable goal, and instead do what you can to move closer to your ideals.

Letting go of perfection and instead setting your sights on improvement will allow you to hear both good and bad news. Praise can be satisfying and flattering, but beware of your own eager acceptance of praise. It is easy to react in dysfunctional ways, being too credulous of ingratiation and excessively skeptical of criticism. Leaders who want to hear only positive news will blind themselves to risks and the dangers of failure. Bad news, on the other hand, may be even more valuable, because it can open your eyes to errors and biases. It will reveal where you are at risk of being blindsided, exploited, or defeated.

SUMMIT FEVER

If you are getting serious about clarifying and quantifying your self-assessments, what is the right way to calibrate your optimism? My advice is that you should strive to believe the truth. This is not to say that you are no better than what you have accomplished. Each of us has an enormous amount of untapped potential. There are great things we have not yet accomplished but could, if we pursued them with committed determination.

Angela Duckworth studies grit—the tendency to persist in the face of setbacks and frustration and to keep trying even when it's not easy. Her rigorous research has documented the many ways in which grit can contribute to success. Indeed, those who show the most tenacious grit are most likely to succeed at challenging tasks that require a great deal of effort, whether that is completing a difficult program of graduate study, finishing military training, or leading a startup firm. But dogged persistence need not always contribute to success. The advice to show greater persistence is good only for those who otherwise would have given up too quickly. It is terrible advice for those who might persist too much or who are at risk of escalating their commitment to a losing course of action.

Jeffrey Rubin was a professor at Tufts University who studied the escalation of commitment. He was also an avid mountain climber.

He had set himself the ambitious goal of climbing all of the one hundred tallest peaks in New England. Rubin had already succeeded in summiting the other ninety-nine peaks, and Mount Katahdin was the only one left when he set out with a fellow climber, Daniel Lieberfeld, on June 3, 1995. Achieving his goal energized Rubin as they set out. But as they climbed, a dense fog rolled in. Soon it got bad enough that Lieberfeld recommended they turn around. Rubin was determined to press on. Eventually, Lieberfeld turned back and Rubin continued without him. By persisting, Rubin showed impressive grit. He persisted even though it meant violating the safety rule that recommends climbers never go it alone. He persisted even though it was dangerous.

Jeff Rubin never made it back. Search parties found his body the next day, dead of hypothermia and exposure. A contributing cause was what mountain climbers call "summit fever." It is the unyielding commitment to reaching the top. The most persistent and tenacious mountain climbers are also the most likely to succumb to summit fever by showing a gritty escalation of commitment to reach the summit.

Mercifully, death is only sometimes the penalty for overconfident persistence. As Jeff Rubin's research showed, we pay many other costs for escalating our commitment to a losing course of action. Investors, for instance, are often reluctant to sell losing stocks, because they hope that the stocks will bounce back. By refusing to sell their losers, they escalate their bet and often wind up losing more money. Many aspiring college athletes persist in training and neglecting their studies even in the face of dwindling chances that they will get drafted into the major leagues, or even that they will ever get paid a salary for playing sports. Many people have trouble ending long-term romantic relationships even when those relationships have become negative, destructive, or abusive. And in the heat of the moment, bidders in an auction often get carried away and wind up bidding more than they intended to.

Escalation of commitment is an error when it neglects the opportunity costs of continued persistence. What else could you be doing with your investments and your life? Bidders are most likely to bid too much when they enter an auction without thinking ahead about their maximum bids and alternative uses for their money. Gillian Ku, Deepak Malhotra, and Keith Murnighan dubbed this bidding escalation "auction fever."

If you want to avoid irrational escalation, the first question you ought to ask yourself is, "What will happen if I persist?" In other words, what is the expected value of persistence? How good would success be, and how much would it cost you? In an auction, consider how valuable the prize is and the most you would consider paying for it. Also reflect on how much it is likely to cost you to win. How much are other bidders likely to pay? The next question is even more important: "If I give up on pursuing this goal, what would I do instead?" Then determine the expected value of this fallback. You should choose the alternative with the highest expected value. Crucial to this logic is the choice of *which* alternative you would choose.

GOOD WHICHES AND BAD WHETHER

Paul Nutt has studied how companies make decisions, and he has found that the majority of them are "whether" decisions. That is, the decision is framed as a question of whether the company should take some action, such as acquire another company, undertake a reorganization, or hire a candidate. "Whether" decisions consider these actions in isolation, where each decision is a go/no-go choice. Nutt has attempted to understand whether the outcomes of these corporate decisions are successful, according to the ambitions and aspirations of the decision makers. He concludes that the majority of these decisions are failures. Many of the worst decisions are "whether" decisions. Jeff Rubin decided whether to persist in his ascent of Katahdin. Investors decide whether to sell their losing stocks. When you're making a "whether" decision, you fail to specify the alternatives. What could you do if you didn't take the action you're considering? "Whether" choices tend to neglect opportunity costs.

Instead, you ought to be making "which" decisions. That is, you should be choosing from the full set of possible alternatives. Choosing among alternatives opens your mind to the other options and also to the opportunity costs of any single choice. The research of Shane Frederick highlights how easy it is for people to neglect opportunity costs. In one study, he asked half of his volunteers whether they would be interested in purchasing a DVD movie they had been wanting to see for $14.99. The other half of his volunteers were in the "which" condition. They chose between the movie or keeping the $14.99 to use some other way. Even though the choices were identical, the proportion of people who bought the movie dropped significantly, from 75 percent in the "whether" condition to 55 percent in the "which" condition.

The advice to consider the alternative may make you think of chapter 4's recommendation that you remember your BATNA when negotiating. Negotiators can make deals they subsequently regret when they fail to consider what they will do if they walk away. Instead of deciding whether to take the deal the other side is offering, you want to consider instead which of your various options is best and how you might improve them. This comparison is, of course, facilitated by having thought through your BATNA before you start negotiating and scoring it according to your own values, interests, and utilities.

One of the obvious benefits of keeping score and assessing the expected values of the alternatives is that it allows you to compare them. Sometimes those alternatives are obvious, such as when a moment's reflection reminds you that not spending money means you have it available to use another way. But other times, it will prompt you to consider other possible choices or think of your choices in a new light. This happened to me when my wife and I were considering whether to have children. My wife, Sarah, was pretty sure she wanted kids. I knew I wanted to be with Sarah, but I wasn't quite as excited about spending my time at the zoo, the pumpkin patch, and the playground.

My reluctance to complicate our lives with children arose, in part, from the life of childless freedom that existed in some fantasized future. In this future, I imagined going out to fancy restaurants every night, seeing all the latest movies and plays, and traveling as much as we liked. But when I reflected on our childless life together up until that point, I realized that Sarah actually didn't like going out or staying up late that much, and for that matter neither did I. I also had to confront the realization that Sarah, the planner and organizer in our family, already brought me to plenty of zoos, parks, and pumpkin patches. And then there was the issue of the possible remorse we could experience. I began to imagine a lifetime of marital tension played out at parks where one or both of us gazed regretfully at other people's adorable children and imagined what we had missed.

By moving my perspective from the question of whether we should have children to the choice of a life with children versus a life without children, I was better able to envision the alternatives and compare them. These considerations convinced me, and we began to get serious about the undertaking. I was then able to confirm for myself what I had been told in graduate school: conceiving a baby is way more fun than conceiving a dissertation topic. And I am furthermore happy to report that zoos and pumpkin patches are more fun with your children.

DOWNSIDE RISK

So far, this chapter has contained cautionary tales of overconfidence. Now I want to remind you of the risks on the downside: overly pessimistic views. As dangerous as it is to be deliriously optimistic, it's also dysfunctional to ruminate on bad news, and to see failure around every corner. I urged you to force yourself to listen to your critics. There is a flip side to this advice, too, since it is possible to go too far. We attend too much to our critics when we ruminate on that criticism. I know for myself how easy it is to obsess about critical feedback on student evaluations or the one student who falls asleep in class. Even if there are seventy other students who are alert, interested, and participating enthusiastically, the image of that one sleeping student will replay in my mind over and over.

My father, the inveterate pessimist, taught me all about negative rumination. He was perennially gloomy about the stock market, sure that the next big crash was just around the bend. So he kept his money far away from the market. He would have kept it in bills under his mattress, except he was sure that hyperinflation was ready to take off any time. Gold, too, seemed too risky—the prices fluctuated too much. Instead, he put his money in investment-quality gemstones. Although a plastic pocket protector was the closest he ever got to personal adornment, we had a safe at home filled with spectacular diamonds.

My father lacked the confidence in the stock market to invest his hard-earned money there. It would have been better for my father if he had been more optimistic about the market. As it was, he missed out on substantial gains he could have enjoyed had he invested his money there. So what's the difference between being optimistic about your chances of winning the lottery and being optimistic about the chance that the stock market will go up? The difference is that there is good reason to expect the market to go up, at least over the long term. It is a bet with positive expected value. And there are even more reasons to believe that lottery tickets have a negative expected value. On average, you can expect to pay more for lottery tickets than you will win.

Perfect confidence is well calibrated. It is based on reason and evidence. Without knowing whether you will win the lottery or what the market will do this coming year, how are you to calibrate your confidence in its prospects? I offer three answers to this important question about quantifying vague probabilities. The first answer is that we have excellent data on the long-term performance of both the stock market and lottery tickets. But I must concede that sometimes there is a shortage of evidence. What should you do if, for example, your prospective investment is neither the stock market nor the lottery, but an exciting new business startup for which there is no historical track record?

The second answer relies on logic and reason. Few sensible investors would consider giving money to an entrepreneur with nothing more than an idea and a dream. Again, wise investors rely on evidence. Don't content yourself with woolly-headed optimism that is not based on facts. What reason is there to think that a given product will have a market? What is an entrepreneur's idea for making her business profitable? Can the operation scale up to capitalize on her good idea and actually make money? What percentage of similar entrepreneurs who were just as confident in their ideas wound up being successful? Answers to these questions can help point the way toward computing expected value in a manner that can guide your decisions.

The third answer is that thinking through an expected value calculation can be helpful for structuring your decision and informing the criteria you will use. This can even help with personal decisions such as choosing among jobs, college majors, or romantic partners. What would it take to compare the expected values of different job opportunities? First you would have to identify the key dimensions on which they differ, such as pay, advancement opportunities, personal fulfillment, and so on. Then you would have to score each of the jobs on each of these dimensions, taking into account the uncertainties. Imagine one job offers a bonus whose value depends on your future performance. Make a realistic estimate of the probability that you will achieve it. You're not sure how fulfilling the work would actually be at job number two? Make some guesses about the range of possible outcomes, how good and bad they would be, and their probabilities. Then add up the different components whose expected values you have calculated.

Admittedly, there is some potential vulnerability in expected value calculations. It is possible to manipulate the numbers by tweaking the underlying assumptions. Someone determined to claim that her business idea is a great investment needs only to build in sufficiently grandiose assumptions about future revenues and costs. I will readily concede that formulas and calculations are only as good as the numbers that go into them. Nevertheless, engaging in a conversation about the accuracy of underlying forecasts and statistics is more productive than arguing about feelings, hunches, and intuitions. We can audit the numbers, assess their plausibility, and consider ways to improve them using better data. I recall the words of the statistician Frederick Mosteller: It is easy to lie with statistics, but easier without them.

CHAPTER 6

Forecast

On October 29, 2018, Lion Air flight 610 crashed twelve minutes after takeoff from Jakarta, Indonesia, killing all 189 people aboard. The plane was a nearly new Boeing 737 Max 8. The weather conditions were good and the pilots were experienced. But nearly immediately, the pilots struggled to control the aircraft. The plane's automatic flight control systems kept pushing the plane's nose down. The pilots radioed the control tower in Jakarta two minutes after takeoff, asking to return to the airport. As they tried to keep their plane aloft, the pilots frantically searched for information to understand the behavior of their aircraft. They were reading the plane's manuals when they crashed into the Java Sea.

The first thing to note about the Lion Air crash is that it is so exceptional. There are over one hundred thousand airplane flights each day, but crashes are so rare that they make front-page news around the world. The Lion Air crash represents a blemish on a spectacularly impressive long-run record of safety for the global airline industry. Since the year 2000, an average of about four hundred people have died in commercial airplane accidents each year. During those years, hundreds of millions of people have taken billions of flights. The fatalities represent less than 0.05 deaths per billion kilometers traveled, which is less than a tenth of the risk associated with other modes of transportation such as bus, train, car, or walking. It turns out that hurtling through the stratosphere in a metal tube filled with jet fuel can be safer than crossing the street. The stupendous safety record of commercial air travel is at least in part attributable to the rigorous system of accident investigation and reporting.

In Latin, *postmortem* means "after death." Coroners conduct postmortem analyses to understand why someone died. But use of the term "postmortem" has expanded to include other sorts of tragedies. Understanding the cause of death is useful information for anyone who wishes to avoid a similar fate. The airline industry has gotten particularly good at conducting postmortem analyses and learning from them. Safety commissions like the US National Transportation Safety Board and the European Aviation Safety Agency perform detailed postmortems that make sense of crashes and thereby help design systems and aircraft that will avoid similar tragedies in the future.

Each accident represents an opportunity to learn about the weaknesses of aviation systems. Fixing those weaknesses increases the safety of the overall system and reduces the risk of subsequent accidents. There are active regulatory agencies that implement system-wide rules designed to minimize the risk of future accidents. And the airline industry has made safety a top priority. Frequent safety checks, extensive backup systems, and rigorous training are all expensive—but aircraft accidents are even more costly. The big players in the industry have supported strong regulation that has forced all airlines to invest in safety even when they might have been tempted to cut corners for the sake of short-term profits.

Not only is there a meticulous system of accident investigation, there is also a system for tracking and learning from accidents that *didn't* happen. The Aviation Safety Reporting System (ASRS) was established by the US Federal Aviation Administration (FAA) to investigate situations that almost resulted in tragedy. Pilots and aviation personnel can report near accidents in the ASRS. The FAA reviews these reports, follows up to ask for more detail when needed, strips the report of identifying information, and then makes it available to pilots and airlines. The FAA uses these reports in its monthly newsletter highlighting current safety issues. You may be wondering why anyone would share the news of a near accident with which they were involved. The reason is that the FAA grants immunity from prosecution of most errors, omissions, and failures reported in the ASRS.

Even though it doesn't grant its employees immunity for errors, Google seeks to understand and learn from its failures. Each failure prompts a postmortem intended to reduce the chances it makes a similar mistake again. There is, in fact, a postmortem form used at the company. The two questions on the form are intended to help guide Google's postmortem discussion. The first is: What happened? Identify what went well, what didn't, and where luck might have played a role. The second question is: What can we do differently next time? Identify lessons for how to avoid the same problems in the future. Consider what else we could have done to improve the project's chances of success. Finally, reflect on what the failure implies about what we should be doing instead. By way of inspiration, the form also includes a quote from Henry Ford: "Failure is only opportunity to begin again. Only this time, more wisely."

Even the most capable entrepreneurs and successful businesses will have their share of failures. Google is one of the largest, wealthiest, and most successful companies in the world, and it can boast an impressively long list of failures. Remember Google+, the company's attempt to build a social network? By some estimates, Google spent over $585 million on the product before closing it down in early 2019. Anyone remember Google Video? The company attempted to compete with YouTube but ultimately just decided to buy YouTube and quietly scuttle Google Video. Remember Google Glass, the intelligent eyeglasses? They faced such a hostile reception that they were available only briefly before Google stopped selling them to the public.

Rather than attempting to cover up failure, it is better to face it and learn from it. "Fail fast, fail often" has become a mantra for Silicon Valley entrepreneurs. Nevertheless, in their pursuit of success, too many organizations punish and stigmatize failure, making it harder for employees to admit that a project has failed and to cut their losses. In an attempt to help counteract this pressure, some companies help their employees accept failure, encouraging them to use failures to learn about their products, their customers, and the marketplace.

Bessemer Venture Partners, one of the oldest venture capital firms, commemorates its failures prominently on its website, telling the stories of its worst funding decisions: the opportunities it missed. David Cowan, a celebrated Silicon Valley investor, gets credit for the biggest failure in Bessemer's "antiportfolio." At the time when Google's founders, Sergey Brin and Larry Page, were just kids operating out of a rented garage, Cowan declined to meet them. Cowan was visiting his college friend who was renting out her garage and offered to introduce the venture capitalist to the two ambitious graduate students with an idea for internet search. "Students? A new search engine?" Cowan asked dubiously. "How can I get out of this house without going anywhere near the garage?" By publicly acknowledging its greatest failures, Bessemer admits the reality that venture capital is beset by uncertainty and gives its employees permission to take risks that might not always pan out. These same risks have also produced Bessemer's greatest successes, including investments in Yelp, Pinterest, LinkedIn, and Wix.

While Lion Air's Indonesia crash was under investigation, another Boeing 737 Max 8 went down. Ethiopian Airlines flight 302 crashed in a field six minutes after takeoff from Addis Ababa, killing all 157 people aboard. Before the crash, the plane's pilots fought to override an automated system that kept lowering the tail flaps and pushing the plane's nose down. The similarities between the Ethiopian and the Lion Air crashes were unmistakable. The investigation of both crashes then turned to the plane's software systems. In particular, the Maneuvering Characteristics Augmentation System (MCAS) was programmed to, among other things, lower the plane's tail flaps and turn its nose down to avoid climbing into a "stall." Boeing, the plane's manufacturer, had intended the MCAS system to operate unobtrusively in the background and had not seen the need to explain the system to pilots of the new planes.

Airlines worldwide reacted to the Ethiopian crash by grounding their new 737 Max aircraft and asking tough questions. Had Boeing given sufficient time for safety testing? Boeing's CEO, Dennis Muilenburg, had boasted about the speed with which the company had brought the new 737 aircraft to market. Investors had rewarded Boeing, which was locked in a fierce competitive battle with its

European rival Airbus, pushing Boeing's stock up 40 percent over the space of a year. But speed came at a cost. The safety assessment Boeing assembled on the new 737 Max aircraft for the Federal Aviation Administration contained a few critical errors, including an underestimate of the power of the MCAS flight control system.

Boeing's stock fell 11 percent immediately following the Ethiopian crash. Airlines and the flying public demanded that Boeing investigate the accidents and address their cause. The postmortem analysis led Boeing to the conclusion that the MCAS system was indeed to blame, and the company promised a software update that would solve the problem. In the meantime, expensive new 737 Max aircraft sat idle, and Boeing was compensating its customers for the costs. Orders for new 737 Max aircraft dried up, and Boeing's stock continued to decline as 2019 dragged on without the company providing a safety fix that would allow the grounded fleet of 737 Max aircraft to fly again. Estimates of the ultimate cost to Boeing's bottom line run as high as $8 billion.

PREMORTEM ANALYSES

Better than understanding a tragedy is anticipating it and avoiding it altogether. The psychologist Gary Klein has proposed the "premortem analysis," in which people imagine that a given project has failed spectacularly. Klein recommends that planners write down every reason they can think of for failure—"Especially the kinds of things they ordinarily wouldn't mention as potential problems, for fear of being impolitic." Klein tells of a premortem meeting for a billion-dollar environmental sustainability project. The discussion revealed a new concern that no one had had the courage to raise earlier. The project was driven, in part, by the passionate support of the CEO. At the premortem, an executive noted the risk of failure should the aging CEO retire before seeing the project through.

You may be thinking that the premortem is inconsistent with an optimistic organizational culture. Many organizations celebrate the can-do attitude that motivates workers to do their best to make the company, and its initiatives, succeed. Undoubtedly, there is value in motivated employees. But no leaders should want a team of spineless wimps who say yes to every idea, no matter how hare-brained or ill conceived. If my project to terraform and colonize Halley's comet is doomed to fail from the start, it would be better not to undertake it in the first place.

There is a time for cautious deliberation and a time for energetic implementation. When a company is formulating strategy, it is useful to consider critiques, problems, and likely reasons for failure. Projects planned around these risks stand a better chance of being successful, because they will be more resilient to failure. In the deliberative phase of strategy formulation, critical perspectives are essential for anticipating problems and developing plans to avoid them. Once the strategic direction has been set, it then becomes more useful to have everyone marching in the same direction. The can-do attitude is most constructive when everyone is working together toward implementing the same well-planned strategic objectives that have been robustly designed against failure. In the words of the World War II general George Patton, "The time to take counsel of your fears is before you make an important battle decision. That's the time to listen to every fear you can imagine! When you have collected all the facts and fears and made your decision, turn off all your fears and go ahead!"

Daniel Kahneman recommends premortems as a remedy for overconfident optimism in forecasting the outcomes of our decisions. As he describes them, premortems invite people to imagine that they are a year into the future: "We implemented the plan as it now exists. The outcome was a disaster. Please take 5 to 10 minutes to write a brief history of that disaster." It is an invitation to reflect on the potential for failure and to consider how to prevent it. Sometimes a premortem analysis will reveal risks or weaknesses against which it is possible to protect yourself. For instance, it may well be possible to hedge against the risk you anticipate.

Brett Brown, the coach of the Philadelphia 76ers, has used premortem analyses to help anticipate his team's weaknesses on the basketball court. He asked himself, "If we're going to die, what's it going to look like? It looks like jacking up bad shots, turning the ball over a lot." Opening up this conversation with the entire team helped them anticipate weaknesses and think about strategies less vulnerable to failure. Engaging in premortem analysis is particularly useful because it runs against your natural inclination to think in positive ways about the successes you desire and intend.

DISASTER PREPAREDNESS

Anticipating disaster so as to avoid it is a celebrated psychological strategy. Julie Norem calls it defensive pessimism. Defensive pessimists focus on the risks of failure to motivate themselves to avoid those risks. I suspect that many of the best students in my classes drive themselves with defensive pessimism. Before every exam, they vividly imagine failure. They anticipate their guilt at having disappointed their teachers, their parents, and themselves. This fear motivates them to work harder and thereby increases the chances that they will, in fact, do well.

Often, the hardest workers are motivated by the potential guilt they envision. They show up and pick up the slack left by others, fearing that failure to do so would leave them feeling even worse. Defensive pessimism is a personal form of premortem. Thinking ahead with defensive pessimism can inoculate individuals against predictable misfortunes. Teams and organizations use planning meetings at which the group explicitly considers the possibility of failure, maybe by asking questions such as those Klein and Kahneman recommend: "What are the most likely reasons we will fail?" "What can we do to mitigate those risks and increase our decision's expected value?" Vividly imagining the possibility of failure—alone and together—is crucial for figuring out how to avoid it.

Charlie Munger, Warren Buffett's longtime business partner, noted the value of both considering the opposite and disaster preparedness when he described his investing strategy: "Invert, always invert: Turn a situation or problem upside down. Look at it backward. What happens if all our plans go wrong? Where don't we want to go, and how do you get there? Instead of looking for success, make a list of how to fail instead—through sloth, envy, resentment, self-pity, entitlement, all the mental habits of self-defeat. Avoid these qualities and you will succeed. Tell me where I'm going to die so I don't go there."

As with premortems, disaster preparation invites organizations to anticipate calamities, both natural and man-made, and plan for them. Ian Mitroff, one of the fathers of modern crisis management, studied engineering but went on to advise companies on disaster preparedness. Mitroff warns that the main impediment to adequate preparation is wishful thinking. The reluctance to invest in disaster preparedness is based on the optimistic belief that "it can't happen to us." Mitroff's work builds on that of the sociologist Charles Perrow, whose research explores the risks of living with modern technologies. Nuclear power plants, air travel, and artificial intelligence have multiplied human influence. Our tool-making ingenuity allows us to accomplish much, but that power increases the risk when things go wrong.

Many companies and governments have taken Mitroff's advice to heart. They conduct drills that test the resilience of their systems to possible disaster. My hometown of Berkeley, California, is vulnerable to earthquakes, and so the city takes part in the Great California ShakeOut, in which millions of people practice what they will do when the Big One hits. Facebook created a team named Project Storm whose job it is to plan for natural disasters that could disable the company's computer installations around the world. They have conducted storm drills that shut down Facebook data centers to test the resilience of their systems.

Here I would like to pause to acknowledge the unsung heroes who work to anticipate disaster and avert it so that the rest of us can continue blithely on, utterly unaware of how much we owe them. This list includes airline safety inspectors, counterterrorism agents, and enforcers of environmental regulations. The one person who stands atop this list is the former Soviet submarine captain Vasily Arkhipov. Arkhipov was second in command on a nuclear-armed submarine on a secret mission in the Caribbean Sea near Cuba in October 1962, at the height of the Cuban missile crisis. The sub's crew was authorized to launch a nuclear weapon if they learned that the Soviet Union was under attack or if their submarine came under fire. When the sub drew near the US naval blockade of Cuba, it dove deep in an attempt to avoid detection, but a group of American destroyers located the Soviet vessel and began dropping depth charges, explosives intended to force it to the surface.

Tensions heightened as the sub's crew grew more and more fearful. At depth, the sub was cut off from radio communication. Conditions in the sub deteriorated as it remained unable to surface for several days. The air grew so bad and the heat grew so intense that sailors aboard started passing out while on duty. In some parts of the sub, temperatures exceeded 120 degrees Fahrenheit. Alone and under threat, the captain would have found it easy to imagine that what he was facing down below was a reflection of an intensifying conflict on the surface. He decided it was time to launch the sub's nuclear weapon. He had the support of the sub's political officer. But Vasily Arkhipov refused. Afraid that striking would trigger a nuclear confrontation if it was not already under way, Arkhipov put his career and his life on the line by refusing to launch without an order from Moscow.

Eventually the sub was able to surface, take on fresh air, establish radio contact with Soviet command, and evade the American destroyers. Looking back at that moment years later, Arthur Schlesinger Jr., a close adviser to US president John F. Kennedy, said, "This was not only the most dangerous moment of the Cold War. It was the most dangerous moment in human history." For his courageous act, many credit Arkhipov with averting a nuclear catastrophe. But he also faced criticism from his superiors, since, by surfacing, his sub had violated its order to maintain secrecy. One Soviet admiral told him, "It would have been better if you had gone down with your ship." Arkhipov himself was ambivalent about what had happened. His widow said that "he didn't like talking about it." The man who saved the world died in obscurity in 1998 at the age of seventy-two.

Those who avert disaster will always be unsung heroes. Their success is a nonevent. All the rest of us can go on living happy lives, oblivious to the protection of guardian angels intercepting dangers before they strike. Consider counterterrorism. Since the terrorist attacks of September 11, 2001, there have been no more attacks of such a scale or impact. We can be sure that this is not because there are no more terrorists. Instead, credit goes to the counterterrorism forces at law enforcement agencies around the world. How many attacks have been thwarted? How many disasters averted? We will probably never know. The agents involved in those actions cannot boast about their successes, since their stories could compromise their ability to use those informants, techniques, or technologies in the future; their successes will remain a secret.

BACKCAST

I have been focusing on postmortems and premortems as tools for averting disaster, but it is also worth thinking about how to maximize the chances of success. In 1982, John Robinson coined the term "backcast" to describe an analysis that begins at the desired end state and works backward. Robinson is a professor at the University of Toronto's School of the Environment. His interest is in energy consumption, so he began by imagining a world in which renewable sources supply all our energy needs and have phased out fossil fuels. From that goal, Robinson attempted to backcast the conditions, projects, and initiatives that might bring about the state he imagined.

Backcasting differs from forecasting in that forecasting attempts to predict the most likely futures. Backcasting, by contrast, seeks to identify a path to a desirable future, even if it is not the most likely path. What would we like to be able to achieve success, and how do we do it? The risk of backcasting is that it can become simple fantasy based on wishful thinking and implausible assumptions. Backcasting is most likely to be useful when it anticipates all the ways in which things could go wrong, deviating from the preferred path and failing to achieve the desired end state. In this sense, backcasting is entirely compatible with conducting a premortem that anticipates reasons for failure.

Backcasting should help you think through the probabilities of success. If you have conducted a thorough premortem, you will also have estimated the probabilities of failure. Obviously, the probabilities of failure and success must sum to 100 percent. This is a useful check on your calculations. In order to do it, you must establish a clear way to assess success or failure. Sometimes the standard for success will be clear. For instance, SpaceX launched many rockets that failed before successfully sending up a rocket that delivered a payload into earth's orbit. For any given launch, the probability of success and the probability of failure must add up to 100 percent. If you have performed this calculation and your figures do not sum to 100 percent, this represents an opportunity to go back and correct your calculations.

This calculation is made more difficult when success is a matter of degree and not a simple dichotomous outcome. When launching a new product, how many sales does it take to qualify as success? Any specific number will necessarily be arbitrary here, and a more useful forecast might be a probability distribution—that is, a prediction of how likely sales are to reach each of several possible milestones. How likely is it that sales will reach one thousand units? Two thousand units? Three thousand? This exercise will produce a histogram probability distribution, as chapter 3 recommends. In the interests of fully exploring both successful and unsuccessful outcomes, you might find that it makes more sense to employ different premortem and backcasting teams, each specifying its own probability distribution. The distributions they produce will not be identical. Forcing them to reconcile their discrepant predictions will likely provide useful insights.

It is possible that those on the backcasting team will have more fun imagining rosy scenarios and successful results. Although it may feel good to anticipate the possibility of success, do not let your glorious visions become delusions of grandeur. There are many reasons why we might be tempted to overestimate our chances of success, for the same reasons people prefer to be optimistic.

OPTIMISM'S IMMEDIATE BENEFITS AND DELAYED COSTS

Chapter 4 recounted research by Armor, Massey, and Sackett in which they invited their research volunteers to choose between holding accurate and optimistic beliefs. Those volunteers endorsed optimism over accuracy nearly two to one. Asked to justify this belief, people offer two reasons. First, it just feels good to be optimistic. Second, optimistic beliefs produce better outcomes. I want to consider each of these reasons in turn, because they are both partially true and partially false. Both are truer in the short term than in the long term. The benefits of optimistic beliefs are more immediate, and the problems they create come later. Consequently, optimism pits one's immediate and future interests against one another.

The first reason to be optimistic is that it feels good. This is undeniably true, at least in the short term. Here I have to think of the cartoon showing two competing services, one providing "Unpleasant Truths" and one providing "Comforting Lies." There is a long line of people eager for the comforting lies, while the provider of unpleasant truths sits alone and dejected. Comforting lies may include the promise that your future is assured, that you can achieve anything, or that you can have all that you desire. *The Secret* has sold some thirty million copies with its promise that wishful thinking makes itself come true.

Optimistic forecasts of a bright future allow you to savor the anticipated pleasure. However, savoring optimistic anticipation comes with risks. The greater the optimism, the greater the prospects for disappointment. Delusional optimism just makes reality more disappointing when it falls short of our grandiose expectations. My optimistic belief that I will be crowned emperor is likely to be dashed. And because people experience the pain of losses more acutely than the pleasure of gains, excessively optimistic beliefs might ultimately make them worse off.

One way to avoid disappointment is to strategically deflate our optimism right before the moment of truth. College students seem to do this with their forecasts of exam performance. If you ask them how they will perform on their final exam, you'll find that students are more optimistic at the beginning of the semester than when they are sitting down to take the test. Companies play the same game with their earnings forecasts. Forecasts are invariably optimistic about how profitable a given company will be five or ten years in the future. But the quarterly earnings forecast is always more circumspect. As the moment of truth approaches, companies "walk down" forecasts so that when they announce the actual number, they are less likely to fall short of analysts' expectations. Even if you are comfortable with the hypocrisy inherent in this strategic approach to manipulating expectations, it can work only as long as you can fool yourself or your investors.

Obviously, there is a trade-off here between the duration of anticipation and recall. If an event is occurring presently and I must live with its memory the rest of my life, optimism is unwise. I will get to savor the anticipation only for an instant, and then I will forever remember the disappointment when I was not crowned emperor. On the other hand, if an event will occur far in the future, it is possible that a lifetime of savoring can tip the scale toward optimism. A belief in heaven might be the best case: you get to look forward to heaven your whole life, and if your belief happens to be wrong—what do you care? You'll be dead. Despite this, there are many among us who forswear heaven's pleasurable anticipation. Most atheists will concede that their belief in the finality of death provides less to look forward to than does the belief in an eternal paradise, lounging around on clouds and strumming harps. Nevertheless, they cannot fool themselves into believing something so at odds with everything else they know to be true.

If you decide to believe a comforting lie, you are then confronted with the vexing problem of how you should go about fooling yourself. What part of your brain will be fooling which other part? It works best when the self-deception is complete, but how can you maintain the optimistic charade and prevent yourself from figuring it out? And then of course there is the problem of exactly how much you should delude yourself. Ten percent? Twenty percent? The more you loosen your tether to reality, the greater the risk that your delusional beliefs can get you into real trouble.

If you object to the idea that optimism need be self-deceptive, then you would probably endorse the second reason people give for preferring optimism: that optimistic beliefs make themselves come true. As I noted in chapter 4, good evidence exists to support the notion that confidence and success go hand in hand. We observe a close association between confidence and success all around us. More-confident athletes win, more-confident politicians get elected, and more-confident businesspeople succeed. When we are confident, performance feels effortless. These feelings can make it difficult to disentangle which came first—was it the confidence that helped you succeed, or were both your confidence and your success the result of your skills, preparation, and abilities?

Helen Keller believed that optimism was self-confirming: "I demand that the world be good, and lo, it obeys. I proclaim the world good, and facts range themselves to prove my proclamation overwhelmingly true." I must concede that there are instances in which positive expectations produce better outcomes than negative expectations. You will make more friends if you go into the world expecting friendship than if you expect betrayal.

According to Merriam-Webster, optimism is the inclination to anticipate the best possible outcome. This definition is problematically vague, because it fails to tie beliefs to reality. It allows me to be optimistic even when I am underconfident, such as when I believe that there is a 95 percent chance I will live another day. In reality, however, that belief would make me underconfident, because I stand a better than 99 percent chance of seeing the new dawn. Conversely, I could be pessimistic by Webster's definition if I expect only a 5 percent chance I will win the lottery. But I would still be overconfident because that is about a million times larger than the actual probability.

We can clarify things by defining overconfident optimism as an *exaggerated* belief in the likelihood of a desirable outcome. This definition also clarifies the claim that optimistic beliefs make themselves come true. If confidence enables me to jump the chasm or win the race, then my beliefs are not overconfident; they are accurate. Insofar as beliefs can influence outcomes, then, I can enthusiastically endorse the empowering belief. Given the choice between enacting success and enacting failure, I'll go with success any day of the week. But self-fulfilling expectations of your success are not overconfident. They are accurate and they are wise.

It does not follow from this fact that more confidence is better. In fact, confidence can be a self-negating prophecy when performance depends on effort. Just think of the work of Jeffrey Vancouver, discussed in chapter 1. The political candidates who are surest they are going to win, and who therefore think they do not need to campaign, can thereby decrease their chances. In October 2016, most pollsters gave Hillary Clinton a better chance than Donald Trump of winning the presidency. The forecaster Nate Silver was derided ahead of the election for giving Donald Trump even a 30 percent chance. Sensing a victory at hand, Clinton modified her campaign strategy in the final weeks before the election. She turned her attention from Wisconsin, Michigan, and Pennsylvania, states that she thought she had a good chance of winning, and instead campaigned in Arizona and North Carolina, hoping to expand her win in the Electoral College into a powerful mandate that would serve as an effective rebuke to Trump's vulgar and divisive campaign. Clinton lost not only Arizona and North Carolina, but also Wisconsin, Michigan, and Pennsylvania in close votes.

Overly confident beliefs can also have profound effects at the level of a national economy. Central bankers base their policy recommendations on forecasts of the economy's future direction. Expecting an economic boom, they might raise interest rates to head off the risk of an overheated economy and inflationary pressure on prices. On the other hand, anticipating a decline in economic activity might prompt a cut in interest rates or increases in fiscal expenditures to stimulate the economy. When forecasts of the economy are too rosy, it biases our policies. If optimistic forecasts of economic booms dissuade policy makers from the need to stimulate the economy, they might actually increase the risk of a recession.

In the fable of the tortoise and the hare, the hare is so confident that he is faster than the tortoise that he believes he can lollygag and still win. So he takes a break, relaxes, does a little shopping, goes for a massage, stops by his favorite bar for a drink, and takes a nap while the tortoise passes him. When performance depends on effort, being too sure of yourself can be a self-negating prophecy. This is also true for organizations: success can breed the type of inertia that prevents corporations from exploiting the innovative opportunities of tomorrow. Successful firms often find themselves blindsided by smaller, fleeter rivals. Just think of Kodak's loss of the photography business, Sears's decline in the mail-order clothing business, Motorola's loss of its leadership in cellular telephones, or GM's loss of market share to foreign competitors.

In addition to jeopardizing success, overconfidence can make failure more difficult to bear. Consider how terminally ill cancer patients hold out hope for a cure despite its minuscule probability. A *New York Times* op-ed entitled "The Cancer of Optimism" highlighted the costs of such unrealistically optimistic beliefs. Patients hoping for a cure often submit to unpleasant and expensive experimental treatments, such as infusions of toxic chemotherapies that will not cure their illnesses. This is an enormous problem, given that as much as half of all health-care expenses in the US are incurred by those with terminal illness in their last months of life. Too many people spend their final days suffering through expensive treatments that increase their pain but cannot cure them.

Dying overconfident does have the advantage that it gets you out of a problem with which the living must contend: intertemporal inconsistency. Deciding to delude yourself about the future sets you up for disappointment. Repeated self-delusion with repeated disappointment is hard to sustain, because experience helps correct erroneous beliefs. Sustaining delusional confidence depends on *not* learning from experience. That is not just irrational; it comes perilously close to how Albert Einstein is said to have defined insanity: "Doing the same thing over and over again, but expecting different results."

THE PLANNING FALLACY

The California High-Speed Rail Authority was established in 1996 with the mission to build a train line between the state's largest cities. Once completed, it would whisk travelers the 442 miles from Los Angeles to San Francisco in just two hours, rivaling the convenience of air travel. Its initial plan, released in 2000, estimated the project would take until 2016 and cost $25 billion.

The project was to be a shining example of progress in a rail system that otherwise serves as a national embarrassment. In the United States, rail travel constitutes less than 1 percent of passenger-miles, and for good reason. Schedules are sparse and delays are commonplace. Because trains run on tracks owned by freight carriers, passenger trains are routinely forced to wait for freight trains to pass ahead of them. Even when there are no traffic problems, the existing passenger trains' maximum speeds are a measly eighty miles per hour over much of the rail network, and considerably slower than that in many places. Because there are so few travelers, few trains run. China alone has a high-speed rail network forty times as extensive as that of the United States.

As the California project progressed, estimates for its cost and completion time grew. A 2018 plan estimated the price at $77.3 billion for a scaled-back project that would not be complete until 2033. Moreover, the plan gave up on the dream of a line dedicated to high-speed rail, and instead conceded to share the tracks with other trains. In May 2019, California governor Gavin Newsom publicly abandoned the goal of connecting San Francisco and Los Angeles by rail. The High-Speed Rail Authority aspired only to complete the 171 miles of track between the cities of Merced and Bakersfield at a price of $20 billion.

California's experience with the high-speed rail project would not be the first major development project that fell short of its initial promise. Boston's "Big Dig" project rerouted 1.5 miles of Interstate 93 from an aboveground causeway into a subterranean tunnel. When work on the project began in 1991, it had a budget of $2.8 billion and was scheduled to finish in 1998. It was actually completed nine years late, about $20 billion over budget. Other infamous examples include the Sydney Opera House and the Channel Tunnel through which trains travel between England and France.

In 1977, Daniel Kahneman and Amos Tversky explored the psychology behind what they called the planning fallacy. They noted how common it is for people and organizations to underestimate how long it will take them to get things done. I illustrate the planning fallacy in my classroom with an exercise on the first day. My students work in teams to complete a model made of Lego bricks. They have fifteen minutes to plan their work together and to formulate a prediction for how long it will take them. At the end of these fifteen minutes, the teams submit their predictions. The incentives reward accurate predictions and punish overconfidence. Teams expect the task to take them, on average, about eight minutes.

When the clock starts, people eagerly rush forward to inspect the prototype at the front of the classroom. They jockey for the best viewing position. They do their best to take notes on what they see since photos are forbidden. They then run back to where their team is working and do their best to build what they saw. It quickly dawns on the teams that their planning could have been better. Tasks that seemed so simple in the abstract are dauntingly complex in reality. It is difficult to hold a notepad while standing and trying to view the prototype from all angles. Developing useful schematic diagrams is not easy. Fitting together the arms, legs, head, and torso of the model turns out to be trickier than expected. In fact, it takes teams more like fifteen or twenty minutes to complete the job, with some teams taking over thirty minutes. Because the incentives punish overconfidence, teams lose points on the exercise. This is a painful lesson, since the points count toward their grade in the class.

At the start of the Lego-building exercise, when I hold up the prototype to show them what they will be building, most of the students think, "Building Legos? How hard can it be?" They imagine the project in the abstract. At this stage, many fail to anticipate potential problems like crowding around the prototype. As with other development and construction projects, there is a long list of things that could go wrong. Even when you can anticipate them, the probability of any one problem actually occurring is likely small. Nevertheless, if there is only a small probability of each, the joint probability that at least one of the problems will occur is high.

The personal consequences of the planning fallacy can be painful. At times, every one of us has been overwhelmed by life. That happens to me when I have made more commitments than I can keep. I get anxious, knowing that I will disappoint someone who is counting on me. Time is too short to accomplish it all, and so something must suffer—I hurry through the work, sure that I'm missing something or making mistakes. I am faced with impossible choices between neglecting my research collaborators, my students, or my family. I work late and rise early, trying to catch up. The sleep deprivation worsens my mood, leaves me feeling more overwhelmed, and it runs down my immune system. I get sick and fall further behind. In that desperate quagmire, I cannot help wondering whether I could have avoided the whole mess and what I can do to avoid being late again.

IF YOU DON'T WANT TO BE LATE, ENUMERATE

The way most of us wind up overcommitted is that we underestimate how long things will take. Like my students, who see the Lego model and think, "How hard can it be?" we are all prone to considering prospective projects from afar and in the abstract. The students who do a better job of estimating how long it will take them to build the Lego model are those who think ahead to mundane frustrations, make detailed plans of the different components, and anticipate the problems and impediments that will arise. Where will the team run into obstacles? Where will coordination be difficult? The smaller the components into which you can break your plans, the less likely you will be to underestimate the total time.

For instance, when my boss comes to me and asks me whether I will serve on some committee or another, I think about the work that such a project will entail, and I imagine how much time it will take to write up the final report. My estimate of the time commitment will be best if I consider not only how much time things will take if everything goes smoothly, but also some of the many problems that could arise. Some of these problems are unlikely, such as the committee chair being struck by lightning. But others are nearly assured, such as the committee members' getting distracted while drafting the report and checking their Twitter feeds too frequently.

The bigger the project, the more the components, the longer it will take, and the greater the tendency to underestimate its full duration. There is always the temptation to leave your armchair planning at the abstract level. You think of the project's major components and imagine how long each will take. But your time estimate will be better if you get down into the weeds and vividly imagine all the small parts and how they could go wrong. People are less likely to underestimate the duration of short and simple tasks than long and complex ones. When your boss asks you to consider taking on a new project, it is in your interest to make an accurate forecast of how long it will take. How often have you actually stopped to reflect on what you are committing to when you accept responsibility for a new project, how many hours it will consume and what other work you will be unable to accomplish because of it?

Sometimes the incentives actually may push people toward overconfidence. You may have noted the dysfunctional incentives associated with bidding and budgeting. If rivals for a railroad construction contract suspect that lowering their cost estimates will increase their chances to win the bidding, they might intentionally underestimate it. This is obviously a dangerous strategy, since it means the contractor will have committed to lose money on the project. Making this strategy profitable relies on the dubious and deceptive intention to hold the project hostage to a renegotiation for more money later. This usually produces accusations of contract violation and lawsuits, which can add substantially to costs and delays for both sides. Moreover, it can do real harm to your reputation in the industry as a reliable partner.

The alternative is to accurately forecast the costs and delays on the way to a project's completion. Such honesty may seem risky if you believe you will be competing with others whom you know will submit recklessly optimistic bids. I can assuage your fears somewhat by letting you in on a little secret: in auctions like this, buyers rarely select the lowest-cost bid. Why not? Savvy buyers realize that inexperienced and unethical sellers will promise to complete a project for less money and in less time than they can, hoping to extract concessions under duress later. Instead, buyers generally prefer the competent and experienced provider, but they will be happy to use the lowball bid as a cudgel with which to extract concessions and a lower price from their preferred provider.

If you have done your homework preparing a bid, you can justify it with details on the components, their costs, and their durations. In other words, you can enumerate the steps to completion for the buyer to help her understand the wisdom of your proposal. If you are thinking realistically, each of these estimates will come with a range of possible completion times, depending on how the project proceeds. If, for example, you are remodeling a kitchen and find throngs of well-fed termites when you open the walls, it will reveal the need for additional work. Therefore, an estimate of completion times will be more accurate if it presents a probability distribution—a range of completion times, with associated probabilities. (Think back to chapter 3's discussion of probability distributions.)

The range of durations on a renovation project also implies a range of possible costs. There are two basic ways in which sellers can manage these costs. The first is by bidding a fixed price. A fixed price puts the risk of cost overruns on the seller. If sufficient unanticipated expenses drive the cost over the agreed-on price, then the seller takes a loss on the project. On the other hand, if the seller manages to complete the project more cheaply than expected, then the seller earns a greater profit. The second approach is to offer "time and materials" pricing, in which the price depends on how long the work takes and how much it costs. Typically, buyer and seller would agree on how to account for all the relevant costs. Fixed prices are more common because they do not require as much trust in the seller's accounting systems. But if the seller is risk averse and the buyer is risk tolerant and trusting, it may make sense to consider time and materials pricing.

If you find yourself choosing among competing bids, it is worth considering the role the planning fallacy may play in the bids you receive. Selecting the lowest bid to put up your building, revamp your website, or to remodel your kitchen runs the real risk that you have selected the most overly confident bidder, whose work is most likely to go over budget and past deadline.

When my family remodeled our kitchen, I asked the contractors many direct questions about their forecasts for the project's cost and duration. Our favored contractor was not the cheapest, but they had a long track record of experience and good answers to my questions. When I asked how long their other kitchen remodels had taken relative to the initial forecast, they could give me numbers. When I asked how long ours would take, they said it would take three weeks. Three weeks? I was stunned. I had friends whose kitchen remodel was supposed to take six months but were still cooking on a hot plate in the dining room and washing dishes in the bathroom sink nine months later. I told our contractor that I was delighted by the three-week estimate and that I wanted to write it into the contract. I would pay an additional bonus if they finished their work sooner than three weeks. Also, for each day their work went past the three-week deadline, I would reduce my payment. I set this penalty at roughly the daily inconvenience I expected we would endure without a kitchen. The result? The contractor finished the remodeling work in just over two weeks, and I happily paid him the bonus after confirming that the work met our satisfaction.

CHAPTER 7

Consider Other Perspectives

In November 1982, Ray Dalio bet that the US economy was going in the tank. He went on television and predicted an impending depression: "There'll be no soft landing. I can say that with absolute certainty, because I know how markets work." His investments reflected his certainty. His young hedge fund, Bridgewater Associates, bought gold. He expected gold would hold its value, especially when stock markets declined in the presence of inflation. Instead, the US economy experienced, in his words, "the greatest noninflationary growth period in its history." Stocks went up, the price of gold fell, and Dalio was devastated: "Being so wrong—and especially so publicly wrong—was incredibly humbling and cost me just about everything I had built at Bridgewater. I saw that I had been an arrogant jerk who was totally confident in a totally incorrect view."

Bridgewater lost so much money that it could not afford to meet payroll. Dalio had to let everyone else go, and he remained the company's sole employee. He sold his car and borrowed money from his parents. He came close to giving up and taking a job at a bank. Instead, he tried to learn from his failures in order to do better in the future. And he has. Dalio credits his subsequent success to the hard lessons he learned in 1982. "In retrospect, my crash was one of the best things that ever happened to me," he wrote. He let go of his attachment to feeling right and sought critical reflection. "How do I know I'm right?" he asked himself. Instead of just seeking confirmation for his views, he actively sought out other independent thinkers who saw things differently. "By engaging them in thoughtful disagreement, I'd be able to understand their reasoning and have them stress-test mine. That way, we can all raise our probability of being right."

He built a culture at Bridgewater that, in his words, sought to "embrace reality and deal with it." It advocated radical transparency in the search for truth. His goal was to create an idea meritocracy in which the best ideas, supported by the best evidence, would rise to the top. Everyone, from the lowliest intern up, was encouraged to challenge others' views using logic and evidence. In order to facilitate open communication and transparency, most meetings were videotaped and available to everyone within the company. Many at Bridgewater credit the company's success to this unique culture. The company Dalio created has made some extraordinarily successful investment decisions that have paid off handsomely. Today, Bridgewater is, by many measures, the world's most successful hedge fund, with something like $160 billion under management.

The practices that Dalio has put in place at Bridgewater represent the sorts of things that research suggests ought to help reduce the natural human tendency toward overprecision. It's easy to be too sure of your beliefs if you never encounter disagreement. When you confront a smart person who disagrees with you, you can't both be right. What, exactly, is the heart of the issue on which you disagree? What are the assumptions underlying your differing beliefs? Can evidence resolve the disagreement? Who has the better evidence? As chapter 2 advised, considering others' perspectives opens up your mind to consider the ways in which you might be wrong and to critically examine the evidence for your beliefs.

WANNA BET?

Annie Duke tells how playing poker helped make her comfortable with life's inherent uncertainties, with learning from evidence, and with disagreeing productively. Some of these lessons came from other poker players asking her, "Wanna bet?" Players issued this challenge in response to another's dubious claim. The invitation to bet on disagreement exploits the profound insight that when two people have different beliefs, a wager can offer positive expected value to both sides. There are many stories of "proposition betting" by professional poker players placing such bets with one another. They include games of golf, eating one hundred White Castle hamburgers at a sitting, or losing sixty pounds in a year. But perhaps the most famous was John Hennigan's bet that he could survive life in Des Moines.

Hennigan, a professional gambler, lived in Las Vegas. Most days, he played the high-stakes poker tables at big casinos late into the night. He was not answerable to any bosses. He played on his own schedule and never had to punch a time clock. One night, conversation with other poker players turned to what it was like living a "normal" life in the country's heartland. Hennigan speculated about the Iowa city of Des Moines. "This led to some good-natured ribbing as the other players in the game imagined the prospect of a nocturnal action junkie like Hennigan in a place that seemed, to them at least, like the opposite of Las Vegas." Hennigan insisted he would do just fine in Des Moines.

"Wanna bet?" his poker pals taunted him. He did. They then worked out the precise terms of the bet: Hennigan would have to confine himself to living on one particular street in Des Moines—a street with a single hotel, restaurant, and bar, all of which closed by 10 p.m. If he stayed there for thirty days, his poker pals would pay Hennigan $30,000. If he could not do it, Hennigan would owe them $30,000. Hennigan took the bet. He got on a plane to Des Moines the next morning.

Before revealing whether Hennigan survived Des Moines, I want to tell you about another proposition bet with substantially higher stakes. In 2007, the investing guru Warren Buffett bet a million dollars that passive investing would beat active investing. In particular, he bet that, over the next decade, the boring old Standard & Poor's 500 stock index would outperform a set of elite hedge funds. Taking the other side of the bet was Ted Seides, a partner at Protégé Partners, a New York City money management firm. Protégé invests its clients' money in hedge funds. The question of whether passive beats active management is a question of monumental importance. It has implications for how the trillions of dollars invested in the markets, including most retirement savings, are managed. It has implications for economic theories of efficient markets. And it has implications for the livelihoods of the many people, like those at Protégé Partners and Bridgewater Associates, who make their living selling financial services.

Hedge funds aim to hire only the smartest and most talented people to help them make money investing. These people are paid well for their efforts, and management fees at most hedge funds can be hefty. It was not obvious that Buffett would win his bet against this sort of talent. Buffett was betting on the S&P500 index, which mindlessly tracks the performance of the five hundred largest companies in the United States. It does not adjust its holdings based on news about companies or their future prospects. Buffett also began the betting period with a handicap. The 2008 financial crisis sent the S&P500 index into a deep dive, which erased nearly half its value. Nevertheless, the S&P500 came back and returned an average of 7.1 percent over the ten-year period covered by the bet. The best Protégé's hedge funds could manage was a 2.2 percent annual gain. Buffett donated the money he won to Girls, Inc. of Omaha, Nebraska. At last report, the charity did not plan to invest its newfound wealth in hedge funds.

If you think you can beat the index with clever investment decisions, you might want to reconsider in light of Buffett's bet. In fact, anytime someone is eager to take the other side of a bet with you, especially someone like Warren Buffet, it is worth asking why. Chapter 2 introduced "consider the opposite" as the best, most useful, all-purpose debiasing strategy. Ask yourself why you might be wrong. This simple question can go a long way to helping you uncover and correct your biases. Other people can also help you reconsider your beliefs by disagreeing with you. Others' disagreement is therefore a gift of great value, but it is not always easy to appreciate it. This is especially true when they disagree with you about something that you hold dear. Your grouchy uncle, who disparages your political views and who voted for the candidate whom you despise, may make conversation at family gatherings awkward. But if you care about understanding your uncle, the flaws in your own political perspective, or the partisan rift that is tearing apart the civil fabric of our great nation, you have something to gain by listening.

Few people actually believe that they are inerrant, but we are nevertheless often so wedded to our own perspectives that we are reluctant to consider the possibility that we might be wrong. Psychologists call this tendency "naive realism." It leads us to assume that the way we see the world is the only sensible way to see it. Those who disagree with us must be either stupid or evil. Stupidity could account for their inability to recognize the facts right in front of them. But if they see the facts and deny them, diabolical motives seem more likely. In reality, however, perspectives different from our own are the opposite of evil. They can help us appreciate what we have missed, glimpse new opportunities, and understand our own propensity for error. In the words of John Stuart Mill, "It is only by the collision of adverse opinions that the remainder of the truth has any chance of being supplied."

After two days in Des Moines, John Hennigan called his friends in Las Vegas to tell them how much fun he was having. He would be happy to stay a month in Iowa. But because he was a nice guy, he would be happy to let them off the hook. He suggested that they pay him just $15,000 and he come back to Las Vegas. His friends weren't having it. They smelled his desperation. He was trying to get out of the bet after just two days? He must really be suffering. After a little negotiation, Hennigan was able to convince them to let him out of his one-month commitment if he would pay them $15,000. He got on the next plane back to Vegas, paid $15,000 to his poker buddies, and his story became part of poker-player lore.

Let's say that when Hennigan took the bet, he estimated a 70 percent chance he could last a month in Des Moines. That 70 percent multiplied by the $30,000 stakes yielded an expected benefit of $21,000. Hennigan would have to subtract from that the expected loss if he bailed out. That was $30,000 multiplied by the 30 percent probability, or $9,000. Given this, Hennigan could have expected to make $12,000 on the bet, if we ignore his ability to renegotiate the deal. If his friends guessed there was only a 30 percent chance Hennigan would make it, following similar logic, the bet also had a $12,000 expected value for them. When they made the bet, both parties could be pleased at having made bets with positive expected value.

Of course, the bets are positive only with respect to *expected* value. Only one can be right, and one person's gain comes at the other's expense. Anticipating this, the logic of the betting falls apart if both bettors are perfectly rational. If everyone's rationality is common knowledge, they cannot agree to disagree about the probability of future outcomes. The fact that another rational person is ready to take the opposite position represents useful information that must move both from their prior opinions. When both think this way, their views will move toward consensus, undermining their interest in betting.

Chapter 4 recounted how my PhD advisor, Max, offered me an insurance policy: In exchange for my paying him an insurance premium, he would pay my salary if I didn't get a job. If the probability of being unemployed was high enough, then I should have been interested in taking Max's insurance. But Max may be the most rational person I know and is good at thinking about probabilities and uncertainty. I aspire to rationality, even if I routinely fall short. If Max was offering me this bet, it must have been in his interest to do so. He was also more informed about the job market for new PhDs than I was, so there was useful information in his bet. I happily up-dated my beliefs to increase the subjective probability of getting a job offer, and I declined Max's bet.

DAY TRADING

Day trading is an excellent way to lose money. Day trading is the practice of betting on short-term movements in stock prices by trading frequently to try to buy low and sell high. Day traders follow the business press closely and look for the stocks that will go up or down in response to the day's news. They also try to figure out which stocks are undervalued or overvalued. They might conduct sophisticated calculations comparing a stock's valuation with its earnings and prospects for growth.

Every time you trade a stock, you're trading with someone. It is worth considering who is likely to be on the other side of the trade. Are you more informed than they are? You probably choose to trade in equities for which you know enough to hold an informed opinion. How much do others know? On average, others probably know less than you do about that one stock. But you are not trading with the average investor—you are trading with someone who, like you, thinks she knows enough about this particular asset and its future value to trade on that knowledge. Why is she trading with you? What does she know that makes her think she should sell, at the very time you are trying to buy?

Perhaps you were moved to buy Apple stock, for example, when you learned that customers were waiting hours in line to buy the latest iPhone. It seems reasonable to expect that the demand for its products will portend an increase in Apple's stock, but how much? The people waiting in line were clearly dedicated Apple customers.

Some were wearing Apple apparel, and one of them even sported an Apple tattoo on her shoulder. However, it may also be worth asking whether the person selling you Apple stock also saw the lines outside the Apple Store. Does her asking price already factor in anticipated future demand from customers with Apple tattoos?

If both buyer and seller are perfectly rational and both know that the other is perfectly rational—that is, that their rationality is common knowledge—then they will ultimately agree on what an asset is worth. If the seller encounters a willing rational buyer, it must follow that the buyer knows something that leads her to a higher estimate of the asset's value. Knowing this, the rational seller will adjust his valuation upward. The buyer, observing a willing rational seller, will adjust his valuation downward. In the end, rationality demands that they will come to agreement regarding the asset's value. This is likely to dampen their interest in trading. In fact, so long as there is any cost to trading, they will not want to trade.

Yet billions of shares continue to trade on stock markets around the world each day. Why? If buyers and sellers disagree about how much a stock is worth, they can't both be right. And trading incurs fees. One explanation centers on overconfidence: if both sides believe they are right and the other side of the trade is wrong, they can both see the trade as having positive expected value. Research in behavioral economics that seeks to apply what we know about the biases in human judgment to understanding economic behavior has considered these issues. There is strong evidence that the more investors trade, the worse their investing returns. Scholars who study behavioral finance have suggested that overprecision might account for so many investors' willingness to trade, despite the fact that half of them are probably making a mistake.

If stock market participants are too sure they have correctly estimated how much a stock is worth, they will be interested in trading despite the clear evidence that there are people who disagree, and who are therefore ready to take the other side of the trade. Investors who overestimate the accuracy of their valuation will be tempted to believe that they are more rational, or know more, than the person on the other side of the trade. This may manifest itself as a failure to appreciate the imperfections in their own information or opinions about a stock's value, or a failure to appreciate the value of knowledge that others possess. They may be too willing to believe in their own perspicacity or too quick to denigrate others' wisdom.

If you own individual stocks, did you think about who was selling the stocks you bought? It is possible you were trading with an unsophisticated rube who lacked your keen insight into the stock's true value. But most trades are not conducted by unsophisticated rubes. Most of the trading volume in the stock market is by banks, hedge funds, sophisticated money managers, and algorithms. It is, in theory, possible for a well-informed individual to outsmart these savvy professionals. But don't bet on it. In every stock trade, one side has less information than the other, just as in every poker game there is a worst player—the patsy whose wallet is most likely to be lightened. Warren Buffett quotes the adage, "If you've been playing poker for half an hour and you still don't know who the patsy is, *you're* the patsy." If you don't know why the person on the other side of the trade is trading with you, consider the possibility that you are the patsy.

Sophisticated institutional investors like banks and hedge funds rarely engage in day trading. By one estimate, over 99 percent of day traders are individuals investing their own money. On average, day traders lose money. Evidence suggests their efforts deliver an annualized 23 percent loss, after fees. That is, for every dollar you begin investing in day trading, you should expect to have only 77 cents after a year of work.

If trading your own stocks is a sucker's bet and you are apprehensive of paying hefty fees to money managers who will fail to deliver stellar returns, what should you do? Warren Buffett's advice to individual investors like you and me is simple. Many wise advisers and finance professors offer the same advice: put your money in index funds. Index funds have low fees because they don't need to pay lots of expensive money managers to pick stocks—they just invest in the index. You can join Buffett in his bet on the performance of passive investing. In so doing, you are capitalizing on the collective wisdom of the crowd participating in the market.

WISDOM OF THE CROWD

Collectively, a crowd can be wiser than the individuals within it. The classic parable comes from Sir Francis Galton's visit to the West of England Fat Stock and Poultry Exhibition in 1907. There Galton witnessed a competition in which 787 visitors to the fair each guessed the weight of an ox. Some of these guessers were on intimate terms with oxen; others hadn't a clue. Each guess included some useful signal of the true weight. But they also included what statisticians call noise—errors that deviate from the truth. Some noise increased estimates, some decreased it. To Galton's great astonishment, the average guess was only a pound off of the ox's true weight of 1,198 pounds. The average was more accurate than virtually all the individuals. How was it so close? When averaged, individuals' errors tended to cancel each other out.

In chapter 2, I mentioned the wisdom of the crowd. We capitalize on the crowd's wisdom when we collect a diversity of viewpoints with the goal of averaging across them. These lessons have been reprised many times in contexts as diverse as stock market valuations, geopolitical forecasting, and organizational decision making. Averaging across people cancels out noise and preserves signal. However, the crowd's wisdom depends on the independence of its members from each other. Correlated error cannot be averaged out. That is, the crowd is wise so long as different people possess at least some accurate information and their errors are uncorrelated with one another. For every person who errs high, another will err low, and so averaging across them will cancel out their errors.

An analogy might help illustrate how this works. If we want to forecast vote shares in an election, asking voters is useful. But like the individuals in Galton's weight-guessing contest, any one voter provides only limited information. So we ask more. The more voters we ask, the better the forecast we will get. No one individual knows the vote share each candidate will receive, but each one has a little bit of information. The average poll includes a thousand registered voters. A poll of that size comes with a 95 percent confidence interval of plus or minus 3 percentage points. In other words, our statistician friends tell us that we can be 95 percent certain that the actual vote, should it occur at that time, would fall within 3 percentage points of the estimate we got from our sample.

You may be surprised to learn that the wisdom of the crowd extends to the crowd within. A clever technique capitalizes on the fact that each of us, in Walt Whitman's words, "contain multitudes." Researchers familiar with the wisdom of crowds have asked individuals to provide multiple estimates of the very same thing. One study asked volunteers to estimate the dates for various historical events, such as the discovery of electricity. Their first estimates were off by an average of 130 years. After answering, volunteers read: "First, assume that your first estimate is off the mark. Second, think about a few reasons why that could be. Which assumptions and considerations could have been wrong? Third, what do these new considerations imply? Was the first estimate rather too high or too low? Fourth, based on this new perspective, make a second, alternative estimate." On average, these second estimates were better—they were off by only 123 years. But averaging the first and second estimates improved their accuracy even more.

This result underscores the value of asking why you might be wrong. Embracing this self-diversity acknowledges the complex reality of the human mind. In his poem "Song of Myself," Walt Whitman pays homage to the diversity within:

Do I contradict myself?
Very well then I contradict myself,
(I am large, I contain multitudes.)

If the inner multitudes can disagree, there is even greater potential in the diversity among different people, their experiences, their beliefs, and their perspectives. Effective leaders capitalize on diversity to help them make better decisions.

DIVERSE CROWDS AND BIASED MOBS

Alfred P. Sloan was one of the most respected business leaders in American history. Under his leadership, General Motors went from a small upstart to the largest auto manufacturer in the world. His management style has been widely admired, studied, and imitated. One particular story recounts a meeting of senior executives at which they had come to consensus: "Gentlemen, I take it we are all in complete agreement on the decision here." They looked around at one another and nodded. The next thing Sloan said was not what they expected: "I propose we postpone further discussion of this matter until the next meeting to give ourselves time to develop disagreement, and perhaps gain some understanding of what the decision is all about."

Fully informed decisions require diverse inputs that reflect all the relevant considerations. Courageous leaders like Sloan will seek out or intentionally inject diversity to avoid prematurely ending debate before all useful perspectives have been aired. US president Abraham Lincoln intentionally constituted a cabinet of people who disagreed with one another. He wanted his advisers to represent the diverse perspectives of the nation he served. Those diverse perspectives increased the chance of the team finding their way to the truth.

The crowd is wise when it is diverse. A variety of perspectives is useful because it reduces the risk that they share the same bias. When everyone shares the same bias, then, in James Surowiecki's words, the crowd becomes a mob. Their errors are correlated, and they may reinforce each other's biases. For example, if everyone who answers your political opinion poll is from Berkeley, California, the results might be a bit more liberal than the nation overall. Discussion within a biased group does not reliably reduce the members' bias. Instead, the participants tend to talk about the information they share and emerge from discussion even more biased than they went in. Psychologists call this "group polarization."

One study compared the famously liberal residents of Boulder, Colorado, with the conservative residents of nearby Colorado Springs. Groups from each town reported their attitudes toward the charged political issues of global warming, affirmative action, and same-sex marriage. They then met to discuss the issues, and afterward reported their attitudes again. People emerged from their discussions more polarized than they went in. That is, the conservatives came out more staunchly conservative and the liberals became more flamingly liberal. They reinforced their shared views and helped reassure each other of the wisdom of their common inclinations.

You want to preserve the diversity of your work teams by reducing mutual influence ahead of a decision or meeting. That means preventing people from lobbying, persuading, or influencing each other before they have had a chance to formulate their opinions. For instance, when my department is considering a hiring decision, we collect everyone's views prior to the meeting. The simple way to do this is by having everyone submit a ranked list of the job candidates via some online survey. If everyone favors hiring the same person, then the meeting can be brief. Even when there is disagreement, aggregated rankings yield a ranked list of candidates, usefully ordering the discussion. Forcing people to state their views at the outset is especially helpful in drawing out the views of the newest members, who might otherwise be reluctant to contradict a more powerful senior colleague who has spoken first.

Collecting the views of the group in this way might lead you to question the value in holding the meeting at all. Many studies of group dynamics suggest that discussions can actually be detrimental to the quality of a decision. Unless the wisest individuals are also the loudest and most persuasive, group discussion can easily draw consensus away from the truth. Studies of grant funding committees show how this can occur. Granting agencies like the National Science Foundation (NSF) expend great effort assessing grant applications with the goal of selecting the most meritorious. The agency enlists several eminent and experienced scholars to review each proposal and submit their ratings to the NSF. The NSF wants to get these decisions right. Grants are regularly hundreds of thousands or millions of dollars, and they can make or break the career of a young scientist.

So the NSF flies the grant review teams from around the world to its headquarters, where they meet to discuss each proposal. The team then makes recommendations to the NSF regarding which proposals deserve funding. The thing is, analysis suggests that the teams would have selected better applications if they had not bothered to meet at all. Instead of flying everyone to Alexandria, Virginia, and spending several exhausting days in meetings, if the NSF had just chosen those applications with the top ratings, they would have made better decisions. Getting everyone together to discuss did not, on average, allow them to select better applications.

INDIVIDUAL DIFFERENCES

While we are on the subject of diversity, we should consider the question of whether some types of people are more overconfident than others. Much has been made of male overconfidence, for instance. However, the evidence supporting these claims is weak and inconsistent. It is difficult to tell, based solely on someone's race, gender, culture, or age, whether he or she is likely to be overconfident. In the popular imagination, men are more overprecise—that is, more confident in their inaccurate knowledge. That is why, for instance, there are so many jokes about men's reluctance to stop and ask for driving directions. The problem is that there is just about no systematic evidence showing that men actually display more overprecision than women. There are some published claims that men are more likely than women to believe that they are better than others. However, these beliefs appear to be restricted to particular stereotypically male domains such as sports and auto repair and are not consistently replicable. Furthermore, women show more overplacement than men in stereotypically female domains.

Some books that discuss gender differences in confidence advise women that they need to step up their confidence to compete with men. However, if men are, on average, overconfident, it seems problematic to instruct women to be more biased. Telling women to make more errors is bad advice. If women are less biased than men, there are many ways in which they could stand to benefit. For instance, if being overconfident about stock valuation leads people to trade too much, women might make better investment decisions. If being too sure of themselves leads men to denigrate others' opinions, women might make better leaders. In sum, even if men are more confident than women, it is not at all clear that women would do well to make themselves more confident.

One woman who brought an enormous amount of confidence to her work was Elizabeth Holmes. Holmes's entrepreneurial vision motivated her to drop out of Stanford University to found the biotechnology company Theranos. Holmes held her own in the male-dominated world of entrepreneurship. It is a world where, in the words of the venture capitalist Randy Komisar, leaders "believe, irrationally, that they are immune to the forces that defeat the normals every day and that they can succeed where others have failed." From a young age, Holmes wanted to "discover something new, something that mankind didn't know was possible." Her high school yearbook identified her ambition to "save the world." When she took classes in chemical engineering and microfluidics at Stanford, she envisioned an opportunity to test blood in a new way.

Holmes built an idealistic vision of a simple, widely accessible blood test that would enable timely health screenings. Her vision inspired powerful luminaries including Henry Kissinger, George Shultz, James Mattis, and William Perry, each of whom she recruited to serve on her board of directors. Theranos attracted over a billion dollars in funding. Holmes was able to lure excellent employees and put together an impressive team. As her successes multiplied, she confidently asserted her vision for the company. Despite the prominence of her board, she gave them almost no control over the company. Instead, Holmes retained control with a special class of stock that provided her with one hundred votes per share.

Holmes became an inspirational figure who rallied faith in her leadership, not only from a loyal board but from the business press, whose fawning articles celebrated her vision. She wore black turtlenecks like her idol, Steve Jobs. The persona she developed as CEO of Theranos successfully leaned in to the confident impresario role adopted by other Silicon Valley aspirants. Unfortunately, her confidence was built on a lie. Theranos could not deliver on its promise of conducting hundreds of tests using only a drop of blood. Holmes's infectious confidence in her project could not overcome the physical limitations of the technology. Despite her valiant effort to keep the myth alive, Theranos collapsed amid scandal. Holmes was ultimately charged with fraud in federal court.

HOLIER THAN THOU

One of the ways in which Elizabeth Holmes defended her aggressive management and marketing puffery was on the basis of high principle. She saw what she was doing as a moral calling: "I want to create a whole new technology, and one that is aimed at helping humanity at all levels regardless of geography or ethnicity or age or gender." When she accepted the Woman of the Year award from

Glamour magazine, she expressed the hope that she would be a role model "that our little girls will see when they start to think about who do they want to be when they grow up." Her noble mission justified much of what Holmes undertook as CEO of Theranos—even when that meant pushing the boundaries of ethics and the law.

Like Holmes, all of us find it easier to justify our biases when we believe we are serving a noble cause. Excessive faith in your own virtue can blind you to your moral shortcomings. Those most sanctimoniously confident of their own virtue are at the greatest risk of moral downfall. One need look no further than the list of religious leaders and self-proclaimed holy men whose moral failings have brought them low. Here, I think first of the scandals involving the sexual abuse of children by holy men high in the Catholic Church, but they are far from alone.

Perhaps there is no more memorable example than that of Jim and Tammy Faye Bakker, the televangelists whose empire included an ostentatious headquarters complex called Heritage Village and a Christian-themed amusement park, Heritage USA, in South Carolina. Viewers' contributions to their *PTL Club* show exceeded a million dollars a week in the 1970s, revenue that helped fuel ostentatious indulgence by the Bakkers. Jim Bakker reveled in his lavish lifestyle, saying, "God wants his people to go first class." The Bakkers justified much of what they did on the grounds that they were serving God.

It is easy to scorn these leaders who see themselves as morally superior. It is harder to see our own moral failings. Most people think of themselves as more virtuous than others. One reason is that we are usually more aware of our own virtuous thoughts and behavior than of others'. If virtue depends on what you believe in your heart, and most of us intend the good in most things, then most of us will usually be virtuous. Even those who engage in the most reprehensible crimes do so only a minority of the time. Innocent pleasures and virtuous motives are more common for virtually all of us than cheating, deception, and crime. If I am honest 95 percent of the time, then it makes sense for me to believe that I am more honest than others. When I ask the students in my class to rate their honesty compared with that of their classmates, over 90 percent of them claim to be in the top half of the class.

As chapter 1 noted, we are all prone to thinking that we will perform better than others on tasks that are simple or about which we feel capable. We are most prone to believing we are better than others when the task is easy and others' performances are hidden, as is the case with honesty. On the flip side, when we are more keenly aware of our own failings than those of others, we are prone to thinking that we are worse than they are, which is why so many people feel that they suffer more private self-doubts than others do. Taking the outside view can correct these errors and provide a more objective perspective.

TAKE THE OUTSIDE VIEW

Taking the outside view helped Andy Grove make the most important decision of his career. Grove led Intel during some of its most successful years. It was a time when the company was at the forefront of stupendous improvements in computing technology and processing speed. A 1990s publicity campaign advertised Intel's famous microprocessors with the tagline "Intel inside." Some of the ads actually celebrated the microchip manufacturing facilities in which workers wear full-body suits to minimize dust. These ads featured workers clad in their "bunny suits" dancing around the pristine environment of the clean room in which Intel chips are assembled. But clean room break dancing is not where Intel started.

Since its founding in 1968, Intel had built a healthy business selling computer chips that stored data. But Intel's profits had taken a beating from increased competition, and Grove described 1985 as "a grim and frustrating year." Rival producers of memory chips were driving down prices and outcompeting Intel. Grove and his colleague Gordon Moore were wrestling with the difficult decision of whether the company should double down on its memory chip business and build a bigger, more efficient factory. Another alternative was to exit the memory business entirely and pivot to focus on building microprocessors. At one critical juncture Grove asked Moore, "If we got kicked out and the board brought in a new CEO, what do you think he would do?" Moore responded without hesitation, "He would get us out of memories." In that instant, Grove and Moore saw what they had to do. Intel refocused its business on microprocessors, and the rest is history.

Taking the outside view is synonymous with considering other people handling a similar situation. It is a useful antidote to the planning fallacy. Chapter 6 explored how the planning fallacy leads us to build overly rosy forecasts of how quickly we will be able to get things done. Daniel Kahneman illustrates this with the story of a committee on which he served. The committee's job was to design an educational curriculum and write a textbook. When they considered the question of how long they should expect the project to take, each of the members of the committee wrote down an estimate. The group's consensus was that it would take them about two years. Then Kahneman took the outside view and asked how long it had taken other curriculum committees like theirs to complete their work. The answer: most others had given up in failure.

Among the 40 percent that had actually finished, none finished in less than seven years.

By asking about other, similar committees, Kahneman was taking the outside view. Doing so is useful in many circumstances. For instance, talented young athletes can focus on their own passion for the game when considering their prospects for making it in the major leagues. It would help them to take the outside view of their prospects: among all talented and passionate young athletes, only a minuscule minority actually earn a living playing sports. Step outside your first-person perspective and consider the rates of success among others like you. Before you decide to focus on playing football rather than studying for your chemical engineering exam, ask yourself how often others have succeeded at what you are trying to do. How often do middling college players get drafted into the NFL? How often are initial public stock offerings successful? What percentage of corporate mergers ultimately make money for shareholders? You may think that you can fly by flapping your arms, but has anyone ever actually done so?

Taking the outside view can also be a helpful antidote to *under-*confidence. If you feel like an impostor in your new job, ask how many successful people experienced challenges early in their careers. How many of them harbored doubts about their ability to make it? Talk to senior colleagues about their early days on the job. You are likely to find that most of them also faced challenges and self-doubt. They may also have useful advice on how best to overcome those challenges.

Sometimes, taking the outside view is made more difficult by the fact that what you want to do has not been tried before. The Wright brothers had few relevant comparison cases when they put their new aircraft to the test in 1903. In situations like this, reason must inform our views with the perspective of an objective outsider. What are the reasons to expect that our project might succeed? What are the reasons to expect failure? Are the risks worth it, and what can you do to protect yourself from disaster? We can be grateful the Wright brothers took the risk, and we can also appreciate that they had the good sense to do so over sand dunes, where a crash was less likely to kill them.

Taking the outside view can help reduce your vulnerability to being too sure you are right. Indeed, this is Ray Dalio's approach to being less wrong: try to understand the perspectives of others whose views differ from yours. Consider the person who is ready to buy the stock I want to sell. What does that person know? Try to understand the perspective of the person who has just voted for the candidate I oppose. Is there a sense in which this person's position might be justified? Considering the possibility that others' perspectives are true and valid helps us work with them, live with them, understand them, settle disputes with them, and do business with them. Considering other perspectives requires that we admit that there are other valid ways to see the truth. Henry Ford, the founder and visionary leader of the Ford Motor Company, advised: "If there is any one secret of success, it lies in the ability to get the other person's point of view and see things from that person's angle as well as from your own." Considering others' perspectives facilitates more harmonious relationships, greater mutual understanding, and more constructive conflict.

CHAPTER 8

Find the Middle Way

On June 3, 2017, Alex Honnold completed what may be the most stupendous athletic achievement of all time. Honnold was thirty-one years old and already one of the world's best rock climbers. He had climbed some of the world's most difficult routes, in Mexico, Canada, Chad, Borneo, and Argentina. But the ultimate climb, according to Honnold, is El Capitan—a granite monolith, three thousand feet tall, at the heart of Yosemite National Park. "El Cap" is famous among climbers for its size and difficulty. Its first ascent, in 1958, took a team of three expert climbers forty-seven days. Today, with better equipment and extensive knowledge of the route, expert climbers can ascend it in four or five days. When Honnold climbed El Cap, he did it in under four hours.

Rock climbing is a dangerous sport. Injuries and deaths are common. Some life insurers will refuse to cover people who rock climb. For most climbers, getting good at the sport is about getting good at using the protective gear, which includes helmets, ropes, harnesses, carabiners, and anchoring devices. Climbers must know how to tie the knots in ropes that will catch them if they fall. A long climb like El Cap requires hundreds of pounds of equipment that climbers have to haul up. A multiday climb also necessitates supplies of food, sleeping platforms, and toilet facilities.

Alex Honnold is different. What he does is known as free soloing. He leaves behind all the safety gear and climbs alone, without so much as a harness. That means any small slip in his four hours climbing El Cap would have cost Honnold his life. Fortunately, he did not slip. His perfect climb was documented in the film *Free Solo*, which won the Academy Award for the best documentary of 2018. The film's most arresting moments are shot from above Honnold with the spectacularly beautiful Yosemite Valley thousands of feet below. Those gorgeous images are tinged with more than a little terror. In the movie, the filmmakers talk about whether their work could possibly distract Honnold at some crucial moment. They imagine the film rolling as they watch their friend fall to his death. There are long stretches in which the cameramen were afraid to look through their lenses.

It is easy to imagine that it must take enormous confidence for Alex Honnold to do what he does. He agrees that confidence is important but disagrees that more confidence is necessarily better. He sees risks for both overestimation and underestimation. "The best strategy is a deep and well-founded confidence that you can indeed do the thing that you're trying to do," says Honnold. "It's not enough to think that you can, you have to absolutely know on a physical and rational level that the free solo that you're attempting is well within your abilities." Overconfident climbers will take on challenges for which they are not ready. Underconfidence can produce counterproductive risk aversion, such as when climbers tire themselves out by clinging too tightly to a handhold.

You may not be clinging to a narrow ledge thousands of feet up, but you undertake risky activities each and every day. Whether that is driving your car in heavy traffic, making high-stakes investment decisions, or navigating complex relationships, you need to be able to calibrate your confidence. Well-calibrated confidence is the map that can guide your life choices about what to undertake, how to direct your efforts, and what risks might get you killed.

This book has cataloged the situations in which each of us is likely to be either overconfident or underconfident. The following table summarizes some of those situations. It distinguishes among the three forms of confidence:

- Estimation quantifies how good you think you are, how likely you are to succeed, or how quickly you will get things done.
- Placement compares yourself with others.
- Precision assesses the accuracy of your beliefs or how sure you are that you are right.

Both overconfidence and underconfidence are common, each in different situations. The one notable exception is the distinct absence of underprecision. Research has failed to identify situations

	Overconfidence	Underconfidence
Estimation	Wishful thinking (ch.4) Planning fallacy (ch.6)	Rumination and worry (ch.1) Risk exaggeration (ch.4)
Placement	Easy tasks (ch.1) Common events (ch.1) Better-than-average effects (ch.5) Moral superiority (ch.7)	Difficult tasks (ch.1) Rare events (ch.1) Impostor syndrome (ch.1)
Precision	90 percent confidence intervals (ch.1) Ideological certainty (ch.2) Religious zealotry (ch.2) Histogram analyses (ch.3) Equity trading (ch.7)	

in which people are systematically underprecise—that is, insufficiently sure that their knowledge is correct. That is why I have so enthusiastically recommended that you consider why you might be wrong.

You will note, however, that I have not urged you as enthusiastically to think that you might be worse than others. Knowing the risks of the impostor syndrome, I would not want to push you toward underplacement. Since these three forms of confidence are not mutually exclusive, it is possible to be overprecise about underplacement. That happens when you are convinced that you are worse than others when you are not. For each of the three, I have done my best to consider the evidence and have come to the conclusion, in one context after another, that wisdom recommends truth and accuracy. Holding accurate beliefs is useful for making decisions, including decisions about how to improve.

CONFIDENT PERSISTENCE

Some readers may still wonder whether reasonable and well-calibrated confidence might be limiting. If greater optimism, grit, and persistence can improve your chances of success, then why tamp them down? Doesn't confidence promote success? It is easy to think of irrepressible optimists and how their hard work ultimately led to success. Thomas Edison's dogged persistence led to his invention of the lightbulb. From 1878 to 1880, Edison's lab in Menlo Park, New Jersey, worked on creating an incandescent bulb that would turn electricity into light. Edison attempted and then discarded many thousands of different designs and materials. Nevertheless, confidence in his ultimate success gave Edison the courage to respond to those who ridiculed his repeated failures: "I have not failed. I've found ten thousand ways that won't work." Was Edison overconfident?

No, Edison's confidence was justified. He did, in fact, succeed in inventing a commercially viable lightbulb. Edison was right to believe in his ultimate success. As he was working, did Edison know with certainty that he would succeed in finding a workable lightbulb? Probably not. He explored a number of other inventions that did not work out, including a mechanical voting machine, an electric pen, a talking doll, and a movie projector. However, the potential rewards for any one of those devices could easily have justified his long hours of toil for a low probability of success. In other words, investing can have a positive expected value, even if the probability is small, provided the payoff is sufficiently large.

Although entrepreneurs are, on average, overconfident, that doesn't mean they have to be, or that overconfidence makes them successful. One of the most successful entrepreneurs of our time,

Jeff Bezos, did not begin certain of his success. He advised early potential investors, "I think there's a seventy percent chance you're going to lose all your money, so don't invest unless you can afford to lose it." Even now, Bezos does not delude himself about the prospects for the company he leads: "I predict that one day Amazon will fail. Amazon will go bankrupt. If you look at large companies, their lifespans tend to be 30-plus years, not a hundred-plus years." This kind of calibrated confidence helps people anticipate the future and make wise decisions in the face of risk and uncertainty.

How should you calibrate your confidence regarding the risks you take? You ought to base that confidence on hardheaded analysis rather than woolly-headed self-delusion. Chapter 3 encouraged you to think through the range of probabilities and consider all the possible outcomes. Chapter 4 applied the logic of expected value, quantifying both the probability and the outcome. Edison could afford ten thousand failures because each one was cheap. Alex Honnold could not afford to fail once, so he practiced every move on the way up El Capitan, protected by a harness and a rope—until he was sure he could do it. Chapter 6 encouraged you to think through the upside and the downside, enumerating the outcomes and calculating the expected value. And chapter 7 encouraged you to take the outside view, considering comparison cases and getting input from unbiased advisers.

When your confidence is justified by rigorous analysis, it is more likely to contribute to your success. Not only do you then have a solid foundation on which to build your beliefs and expectations, but you can be more convincing to others. Venture capitalists and investors, for instance, are famously skeptical of overconfident entrepreneurs who attempt to oversell their future promise. Being able to explain the basis for your confident beliefs will make them more persuasive to others. Having computed expected value may also help persuade a boss, a colleague, or an investor who is skeptical of your proposal. Nevertheless, you will have choices about how optimistically to portray your venture and how aggressively to sell it.

PUTTING A BRAVE FACE ON IT

Chapter 4 confronted a dilemma for entrepreneurs: the pull between the need to hold accurate beliefs to inform good decisions and the motive to display confidence for the sake of persuading others. This dilemma is just a special case of a more general problem that every leader faces. On the one hand, decisions are best when based on the best evidence, the most accurate forecasts, and the most objective assessments. On the other hand, every business leader would like to attract investors, workers, and customers—and that is easier when a company's prospects are bright. Indeed, each company's future depends on its leader convincing investors, workers, and customers to bet on that future.

The display of confidence is inherent in effective leadership. We look to leaders to inspire and direct the efforts of the team. Displaying confidence in yourself and your abilities helps show off your leadership potential. Some business writers go so far as to say that confidence is the fundamental basis from which leadership grows. In a study I published with Cameron Anderson, Jessica Kennedy, and Sebastien Brion, we found that the display of confidence increases people's influence and social status. We assigned volunteers to work in pairs and randomly assigned one person in each pair to the high-confidence condition. Volunteers in the high-confidence condition learned that they had good reason to be confident they would do well because they had performed well on a pretest. These confident people behaved in ways that produced greater deference from their partners and higher status for them. They were more influential.

Because it is easier to assess someone's outward display of confidence than his or her actual abilities, it is tempting to rely on that display and place our trust in those who seem more confident. But that is an easy way to get conned, because people can fake the display of confidence. The appearance of self-assurance is crucial to the way con men gain our confidence. The notorious con man Frank Abagnale reports that the most important feature of a successful swindler is confidence: "Top con artists, whether they're pushing hot paper or hawking phony oil leases, are well dressed and exude an air of confidence and authority."

The fact that con men, swindlers, and shysters do sometimes succeed is not evidence that fakery is a winning strategy. Even for those who can overcome their moral qualms about deceiving and manipulating others, the approach carries real risks. The con is a problematic long-term strategy because being exposed as a fraud quickly undermines a leader's credibility. Leaders must rely on others' trust in their abilities and confidence in their judgment. Losing credibility can mean leaders lose their followers and their ability to lead.

My research with Elizabeth Tenney, Nate Miekle, Cameron Anderson, and David Hunsaker explores the circumstances under which people can be held accountable for their false expressions of confidence. We find that leaders are more likely to face consequences for specific, factual claims. All of us have seen leaders who avoid accountability by providing more puffery than substance. They may use ambiguity and "weasel words" to make vague promises that do not commit them to anything in particular. Rather than substantive commitments, they may instead adopt confident mannerisms; they have a confident tone of voice, they speak before others, they speak louder, and they talk over others. Even if these confident people fail to deliver a stellar performance, it can be hard to discredit them, since it is hard to identify any particular falsehood.

Abagnale advises that if you want to avoid being swindled, you should look beyond the confidence and try to assess the substance. Be suspicious of confident talk that isn't supported by credible evidence and binding commitments. "We guarantee a zero defect rate in our products" is a more substantive claim than "We will provide a quality product, guaranteed." When testing the claims of someone who you think might be putting on a confident show but who lacks the ability to back it up, remember the recommendation in chapter 7 and ask them "Wanna bet?" Will they back up their claim with a contractual guarantee? Their reluctance to do so could reveal that they do not actually believe what they are saying.

There are many ways to structure bets on others' confident claims. If you think that a colleague is exaggerating the potential market for her new product, you could offer her a bet on future sales. If a potential employee is confident in his future performance, he should be willing to accept more of his pay as a performance-contingent bonus. If a vendor is claiming that her product is better than a competitors', invite her to back up that claim with verifiable quality measures. It is common, for instance, for companies to claim that their products are worth premium prices because of superior quality. If that is true, it ought to be possible to measure it and make payments contingent on the successful delivery of that quality.

This discussion might have you thinking about how you can assert your confidence as a leader. It is not always feasible or desirable to put a bet on every forecast or promise. How can you express enough confidence to give others faith in your leadership but avoid making claims that could get you in trouble? Could your honesty undermine your leadership status? Daniel Kahneman warns, "Experts who acknowledge the full extent of their ignorance may expect to be replaced by more confident competitors, who are better able to gain the trust of clients. An unbiased appreciation of uncertainty is a cornerstone of rationality—but it is not what people and organizations want." You should be concerned about less honest or less ethical rivals who might indulge in more confident claims than you in order to increase their influence.

This was the situation faced by my colleague Rob MacCoun when he testified before Congress on the topic of drug decriminalization. He had studied how decriminalization might affect drug use. In response to questions from members of Congress, MacCoun reported that the available evidence suggested that decriminalizing marijuana was likely to lead only to a modest increase in marijuana usage. However, he also noted that the empirical evidence regarding the decriminalization of harder drugs was limited.

MacCoun was followed in the hearing by a passionate antidrug crusader, Sandra Bennett, who spoke from her own experience: "First and foremost, I'm a mother who, because of illicit drugs, has been subjected to every parent's worst nightmare and ultimate horror, the death of their child, and it's from that perspective that I'm going to address you today." She accused MacCoun of influencing children to take up drugs: "The pro-drug advocates are allowed to operate out of our universities with impunity, and their deceptive and dangerous rhetoric fills the Internet, where it is readily available even to our primary school children." Bennett scorned MacCoun's research and told the members of Congress that decriminalizing marijuana would certainly lead to a spike in usage. Any contradictory evidence was, in her words, "balderdash."

If you suspect that Sandra Bennett was more influential that day, some evidence might confirm your suspicions. Research by Celia Gaertig and Joe Simmons has found that expressing confidence increases advisers' credibility, all else being equal. Volunteers in their studies tried to forecast the outcomes of sporting events. They weren't experienced sports bettors, but they did have the benefit of some useful advice. The researchers manipulated the confidence expressed by advisers and examined its effect on research volunteers. The results showed that advisers' credibility dropped after they admitted that they weren't confident. When advisers began by saying, "I'm not sure," volunteers saw them as less competent, trustworthy, and persuasive. On the other hand, advisers achieved greater credibility when they began by claiming "I am very confident." This result is consistent with a great deal of research showing that the expression of confidence confers credibility and increases perceived competence.

But if you infer that the right way to gain credibility is to provide false certainty, you would be wrong. Advisers in the study actually undermined their credibility by claiming absolute certainty about uncertain events, such as whether the Chicago Cubs would beat the San Francisco Giants. Instead, the adviser who made forecasts like "there's a sixty-four percent probability that the Cubs will win" earned greater credibility. The most respected advisers claimed to be confident in predicting that the Cubs had a 64 percent chance of winning. The least respected said they were not sure but thought the Cubs would win. It was as if volunteers in Gaertig and Simmons's study had taken Voltaire's words to heart: "Uncertainty is an uncomfortable position, but certainty is an absurd one." Volunteers appreciated the honesty in a probabilistic prediction for an inherently uncertain event. To be clear, volunteers preferred advisers who claimed confidence to advisers who confessed to being poorly informed. What they wanted was advisers whose confidence was both well informed and well calibrated.

The lessons offered by this research ought to be comforting to any leader who prefers honesty to puffery. It suggests that good calibration is compatible with earning others' trust. You don't have to profess exaggerated optimism to be influential. Actually being overconfident exposes you, your organization, and your investors to a whole host of risks, especially if you let it bias your forecasts and impair your decisions. On balance, the evidence suggests that achieving leadership credibility does not depend on being either delusional or hypocritical. Honestly communicating the real uncertainty about uncertain things is a viable strategy for aspiring leaders.

OVER OR UNDER?

On August 14, 2018, Ersilia Piccinino, her husband, and their eight-year-old son were headed on vacation. They had packed their car with luggage and beach toys for a seaside holiday. They were crossing the Morandi Bridge in Genoa around noon when it collapsed, dropping the family 150 feet to the ground below. The three were found dead inside the crumpled wreck of their car under the remains of an immense concrete beam. They were among the forty-three people who lost their lives in the bridge collapse.

The celebrated Italian engineer Riccardo Morandi had designed the bridge. An article heralding the bridge's innovative design bragged that the concrete structure would not need any maintenance. Diego Zoppi, a former president of the Genoa branch of the Order of Architects, said, "Fifty years ago, we had unlimited confidence in reinforced concrete, we thought it was eternal." However, the bridge did not live up to the confidence in its durability. Morandi himself noticed the bridge aging faster than he had anticipated and recommended new measures to maintain and reinforce the bridge. Bridge maintenance fell to Autostrade per l'Italia, a private corporation that manages more than half of Italy's four thousand miles of toll roads. Its maintenance program appears to have been based more on early optimism than on Morandi's later recommendations.

It is not always easy to hit the bull's eye of accuracy. There have been some who have argued that, given a choice, it's better to be overconfident than underconfident. The psychologists Shelley Taylor and Jonathon Brown wrote in 1988, "The capacity to develop and maintain positive illusions may be thought of as a valuable human resource to be nurtured and promoted." Their theory of positive illusions argued that a little self-delusion was conducive to mental health. Their work grew out of Taylor's research with cancer patients, in which she observed that those patients who believed in their prospects for recovery actually survived longer.

Taylor's results are of course just one small part of a large literature showing the reliable correlation between confidence and life outcomes. There are innumerable ways in which greater confidence in one's performance is associated with better results. This correlation does not prove that confidence produced those better results. As chapter 4 notes, it is usually plausible to assume that people know something about their future prospects and that this would contribute to their confidence. So long as Taylor's cancer patients had a sense of how bad their cancer was, those with better health would be more confident in their prospects for survival. On the other hand, experimental evidence that employs clean manipulations of confidence and measures its effect on subsequent performance suggests most people are overconfident about the benefits of confidence. It is easy to confuse correlation with causation.

Taylor and Brown argued that if you have to pick either overconfidence or underconfidence, overconfidence has more potential benefits and fewer likely costs than underconfidence. No doubt this is sometimes true. Initiating a friendship, for instance, is risky. A warm greeting or an invitation could result in an embarrassing rejection. On the other hand, the potential benefits of a new friendship are enormous.

However, it is easy to show that overconfidence is not always better. Sometimes overconfidence is worse. For example, being a bit overconfident in your bridge design could result in tragedy. Catastrophic collapse is surely a worse outcome than if underconfidence had led you to reinforce your design with more steel than was absolutely necessary. Overestimating the amount of money in your bank account can be a costly mistake if it leads you to bounce checks. Being overconfident about your skill at rock climbing, driving, or flying can get you killed.

If you indulge in positive illusions, you must confront the practical problem of determining how overconfident you should be. If you're deciding to overestimate your chances of success, how much should you overestimate? Believing that your success is guaranteed, that you are invincible, and that the whole world worships you is more characteristic of mental illness than success. Those who believe they are immortal will not take precautions that can help prolong their lives. And believing that everybody worships you can turn you into an insufferable jerk. To acknowledge the dangers of these sorts of delusions is to acknowledge the dangers of self-deception, even a little bit. The same problems that arise from believing you are invincible also hold for believing you are tougher than you actually are.

The question of whether it is better to be overconfident or underconfident is a particular version of the question of which is worse, false positives or false negatives. Of course, in its general form, there is no one answer—it depends. When it comes to making friends, false negatives (missing out on friendships) are usually worse than false positives (boring encounters). However, when it comes to bridge maintenance, false positives (bridge collapse) are worse than false negatives (excessively diligent maintenance). It will always be possible to imagine particular settings in which overconfidence is the greater or the lesser error. Agreeing that "it depends" then asks whether situations favoring over- or underconfidence are more common in the world. That discussion can go on forever.

Instead of attempting to pick a winner in the competition between overconfidence and underconfidence, I recommend the middle way. If you must commit to a single posture, the only consistently and rationally defensible position is to remain faithful to the truth. The evidence most consistently supports its benefits. But even if you agree that it is best to believe the truth, that leaves open the important issue of how to feel about it.

HOW TO FEEL ABOUT THE FACTS

When I highlight the benefits of having accurate beliefs, it is not my intention to make you feel worse about your life. Go ahead and feel grateful for your good fortune. Please do savor the anticipation of a bright future. Appreciate your good health, your friends, and the many pleasures your life affords. How you choose to feel about your situation is a separate issue from what your situation is. You can, and ought to, choose to feel good about what you have. Just as it would be a mistake to believe that having more money will solve all your problems and make you happy, so is it a mistake to assume that having accurate beliefs about how much money you have (or are likely to have in the future) need determine how you feel about it. It is possible to feel grateful for what you have, regardless of how much or little that is.

My father, as I have already noted, was the consummate pessimist. When attempting to define the difference between optimists and pessimists, he quoted James Branch Cabell: "The optimist believes that he lives in the best of all possible worlds. The pessimist fears that this is the case." This contrast nicely captures what it means to feel positively about life. One way in which some people choose to feel positively about what they have is to imagine how much worse it could be. If this is indeed the best of all possible worlds, then all the other possibilities must be worse than this one.

Vividly imagining what psychologists call "downward counterfactuals"—worse alternative outcomes—is one way to help you feel good about what you have. And the truth is that it is always possible to imagine how it could be worse. Conversely, it is always possible to imagine how it might be better. Even the most fortunate members of society—the richest, most famous, and most successful—can be plagued by feelings of failure and inadequacy if they compare themselves with others who are richer, more famous, or more successful than they are. There is a long list of people who achieved stupendous success yet were so unhappy they chose to take their own lives. Suicide remains one of the leading causes of death among young people, even in the most prosperous nations.

My mother tells me she thinks it is ironic that, in this book, I am playing the role of Debbie Downer about optimism. In her perfectly objective assessment, I am an optimist. I responded by telling my mother that was a mean thing to say and by denying the charge of optimism. She clarified that what she meant to say was not that I always believe good things will happen, but that I manage to put a positive spin on the facts as they are. I guess my mom was echoing German philosopher Gottfried Leibniz when he argued that we live in the best of all possible worlds. He imagined other, less desirable worlds and appreciated how good we have it.

I must agree with my mother and with Leibniz that this is a fine way to go through life. It is easy to find reasons to feel fortunate. We live in a time of outrageous plenty. The world is richer, healthier, better educated, and more peaceful than it has ever been. Most of you reading this book are living lives of ostentatious luxury. You have enough to eat; indeed, your palate is tempted daily by a dizzying variety of delightful cuisines from around the world. You have a bed to sleep in at night. You have trained physicians who minister to your illnesses. You can select from thousands of movies and shows to entertain you at any moment. The internet puts the world's knowledge at your fingertips. You can travel almost anywhere in the world safely and quickly by car, train, or airplane. You have enough free time to fritter it away reading books like this.

On the other hand, it is possible to view the facts but feel bad about them. You might wish you ate less and weighed less. You might wish you were wealthier. You might worry about whether you are getting the best health care available. You might be disappointed by the latest film in the Star Wars franchise. You might worry that technology companies do not do enough to protect your privacy online. You might complain about the amount of leg room on modern planes. And just think about how much you could have gotten done if you hadn't been reading this book. These gloomy assessments all imply upward counterfactuals—they imagine how much better you could have it.

It is hard to argue that either the cheery or the gloomy assessment of the facts is more factually correct. In this book, I have encouraged you to see the facts with clear eyes. I have done so because, as a psychologist, scholar, and decision researcher, I think the evidence demonstrates the benefits of doing so. Being in touch with reality will help you make better decisions and help you achieve your aspirations, whatever they may be. In offering this guidance, I don't intend to imply how you should feel about those facts. If both the positive and negative interpretations of the same facts lead to widely differing feelings about one's life, then it seems to me that the choice is obvious: pick the assessment that delivers more happiness. Choosing misery and regret would simply be a mistake.

REGRET AND UNDERCONFIDENCE

Thierry Magon de La Villehuchet was a wealthy French financier who locked himself in his New York office and slit his wrists on December 22, 2008. He had founded several investment firms and served as the chairman and chief executive of the French bank Crédit Lyonnais. At the time of his death, he had $3 billion under management at his hedge fund, Access International. Impressed by Bernard Madoff's consistent investment returns, La Villehuchet entrusted him with $1.4 billion. Madoff was a confident man who inspired faith in the aristocratic La Villehuchet. When Madoff's massive Ponzi scheme was uncovered, La Villehuchet was devastated. His suicide note to his brother expressed personal responsibility and agonizing regret for having been duped by Madoff and for having lost so much money.

When you take a risk that turns out badly, regret is common. Critical self-reflection can be wise and helpful, as chapter 6 argued.

Postmortem analyses can provide insight into what went wrong and are helpful when they show how to avoid those mistakes in the future. But it is common for postmortem analysis to drift into regretful rumination about what might have been, as it was for La Villehuchet. Regret takes the sharp edge of your prior misfortune and uses it to slice open an emotional wound. That self-inflicted wound is all the more painful if we imagine that we deserve it. Regret can turn postmortem analysis into pathological self-recrimination.

Here again I will steer you away from the quicksand of under-confidence. Just because your invention, your idea, or your trust in another person failed, it does not make you a failure. It does make you unlucky. And if your failure inspires ideas for how you can avoid such failures in the future, then it may wind up having positive consequences. But do not beat yourself up because of some misguided sense that you deserve to be punished. Self-flagellation is unlikely to help you, unlikely to facilitate future success, and unlikely to elicit sympathy from others. Instead, it is better to learn what you can from these failures and avoid overreacting.

The last thing I want to do in this book is to have my message of moderation and truth be mistaken for a discouraging message of pessimism. The truth is that most of us have a greater capacity for achievement, for inspiration, and for joy than we assume. To forgo glorious possibilities in the name of temperance is not virtuous; it is tragic. You may glimpse tremendous, inspiring opportunities that you are apprehensive to take. Think rigorously about the risks that frighten you, and think about how to hedge against them. Calculate the value of their outcomes, and take the course of action with the highest expected value, even when it is risky.

Another way in which many of us are underconfident centers on our fears that the world is going to hell. Public opinion polls reveal that people around the world fear that their politicians are less honorable, their economies are less prosperous, and the world is less safe than it used to be. In fact, the evidence suggests otherwise. Rates of death due to interpersonal violence have declined steadily over time. Economic growth has delivered steadily increasing standards of living throughout the world, lifting vast numbers of people out of poverty. And in truth there was no halcyon time in the past when honest and virtuous politicians presided over broad social consensus on the important issues of the day.

BECOMING PERFECTLY CONFIDENT

The way to wisdom treads the line between overconfidence and underconfidence. It accepts the truth of who we are and what we can achieve. This path of self-acceptance has been described in rich spiritual terms by Buddhists and meditators. It comes with a peace and equanimity that grow from acknowledging the world and our place within it with open eyes and a warm heart. You can regard both yourself and your fellow beings with loving kindness, even as you see them with clear eyes. This acceptance is entirely compatible with an honest assessment and well-calibrated confidence.

I am not the first one to describe the virtues of the middle way. The Greek philosopher Socrates taught that a person ought to "choose the mean and avoid the extremes of either side, as far as possible." Aristotle described the Golden Middle Way or Golden Mean between excess and deficiency. The ancient Greek myths venerate moderation, as in the story of Daedalus and Icarus. According to legend, Daedalus built wings for himself and his son, Icarus, to escape an island. Daedalus warned his son to fly the middle course, between the sea's spray and the sun's heat. Icarus did not heed his father's warnings and flew too close to the sun, resulting in tragedy. And in the ultimate tale of heroism and triumph, Odysseus delivers his ship to safety only by expertly navigating a narrow course between the twin dangers of Scylla and Charybdis.

The Jewish philosopher Maimonides advised balance between care for the body and for the soul. The Bible admonishes moderation: "So don't be too good or too wise—why kill yourself? But don't be too wicked or too foolish, either—why die before you have to? Avoid both extremes." The Islamic scholar Ibn Manẓūr wrote, "Every praiseworthy characteristic has two blameworthy poles. Generosity is the middle between miserliness and extravagance. Courage is the middle between cowardice and recklessness. Humanity has been commanded to avoid every such blameworthy trait."

But nowhere is the middle way more prominent than in Buddhism. Born in the sixth century BC, in what is now Nepal, Siddhartha Gautama was raised in opulent luxury. When he discovered the punishing poverty outside the palace walls, he set out to experience the whole world in all its harsh cruelty. For six years, he lived a life of ascetic penance, fasting and suffering. When misery failed to deliver enlightenment, Siddhartha sought guidance through meditation. Revelation came to him when he realized the middle path of moderation between the extremes of self-indulgence and self-sacrifice. In that moment, Siddhartha became the Buddha. For the rest of his life, he traveled and taught the virtues of the middle path.

I venerate the deep truths these ancient philosophies advise. In every page of this book I have wholeheartedly endorsed the profound wisdom of the middle way between overconfidence and underconfidence. At the same time, it can often be difficult to find the middle path. How is it possible to determine whether you are engaging in too much self-denial or too much self-indulgence? One potential answer is to take social norms as a guide for finding the golden mean. The problem with this is that such guidance, too, is vague. Which society's norms should I follow? I would drink a lot more vodka if I observed the norms in Russia than in Saudi Arabia. Would the world's great religious philosophers have said that the meaning of their teachings ought to change with time or with a plane flight from Moscow to Riyadh? I suspect not.

In greatest humility, I would like to offer a guide to finding the middle way, at least when it comes to calibrating one's confidence. I cannot tell you how much vodka you should drink, but when it comes to confidence, the middle way is clear, simple, and unambiguous: *You should believe the truth.* You should believe in yourself insofar as that belief increases your chances of success. If believing that you can leap the chasm, win the race, or wow the crowd allows you to achieve these things, then you absolutely should believe. On the other hand, to believe that you can jump the Grand Canyon is simple fantasy, and no amount of confidence will change that fact.

Well-calibrated confidence will prompt you to act boldly when your actions are most likely to produce a beneficial result, and to act cautiously when the risks are too great. Yes, you should start your own company to commercialize an amazing new product if that venture is likely to succeed; but you should keep your salaried job if the new product is likely to fail. Overconfident people risk too much, make promises on which they cannot possibly deliver, and fall short of their grand hopes, disappointing both themselves and others. Well-calibrated confidence is therefore good for you, helping you choose wisely in ways that maximize the expected value of your decisions and realize your highest values.

Throughout the foregoing chapters, I have endeavored to bust the myth that confidence is a matter of gut feelings or self-esteem. Instead, it is a practice to be mastered. I have offered research-based tools that can help you develop your ability to calibrate and perfect your confidence. With each personal prediction that you make well, your confidence builds a more solid foundation. This will lead you to the middle way—that Goldilocks zone in which your confidence is just right. The middle way—the only way that is consistent with the wonderful, inspiring truth—balances between excessive and insufficient confidence. It is fundamentally justified by evidence and honest self-examination. And it steers between the perilous cliff of overconfidence and the quicksand of underconfidence. It is not easy to find, for it takes honest self-reflection, levelheaded analysis, and the courage to resist wishful thinking. But it is a valiant and rewarding way to live.

Good calibration is also good for your relationships, both professional and intimate. Research by Elizabeth Tenney and Simine Vazire suggests that the healthiest relationships with friends, family members, and romantic partners are supported by accurate self-knowledge. Eli Finkel has studied what makes marriages successful. His advice is to invest in developing an accurate understanding: "Learn about yourself, learn about your partner, learn about the dynamics between the two of you, and then calibrate your expectations appropriately." This sort of accurate self-knowledge is a cornerstone of good confidence calibration.

Well-calibrated confidence is also good for the broader society. The most dysfunctional and destructive societies are built on lies, delusions, and unquestioning loyalty to dogmatic ideologies. In the words of the historian Yuval Noah Harari: "Modern history has demonstrated that a society of courageous people willing to admit ignorance and raise difficult questions is usually not just more prosperous but also more peaceful than societies in which everyone must unquestioningly accept a single answer." Pluralistic democracies deserve credit for impressive social, economic, and scientific progress. Democracies with market economies have, over the long term, become more tolerant, prosperous, healthy, and peaceful, even as they have endured vigorous public debates and energetic disagreements about optimal public policies and the nature of a good society.

For societies, organizations, groups, and individuals, perfection is unattainable. Nevertheless, it will always be a goal worth striving toward. Seeking the middle way strives toward perfectibility. It takes courage, because the truth is not always easy to uncover, nor is it always pleasing to behold. Well-calibrated confidence is exceptionally rare. It requires that you understand yourself and what you are capable of achieving. It requires that you know your limitations and what opportunities are not worth pursuing. It requires that you act confidently based on what you know, even if it means taking a stand, making a bet, or speaking up for a viewpoint that is unpopular. But it also requires the willingness to consider the possibility that you are wrong, to listen to evidence, and to change your mind. It requires an uncommon combination of courage and humility. It takes the perfect amount of confidence.

Acknowledgments

This book is based on my life's work studying confidence and over-confidence. That work is collaborative, and I owe deep debts of gratitude to my coauthors, students, mentors, and advisors. This is a long list that includes Jenn Logg, Liz Tenney, Derek Schatz, Uriel Haran, Sam Swift, Daylian Cain, Nate Meikle, Francesca Gino, Zach Sharek, Cameron Anderson, Jessica Kennedy, Phil Tetlock, Barb Mellers, Dan Benjamin, Matthew Rabin, Sunita Sah, Rob MacCoun, Terry Murray, Welton Chang, Pavel Atanasov, and many others. But a deeper debt goes to George Loewenstein, my colleague and mentor in my first job at Carnegie Mellon, who encouraged me to follow my hunches to the fertile research topics that have fueled my career. And then there is the deepest debt of all, to my doctoral advisor, Max Bazerman. I aspire to be as great a scientist, as wise a mentor, and as noble a person as Max.

I must also mention my wonderful colleagues at UC Berkeley: Leif Nelson, Ellen Evers, Clayton Critcher, Juliana Schroeder, Severin Borenstin, Drew Jacoby-Senghor, Sameer Srivastava, Andy Rose, Barry Schwartz, Ned Augenblick, Mathijs De Vaan, Laura Kray, Jenny Chatman, Toby Stuart, Dana Carney, and Alain Kesseru, among others. They make it fun to come to work every day. They set a high bar for intellectual rigor and for quality scholarship. I strive to live up to the impressive standards they set. Sameer and Barry deserve a special note of thanks for reading the first full draft of this book and providing me thoughtful and wise feedback.

I must offer my appreciation for the team of students and research assistants who are or have been part of my lab group at UC Berkeley. Thanks to Amelia Dev, Shreya Agrawal, Christina Carr, Mary Ford, Aditya Kotak, Ekaterina Goncherova, Sydney Mayes, Sean Sinisgalli, Maya Shen, Cody Strohl, Mitchell Wong, Winnie Yan, and Andrew Zheng. The first among these is the brilliant Amelia Dev, whom I am fortunate to be able to have as my lab manager.

This book would not have been possible without the heroic efforts of a small village in which I am fortunate to reside. First, I must acknowledge the tireless encouragement and patient support of my agent, Margo Fleming. She convinced me to pick the project back up after I had given up on it. She had confidence when I did not. Margo was my advocate, mentor, and consigliere throughout the process. She made the process a joy. I often wondered whether Margo was overconfident about me and this book's potential.

I could not have hoped for a better editor than Hollis Heimbouch at HarperBusiness. At every point, I expected her to tell me to throw away what I had written and start over. Instead, she provided generous encouragement and the gentle guidance I needed. I will be forever grateful for her faith in my vision and her willingness to bet on this project. I hope that the confidence she and Margo displayed in this book will be borne out.

Most of all, thanks to my family. My mother taught me to see the many facets of optimism, happiness, and confidence. My father served as an inspiration to this book in many ways. First, he personified the high costs of pessimism, caution, and underconfidence. He missed out on many of life's joys, rewards, and surprises because he was so fearful that any risk would turn into disaster. Second, he provided many useful examples for this book. I miss him and his gloomy sense of humor.

My wonderful wife, Sarah, and my fabulous children, Josh and Andy, give my life its most fulfilling purpose. They were able to both buoy my faith in myself when it flagged and cut me down to size when I was getting too big for my britches. Teenage children proved particularly useful for the latter.

Berkeley, California
July 2019

Notes

————

INTRODUCTION

5   power posing: In case you haven't been following the scholarly controversies around power posing, you should know that the original findings have not held up well to replication. When an experimenter tells you to put your body in a confident and expansive stance (like Wonder Woman), it is unlikely to induce hormonal changes. However, it may lead you to tell the experimenter that you're feeling more confident. Whether that increases your ability to repel bullets or fly invisible jets has not yet been tested. Joseph P. Simmons and Uri Simonsohn, "Power Posing: P-Curving the Evidence," *Psychological Science* 28, no. 5 (March 20, 2017): 687–93, https://doi.org/10.1177/0956797616658563.

5   "you can never be too rich": (*Oxford Dictionary of Quotations*, 8th ed. [New York: Oxford University Press, 2014], s.v. "Duchess of Windsor"). But of course being too thin or too confident can be dangerous, for different reasons.

10   Aristotle quotes: *Complete Works of Aristotle*, Jonathan Barnes, ed., vol. 2, *The Revised Oxford Translation* (Princeton, NJ: Princeton University Press, 2014).

10   Roosevelt quote: Theodore Roosevelt, *The Works of Theodore Roosevelt* (New York: Charles Scribner's Sons, 1906).

CHAPTER 1: WHAT IS CONFIDENCE?

16   Musk stories and quotes: Ashlee Vance, *Elon Musk: Tesla, SpaceX, and the Quest for a Fantastic Future* (New York: HarperCollins, 2015).

17   More confident entrepreneurs: Mathew L. A. Hayward, William R. Forster, Saras D. Sarasvathy, and Barbara L. Fredrickson, "Beyond Hubris: How Highly Confident Entrepreneurs Rebound to Venture Again," *Journal of Business Venturing* 25, no. 6 (2010): 569–78.

17   Confident applicants are more likely to get hired: Jack L. Howard and Gerald R. Ferris, "The Employment Interview Context: Social and Situational Influences on Interviewer Decisions," *Journal of Applied Social Psychology* 26, no. 2 (1996): 112–36.

17   confident political candidates are more likely to get elected: Harold M. Zullow and Martin E. P. Seligman, "Pessimistic Rumination Predicts Defeat of Presidential Candidates, 1900 to 1984," *Psychological Inquiry* 1, no. 1 (1990): 52–61.

17   both confidence and success may share: Tomas Chamorro-Premuzic, *Confidence: Overcoming Low Self-Esteem, Insecurity, and Self-Doubt* (London: Penguin, 2013).

17   CHOSEN I tattooed: Khadrice Rollins, "What Is the Origin of LeBron James's Chosen One Tattoo?," *Sports Illustrated*, May 30, 2018, https://www.si.com /nba/2018/05/30/origin-lebron-james-chosen-1-tattoo.

18   "I'm back to sleeping": Kate Samuelson, "Tesla Has Tons of Problems and Elon Musk Says He's Sleeping at the Factory to Fix Them," *Fortune*, April 3, 2018, https://fortune.com/2018/04/03/elon-musk-sleeping-tesla-factory/.

20   overprecision emerges in: Don A. Moore, Elizabeth R. Tenney, and Uriel Haran, "Overprecision in Judgment," in *Handbook of Judgment and Decision Making*, ed. George Wu and Gideon Keren (New York: Wiley, 2015), 182–212.

20   Research on "flashbulb memories": Christopher F. Chabris and Daniel J. Simons, *The Invisible Gorilla* (New York: Crown, 2010).

20   When researchers cross-checked: Jennifer M. Talarico and David C. Rubin, "Confidence, Not Consistency, Characterizes Flashbulb Memories," *Psychological Science* 14, no. 5 (2003): 455–61.

21   World population statistic: U.S. and World Population Clock, U.S. Census Bureau, https://www.census.gov/popclock/.

21   Orville Wright's first powered flight: "The Wright Brothers: The First Successful Airplane," Smithsonian National Air and Space Museum, https:// airandspace.si.edu/exhibitions/wright-brothers/online/fly/1903/.

21   Dean Hovey's hourly wage: Malcolm Gladwell, "Creation Myth," *New Yorker*, July 6, 2017, https://www.newyorker.com/magazine/2011/05/16/creation -myth.

21   Depth of the Mariana Trench: Becky Oskin, "Mariana Trench: The Deepest Depths," *LiveScience*, December 6, 2017, https://www.livescience.com/23387 -mariana-trench.html.

21   Tesla corporation 2018 revenue: Tesla, Inc, *Tesla Fourth Quarter & Full Year 2018 Update*, https://ir.tesla.com/static-files/0b913415-467d-4c0d-be4c-9225 c2cb0ae0.

21   Daniel Kahneman's Nobel Prize: Noble Media AB 2019, "Daniel Kahneman— Facts," NobelPrize.org, https://www.nobelprize.org/prizes/economic-sciences /2002/kahneman/facts/.

21   Price for which Google buys YouTube: Andrew Ross Sorkin and Jeremy W. Peters, "Google to Acquire YouTube for $1.65 Billion," *New York Times*, October 9, 2006, https://www.nytimes.com/2006/10/09/business/09cnd-deal .html.

21   LeBron James's average points-per-game: NBA Media Ventures, LLC, "LeBron James," NBA Stats, https://stats.nba.com/player/2544/

21   William James's first Harvard class: Robert D. Richardson, *William James: In the Maelstrom of American Modernism* (New York: Houghton Mifflin, 2007).

21   Maya Angelou's Presidential Medal of Freedom: World Heritage Encyclopedia, "List of Honors Received by Maya Angelou," http://self.gutenberg.org /articles/list_of_honors_received_by_maya_angelou.

22   "no problem in judgment": Scott Plous, *The Psychology of Judgment and Decision Making*, McGraw-Hill Series in Social Psychology (New York: McGraw-Hill, 1993).

22   "the most significant": Daniel Kahneman, *Thinking, Fast and Slow* (New York: Farrar, Straus and Giroux, 2011).

22   overconfidence is the mother: Max H. Bazerman and Don A. Moore, *Judgment in Managerial Decision Making*, 8th ed. (New York: Wiley, 2013).

22   "Perhaps the most robust": Werner F. M. De Bondt and Richard H. Thaler, "Financial Decision-Making in Markets and Firms: A Behavioral Perspective," in *Finance, Handbooks in Operations Research and Management Science*, ed. Robert A. Jarrow, Voijslav Maksimovic, and William T. Ziemba, vol. 9 (North Holland, Amsterdam: Elsevier, 1995), 385–410.

22   Overconfidence may contribute: Dominic D. P. Johnson, *Overconfidence and War: The Havoc and Glory of Positive Illusions* (Cambridge, MA: Harvard University Press, 2004).

24   Many have noted: Michael Lewis, *The Big Short* (New York: Simon & Schuster, 2015).

25   NINA and NINJA loans: Alex Blumberg and Adam Davidson, "The Giant

Pool of Money," *This American Life*, May 9, 2008, https://www.thisamerican
life.org/355/the-giant-pool-of-money.

27   "But as long as the music": Cyrus Sanati, "Prince Finally Explains His
     Dancing Comment," *New York Times*, DealBook, https://dealbook.nytimes
     .com/2010/04/08/prince-finally-explains-his-dancing-comment/.

27   "I'll be gone, you'll be gone": Barry Ritholtz, "Putting an End to Wall
     Street's 'I'll Be Gone, You'll Be Gone' Bonuses," *Washington Post*, March 12,
     2011,   https://www.washingtonpost.com/business/putting-an-end-to-wall
     -streets-ill-be-gone-youll-be-gone-bonuses/2011/03/08/ABDjpJS_story.html.

28   Kruger showed how easy: Justin Kruger, "Lake Wobegon Be Gone! The
     'Below-Average Effect' and the Egocentric Nature of Comparative Ability
     Judgments," *Journal of Personality and Social Psychology* 77, no. 2 (1999): 221–32.

28   People think they use: Justin Kruger and Kenneth Savitsky, "On the Genesis
     of Inflated (and Deflated) Judgments of Responsibility: Egocentrism Revis-
     ited," *Organizational Behavior & Human Decision Processes* 108, no. 1 (2009):
     972–89, https://doi.org/10.1016/j.obhdp.2008.06.002.

29   "more confidence is placed": J. Meacham, *Thomas Jefferson: The Art of Power*
     (New York: Random House, 2012).

29   "I am not a writer": Josh Jones, "John Steinbeck Has a Crisis in Confidence
     While Writing *The Grapes of Wrath*," Open Culture, 2017, http://www.open
     culture.com/2017/07/john-steinbeck-has-a-crisis-in-confidence-while-writing
     -the-grapes-of-wrath.html.

29   "I have written eleven books": Sanyin Siang, "Got The Imposter Syn-
     drome? Here Are 3 Strategies For Dealing With It," *Forbes*, April 17, 2017,
     https://www.forbes.com/sites/sanyinsiang/2017/04/17/impostersyndrome
     /#49880cc3e5fe.

29   "I thought it was a big fluke": Abel Riojas, "Jodie Foster, Reluctant Star," *60
     Minutes*, July 12, 1999, https://www.cbsnews.com/news/jodie-foster-reluctant
     -star-07-12-1999/.

29   The impostor syndrome was first named: Pauline Rose Clance and Suzanne
     Ament Imes, "The Imposter Phenomenon in High Achieving Women: Dy-
     namics and Therapeutic Intervention," *Psychotherapy: Theory, Research &
     Practice* 15, no. 3 (1978): 241.

29   Currie quote: Katty Kay and Claire Shipman, *The Confidence Code: The Sci-
     ence and Art of Self-Assurance—What Women Should Know* (New York: Harper-
     Collins, 2014).

30   it is the most hardworking: Francis J. Flynn and Rebecca L. Schaumberg,
     "When Feeling Bad Leads to Feeling Good: Guilt-Proneness and Affec-
     tive Organizational Commitment," *Journal of Applied Psychology* 97, no. 1
     (2012): 124.

31   Only a third: Caroline Hoxby and Christopher Avery, "The Missing 'One-

Offs': The Hidden Supply of High-Achieving, Low-Income Students," *Brookings Papers on Economic Activity* 2013, no. 1 (Spring 2013), https://doi.org/10.1353/eca.2013.0000.

31 talented kids from poor families: David Leonhardt, "Better Colleges Failing to Lure Talented Poor," *New York Times*, March 16, 2013, https://www.nytimes.com/2013/03/17/education/scholarly-poor-often-overlook-better-colleges.html.

32 "I suck at writing": Hugh Howey, "I Suck at Writing," hughhowey.com, February 4, 2014, http://www.hughhowey.com/i-suck-at-writing/.

32 "Today will be good": David Rakoff, *Half Empty* (New York: Doubleday, 2010), 59.

33 Jung praises William James: "William James," Harvard University Department of Psychology, https://psychology.fas.harvard.edu/people/william-james.

33 Freud praises William James: Ernest Jones, *The Life and Work of Sigmund Freud* (New York: Basic Books, 1961).

33 "I was, body and soul": Kendra Cherry, "William James Biography (1842–1910)," Very Well Mind, 2018, https://www.verywellmind.com/william-james-biography-1842-1910-2795545.

34 "the first lecture": Ralph Barton Perry, *The Thought and Character of William James: As Revealed in Unpublished Correspondence and Notes, Together with His Published Writings* (Oxford, England: Little, Brown, 1935).

34 James's story of leaping the chasm: William James, "Some Reflections on the Subjective Method," in *Essays on Philosophy: The Works of William James* (Cambridge, MA: Harvard University Press, 1978).

35 study of the effectiveness of visualization: Lien B. Pham and Shelley E. Taylor, "From Thought to Action: Effects of Process- versus Outcome-Based Mental Simulations on Performance," *Personality and Social Psychology Bulletin* 25, no. 2 (1999): 250–60.

35 For visualization to be effective: Shelley E. Taylor et al., "Harnessing the Imagination: Mental Simulation, Self-Regulation, and Coping," *American Psychologist* 53, no. 4 (1998): 429–39.

35 subliminal audio tapes: Philip M. Merikle, "Subliminal Auditory Messages: An Evaluation," *Psychology and Marketing* 5, no. 4 (December 1, 1988): 355–72, https://doi.org/10.1002/mar.4220050406.

36 "Pride goeth before": Proverbs 16:18 (King James Version).

36 being too sure of yourself: Jeffrey B. Vancouver, Kristen M. More, and Ryan J. Yoder, "Self-Efficacy and Resource Allocation: Support for a Non-monotonic, Discontinuous Model," *Journal of Applied Psychology* 93, no. 1 (2008): 35–47, https://doi.org/10.1037/0021-9010.93.1.35.

37 Vancouver's Mastermind study: Jeffrey B. Vancouver et al., "Two Studies

Examining the Negative Effect of Self-Efficacy on Performance," *Journal of Applied Psychology* 87, no. 3 (2002): 506–16.

37   Oettingen's research on how imagining success can lead to failure: Gabriele Oettingen, "Positive Fantasy and Motivation," in *The Psychology of Action: Linking Cognition and Motivation to Behavior*, ed. Peter M. Gollwitzer and John A. Bargh (New York: Guilford, 1996), 236–59.

38   Raynor on overconfident businesses: Michael Raynor, *The Strategy Paradox: Why Committing to Success Leads to Failure (and What to Do about It)* (New York: Crown Business, 2007).

38   On the risks of exaggerating children's talents: Polly Young-Eisendrath, *The Self-Esteem Trap: Raising Confident and Compassionate Kids in an Age of Self-Importance* (New York: Little, Brown, 2008).

39   "I certainly don't try": Vance, *Elon Musk*.

CHAPTER 2: HOW MIGHT I BE WRONG?

41   "For the Lord himself": 1 Thessalonians 4:16–17 (King James Version).

41   "I was an engineer": Michael Gryborski, "Tribute to Harold Camping on Family Radio Network Leaves Out Any Mention of His End Times Prophecies," *Christian Post*, December 30, 2013, https://www.christianpost.com/news/tribute-to-harold-camping-on-family-radio-network-leaves-out-any-mention-of-his-end-times-prophecies-111693/.

42   Rationale behind Camping's prophecy: *Judgment Day*, Family Radio, archived from the original on June 8, 2011, https://web.archive.org/web/201106082 23300/http://www.familyradio.com/graphical/literature/judgment/judg ment.html.

42   "I don't even think": "Harold Camping Interview (Judgement Day)," You-Tube video, posted by "BibleandScience2," April 12, 2011, https://www.you tube.com/watch?v=rlWlcU7UvpU.

42   Economic study of faith in the prophecy: Ned Augenblick et al., "The Economics of Faith: Using an Apocalyptic Prophecy to Elicit Religious Beliefs in the Field," *Journal of Public Economics* 141 (2016): 38–49.

45   the way human minds search for evidence: Joshua Klayman and Young-won Ha, "Confirmation, Disconfirmation, and Information in Hypothesis Testing," *Psychological Review* 94, no. 2 (1987): 211–28.

45   In one classic psychology study: Mark Snyder and William B. Swann Jr., "Hypothesis-Testing Processes in Social Interaction," *Journal of Personality and Social Psychology* 36, no. 11 (1978): 1202–12.

47   radio stations in the Christian Family Radio network: "Find the Nearest Stations," Family Radio, accessed September 29, 2019, https://www.family radio.org/stations/.

47   deaths worldwide due to motor vehicle accidents: "Road Traffic Injuries," World Health Organization, December 7, 2018, https://www.who.int/news -room/fact-sheets/detail/road-traffic-injuries.

47   Jeff Bezos's net worth: Forbes, "Jeff Bezos," *Forbes,* https://www.forbes.com /profile/jeff-bezos/#2dbb1b171b23.

47   Year King Charles I was beheaded: British Library, "Execution of Charles I," The British Library Board, http://www.bl.uk/learning/timeline/item103 698.html.

47   Deaths due to the 9/11 attacks: "September 11 Terror Attacks Fast Facts," CNN, October 22, 2019, https://www.cnn.com/2013/07/27/us/september -11-anniversary-fast-facts/index.html.

47   Amazon revenues: Amazon, *Annual Report to Shareholders,* 2018, https:// ir.aboutamazon.com/static-files/0f9e36b1-7e1e-4b52-be17-145dc9d8b5ec.

47   Year of Oliver Cromwell's death: "Cromwell's Health and Death," The Crom-well Association, http://www.olivercromwell.org/wordpress/?page_id=1757.

47   Deaths at Masada: Abraham Wasserstein, ed., *Flavius Josephus: Selections from His Works* (New York: Viking Press, 1974), 186–300.

48   Bridgewater Associates' assets under management: Tom Huddleston Jr., "Billionaire Ray Dalio Says This Is How to Be 'Truly Successful,'" CNBC, August 22 2019, https://www.cnbc.com/2019/08/22/bridgewater-associates -ray-dalio-how-to-be-truly-successful.html.

48   Saints canonized by Pope John Paul II: Peter Stanford, "How Many Saints Are There?," *Guardian,* May 13, 2013, https://www.theguardian.com/world /shortcuts/2013/may/13/pope-francis-how-many-saints.

48   Instead of reporting the 5th and 95th percentiles from a subjective proba-bility distribution, when asked for a 90 percent confidence interval, people are more likely to report upper and lower bounds on a range of what seem like plausible possibilities. These wind up, on average, being closer to the 25th and 75th percentiles. Karl Halvor Teigen and Magne Jørgensen, "When 90% Confidence Intervals Are 50% Certain: On the Credibility of Credible Intervals," *Applied Cognitive Psychology* 19, no. 4 (2005): 455–75.

48   Fox and Tversky study of probability estimation: Craig R. Fox and Amos Tversky, "A Belief-Based Account of Decision under Uncertainty," *Manage-ment Science* 44, no. 7 (1998): 879–95, https://doi.org/10.1287/mnsc.44.7.879.

49   Stats on causes of death: "Health Statistics and Information Systems," World Health Organization, 2018, http://www.who.int/healthinfo/global_burden _disease/estimates/en/index1.html.

50   Study of social priming: John A. Bargh, Mark Chen, and Lara Burrows, "Au-tomaticity of Social Behavior: Direct Effects of Trait Construct and Stereo-type Activation on Action," *Journal of Personality and Social Psychology* 71, no. 2 (August 1996): 230–44, https://doi.org/10.1037/0022-3514.71.2.230.

50   Failure to replicate social priming: Stéphane Doyen et al., "Behavioral Prim-
      ing: It's All in the Mind, but Whose Mind?," *PLoS ONE* 7, no. 1 (January 18,
      2012): e29081, https://doi.org/10.1371/journal.pone.0029081.

51   "If we are uncritical": Karl Popper, *The Poverty of Historicism* (Boston: Bea-
      con Press, 1957).

51   "consider the opposite": Charles G. Lord, Mark R. Lepper, and Elizabeth
      Preston, "Considering the Opposite: A Corrective Strategy for Social Judg-
      ment," *Journal of Personality and Social Psychology* 47, no. 6 (1984): 1231–43.

52   Cromwell quote: Oliver Cromwell, "Letters and Speeches—Letter 129,"
      The Cromwell Association, http://www.olivercromwell.org/wordpress
      /?page_id=2303#letters.

52   "The human understanding": Francis Bacon, *The New Organon*, Cambridge
      Texts in the History of Philosophy (Cambridge, UK: Cambridge University
      Press, 2000). First published 1620.

53   Zealots fled to the mountain fortress: Historians believe that it was actually
      a radical Zealot splinter group, the Sicarii (the "Dagger-Men"), who holed
      up in Masada. One of their leaders, Menahem ben Judah, claimed to be the
      Jewish messiah, the one who would deliver the Jews from oppression and
      usher in the "world to come." A contest for leadership with Eleasar, another
      Zealot leader, left him dead before the group fled to Masada.

54   "The fundamental cause": Bertrand Russell, "The Triumph of Stupidity,"
      in *Mortals and Others: American Essays, 1931–1935, Volumes 1 and 2* (New York:
      Routledge, 2009).

54   "I'm wrong all the time": Kathryn Schulz, *Being Wrong* (New York: Ecco,
      2010).

55   we believe the things we believe: Lee Ross and Andrew Ward wrote about
      the "naive realism" that leads us to believe that our own beliefs and opin-
      ions are the most rational, reasonable, and defensible. "Naive Realism in
      Everyday Life: Implications for Social Conflict and Misunderstanding," in
      Values and Knowledge, ed. E. Reed, E. Turiel, and T. Brown (Hillsdale, NJ:
      Lawrence Erlbaum Associates, 1996), 103–35.

55   overconfidence may be getting worse: Jean M. Twenge and W. Keith Camp-
      bell, *The Narcissism Epidemic: Living in the Age of Entitlement* (New York: Atria
      Books, 2010).

55   "They don't set": E. J. Mundell, "U.S. Teens Brimming With Self-Esteem,"
      MedicineNet.com, 2008, https://www.medicinenet.com/script/main/art.asp
      ?articlekey=94175.

56   when people force themselves: Don A. Moore, Ashli Carter, and Heather
      H. J. Yang, "Wide of the Mark: Evidence on the Underlying Causes of Over-
      precision in Judgment," *Organizational Behavior and Human Decision Processes*
      131 (2015): 110–20.

56   If I just ask: Uriel Haran, Don A. Moore, and Carey K. Morewedge, "A Simple Remedy for Overprecision in Judgment," *Judgment and Decision Making* 5, no. 7 (2010): 467–76.

56   Amazon's fourteen leadership principles: "Leadership Principles," AmazonJobs, 2018, https://www.amazon.jobs/principles.

56   "People who are right": Taylor Soper, "'Failure and Innovation Are Inseparable Twins': Amazon Founder Jeff Bezos Offers 7 Leadership Principles," *GeekWire*, October 28, 2016, https://www.geekwire.com/2016/amazon -founder-jeff-bezos-offers-6-leadership-principles-change-mind-lot-embrace -failure-ditch-powerpoints/.

57   Amazon's leadership principles: "Leadership Principles."

58   Job description for devil's advocate: *The Catholic Encyclopedia* (New York: Robert Appleton Company, 1911), s.v. "Promotor Fidei," http://www.new advent.org/cathen/12454a.htm.

58   In the next 396 years: David Gibson, "Does Being Pope Give You an Inside Track to Sainthood?," Religion News Service, April 23, 2014, https:// religionnews.com/2014/04/23/analysis-does-being-pope-give-you-an-inside -track-to-sainthood/.

59   he canonized 813 people in a single day: "How Do You Become a Saint? What to Know about Canonization," NBC News, April 25, 2014, https:// www.nbcnews.com/storyline/new-saints/how-do-you-become-saint-what -know-about-canonization-n89846.

60   Research attests to the enormous value: James Surowiecki, *The Wisdom of Crowds* (New York: Random House, 2005).

61   averaging opinions usually winds up being more accurate: Jack B. Soll and Richard P. Larrick, "Strategies for Revising Judgment: How (and How Well) People Use Others' Opinions," *Journal of Experimental Psychology: Learning, Memory, & Cognition* 35, no. 3 (2009): 780–805.

61   "vocally self-critical": "Leadership Principles," AmazonJobs, 2018, https:// www.amazon.jobs/principles.

61   deviance and protest: In 2015, the good people of Berkeley protested a plan to cut down eucalyptus trees in a large county park. Protesters feared if they held their protest away from the park, no one would notice. So they gathered on the UC Berkeley campus, stripped naked, and hugged the trees. Tracey Taylor, "In Berkeley, Protesters Get Naked to Try to Save Trees," *Berkeleyside* (blog), July 18, 2015, https://www.berkeleyside.com/2015/07/18/in-berkeley -protesters-strip-naked-to-try-to-save-trees.

62   Richard Lyons, leadership and feedback: Personal communication with the author, August 10, 2010.

62   The former Minnesota senator: Al Franken, *Al Franken, Giant of the Senate* (New York: Twelve, 2017).

62 courage that Franken again displayed: Jane Mayer, "The Case of Al Franken," *New Yorker*, July 22, 2019.

CHAPTER 3: WHAT IS POSSIBLE?

65 Wright brothers stories and quotes: John Robert McMahon, *The Wright Brothers: Fathers of Flight* (Boston: Little, Brown, 1930).

67 It is the largest chemical producer in the world: "The World's Largest Chemical Companies," WorldAtlas, accessed September 15, 2019, https://www.worldatlas.com/articles/which-are-the-world-s-largest-chemical-producing-companies.html.

67 these point predictions: A "point prediction" is just a simple numerical estimate of an uncertain quantity. In the case of product sales forecasts, a point prediction is a single number intended to represent what really is a distribution of possible sales figures.

71 About 15 percent of participants estimated the risk at 50 percent: Baruch Fischhoff and Wändi Bruine de Bruin, "Fifty-Fifty = 50%?," *Journal of Behavioral Decision Making* 12, no. 2 (1999): 149–63.

71 if their partner had HIV: Susan S. Witte et al., "Lack of Awareness of Partner STD Risk among Heterosexual Couples," *Perspectives on Sexual and Reproductive Health* 42, no. 1 (2010): 49–55.

71 a quarter to half: Seth C. Kalichman and Dena Nachimson, "Self-Efficacy and Disclosure of HIV-Positive Serostatus to Sex Partners.," *Health Psychology* 18, no. 3 (1999): 281; Michael D. Stein et al., "Sexual Ethics: Disclosure of HIV-Positive Status to Partners," *Archives of Internal Medicine* 158, no. 3 (1998): 253–57.

71 the actual risk of infection: "HIV Risk Behaviors," US Centers for Disease Control and Prevention, HIV/AIDS, 2018, https://www.cdc.gov/hiv/risk/estimates/riskbehaviors.html; Pragna Patel et al., "Estimating Per-Act HIV Transmission Risk: A Systematic Review," *Aids* 28, no. 10 (2014): 1509–19.

72 The actual lifetime risk is about 40 percent: "Lifetime Risk of Developing or Dying from Cancer," American Cancer Society, accessed May 17, 2018, https://www.cancer.org/cancer/cancer-basics/lifetime-probability-of-developing-or-dying-from-cancer.html.

72 16 percent: Fischhoff and De Bruin, "Fifty-Fifty = 50%?"

73 The subjective probability weighting function: Daniel Kahneman and Amos Tversky, "Prospect Theory: An Analysis of Decision under Risk," *Econometrica* 47, no. 2 (March 1979): 263–92. In fairness, this figure does not look exactly like the one from their paper.

73 Fossil fuel companies exploit uncertainty: Union of Concerned Scientists, *The Climate Accountability Scorecard (2018)* (Cambridge, MA: Union of Con-

cerned Scientists, 2018), accessed July 16, 2019, https://www.ucsusa.org
/climate-accountability-scorecard-2018.

74 Carnegie Mellon undergraduates: Don A. Moore and Deborah A. Small, "When It's Rational for the Majority to Believe That They Are Better than Average," in *Rationality and Social Responsibility: Essays in Honor of Robyn M. Dawes*, ed. Joachim I. Krueger (Mahwah, NJ: Lawrence Erlbaum Associates, 2008), 141–74.

74 Probability winning the Pennsylvania State Lottery when this study was conducted in 2003: "Powerball Game Information," Pennsylvania Lottery, numbers games, February 2003, http://www.palottery.com/lottery/cwp /view.asp?a=3&q=457089&lotteryNav=%7C29736%7C.

75 "not that many videos": Richard E. Ferdig, *Society, Culture, and Technology: Ten Lessons for Educators, Developers, and Digital Scientists* (Pittsburgh: ETC Press, 2018).

75 Google for $1.65 billion: Dealbook, "Google to Buy YouTube for $1.65 Billion in Stock," *New York Times*, October 9, 2006, https://dealbook.nytimes .com/2006/10/09/google-to-buy-youtube-for-165-billion-in-stock/.

75 Grant Eizikowitz, "How to Get a Billion Views on YouTube," *Business Insider*, 2018, http://www.businessinsider.com/how-to-get-billion-views-viral -hit-youtube-2018-4.

75 a big team of collaborators: This list of collaborators includes Tom Wallsten, Joe Tidwell, Sam Swift, Terry Murray, Emile Servan-Schreiber, Jenn Logg, Welton Chang, Pavel Atanasov, Jason Dana, Liz Tenney, Jonathan Baron, Lyle Ungar, and others.

76 On the liability of experts' ideologies: Philip E. Tetlock, *Expert Political Judgment: How Good Is It? How Can We Know?* (Princeton, NJ: Princeton University Press, 2005).

76 training turned out to be successful: Barbara A. Mellers et al., "Psychological Strategies for Winning a Geopolitical Forecasting Tournament," *Psychological Science* 25, no. 5 (2014): 1–10, https://doi.org/10.1177/0956797614524255.

77 Laplace and his omniscient demon: Pierre-Simon Laplace, *A Philosophical Essay on Probabilities* (New York: Wiley, 1825).

78 The story of Gombaud and Pascal: Dan Ma, "One Gambling Problem That Launched Modern Probability Theory," *Introductory Statistics* (blog), November 12, 2010, https://introductorystats.wordpress.com/2010/11/12/one -gambling-problem-that-launched-modern-probability-theory/.

79 Duke on the difference between poker amateurs and heavyweights: Annie Duke, *Thinking in Bets* (New York: Penguin, 2018).

79 interviews, as they are commonly used: Robert M. Guion and Scott Highhouse, *Essentials of Personnel Assessment and Selection* (Mahwah, NJ: Lawrence Erlbaum Associates, 2006).

80   from .38 to .53: Better methods include objective tests of candidates' abilities
      and structured interviews. Interviews should be structured so that every
      candidate meets with the same interviewers in the same order and each
      interviewer asks each candidate precisely the same questions. The ques-
      tions should provide hard-to-fake tests of work-relevant skills and abilities,
      and each response should be scored accordingly. Don A. Moore, "How
      to Improve the Accuracy and Reduce the Cost of Personnel Selection,"
      California Management Review 60, no. 1 (August 7, 2017): 8–17, https://doi
      .org/10.1177/0008125617725288.

80   Tim Anderson's batting average as of September 15, 2019: "Major League
      Baseball Player Stats," MLB.com 2019, http://mlb.mlb.com/stats/sortable.jsp.

80   an increase in batting average: Mikhail Averbukh, Scott Brown, and Brian
      Chase, "Baseball Pay and Performance" (unpublished manuscript, 2015),
      https://docplayer.net/9999190-Baseball-pay-and-performance.html.

80   Ryan Belz on *The Price is Right*: Erin Nyren, "'The Price Is Right' Contestant
      Breaks Plinko Record, Loses Mind," *Variety*, 2017, https://variety.com/2017
      /tv/news/the-price-is-right-plinko-record-1202445944/.

82   Quincunx experiments: Don A. Moore, Ashli Carter, and Heather H. J. Yang,
      "Wide of the Mark: Evidence on the Underlying Causes of Overprecision in
      Judgment," *Organizational Behavior and Human Decision Processes* 131 (2015):
      110–20.

CHAPTER 4: HOW BAD COULD IT BE?

90   Max's insurance: This analysis assumes risk neutrality, which is usually the
      wisest risk attitude to hold. Matthew Rabin and Max Bazerman, "Fretting
      about Modest Risks Is a Mistake," *California Management Review* 61, no. 3
      (2019): 34–48. However, human intuition can generate strong risk prefer-
      ences based on arbitrary or normatively irrelevant considerations. For in-
      stance, people are often risk averse for gains and risk seeking for losses.
      Daniel Kahneman and Amos Tversky, "Prospect Theory: An Analysis of
      Decision under Risk," *Econometrica* 47, no. 2 (1979): 263–91. Thinking about
      collecting on Max's insurance could feel like a loss relative to getting a real
      job or feel like a gain relative to being unemployed. Wisdom counsels that
      an attitude of risk neutrality is useful for avoiding these biases.

91   Sports fans, for example: Cade Massey, Joseph P. Simmons, and David
      A. Armor, "Hope over Experience: Desirability and the Persistence of Opti-
      mism," *Psychological Science* 22, no. 2 (2011): 274–81; Joseph P. Simmons and
      Cade Massey, "Is Optimism Real?," *Journal of Experimental Psychology: Gen-
      eral* (November 2012): 630–34, https://doi.org/10.1037/a0027405.

91   Partisan political pollsters: Brian Palmer, "Why Are There Democratic and

Republican Pollsters?," *Slate*, April 23, 2012, http://www.slate.com/articles /news_and_politics/explainer/2012/04/partisan_polling_why_are_there _democratic_and_republican_pollsters_.html.

91 Jerry Yang stories: Kate Pickert, "Yahoo! CEO Jerry Yang," *Time*, November 19, 2008, http://content.time.com/time/business/article/0,8599,1860424,00.html.

92 "All of you know": Pickert, "Yahoo! CEO."

92 "Yahoo is positioned": "Yahoo! Investor Presentation Details Financial Plan," Business Wire, March 18, 2008, https://www.businesswire.com/news /home/20080318005764/en/Yahoo%21-Investor-Presentation-Details -Financial-Plan.

92 Optimism won in a landslide: David A. Armor, Cade Massey, and Aaron M. Sackett, "Prescribed Optimism: Is It Right to Be Wrong about the Future?," *Psychological Science* 19 (2008): 329–31.

93 "Your belief that you have it": Rhonda Byrne, *The Secret* (New York: Simon & Schuster, 2006), 92.

93 Confident political candidates: Harold M. Zullow, Gabriele Oettingen, Christopher Peterson, and Martin E. P. Seligman, "Pessimistic Explanatory Style in the Historical Record: CAVing LBJ, Presidential Candidates, and East versus West Berlin," *American Psychologist* 43, no. 9 (1988): 673.

93 Confidence predicts cancer mortality: Joanne V. Wood, Shelley E. Taylor, and Rosemary R. Lichtman, "Social Comparison in Adjustment to Breast Cancer," *Journal of Personality and Social Psychology* 49, no. 5 (1985): 1169–83.

93 Confident entrepreneurs: Pia Arenius and Maria Minniti, "Perceptual Variables and Nascent Entrepreneurship," *Small Business Economics* 24, no. 3 (April 1, 2005): 233–47, https://doi.org/10.1007/s11187-005-1984-x.

93 Confident athletes: Pamela S. Highlen and Bonnie B. Bennett, "Psychological Characteristics of Successful and Nonsuccessful Elite Wrestlers: An Exploratory Study," *Journal of Sport and Exercise Psychology* 1, no. 2 (1979): 123–37.

94 Competence can explain the correlation between confidence and success: Tomas Chamorro-Premuzic, *Confidence: Overcoming Low Self-Esteem, Insecurity, and Self-Doubt* (London: Penguin, 2013).

94 "It's not bragging": "30 of Muhammad Ali's Best Quotes," *USA Today*, June 3, 2016, https://www.usatoday.com/story/sports/boxing/2016/06/03/muham mad-ali-best-quotes-boxing/85370850/.

94 impersonating a doctor: Frank Abagnale, *Catch Me If You Can* (New York: Broadway Books, 2000).

95 In a study I conducted: Elizabeth R. Tenney, Jennifer M. Logg, and Don A. Moore, "(Too) Optimistic about Optimism: The Belief That Optimism Improves Performance," *Journal of Personality and Social Psychology* 108, no. 3 (2015): 377–99, https://doi.org/10.1037/pspa0000018.

97   Americans estimated their chances: Jennifer S. Lerner et al., "Effects of Fear and Anger on Perceived Risks of Terrorism: A National Field Experiment," *Psychological Science* 14, no. 2 (2003): 144–50.

97   Fears of terrorism: Alvin Chang, "Americans' Sustained Fear from 9/11 Has Turned into Something More Dangerous," *Vox*, September 11, 2017, https://www.vox.com/2016/9/9/12852226/fear-witches-terrorists.

98   Iraq war, casualties and costs: Daniel Trotta, "Iraq War Costs U.S. More than $2 Trillion," Reuters, March 14, 2013, https://www.reuters.com/article/us-iraq-war-anniversary/iraq-war-costs-u-s-more-than-2-trillion-study-id USBRE92D0PG20130314.

98   60 percent of men: Laura Blue, "Study Shows More Than Half of All Americans Will Get Heart Disease," *Time*, November 7, 2012.

99   "As soon as you think": Susan Casey, *The Wave* (New York: Doubleday, 2010), 39.

100   "If you want to be a successful entrepreneur": Sujan Patel, "7 Things Confident Entrepreneurs Never Do," *Entrepreneur*, November 10, 2014, https://www.entrepreneur.com/article/238960.

100   advice encouraging would-be entrepreneurs to bolster their confidence: Randy Komisar and Jantoon Reigersman, *Straight Talk for Startups* (New York: HarperCollins, 2018).

100   one-third of them: Arnold C. Cooper, Carolyn Y. Woo, and William C. Dunkelberg, "Entrepreneurs' Perceived Chances for Success," *Journal of Business Venturing* 3, no. 2 (1988): 97–109.

100   "Successful entrepreneurship involves": James Surowiecki, "Do the Hustle," *New Yorker*, January 5, 2014, https://www.newyorker.com/magazine/2014/01/13/do-the-hustle.

101   nearly 80 percent: Jose Mata and Pedro Portugal, "Life Duration of New Firms," *Journal of Industrial Economics* 42, no. 3 (1994): 227–46.

101   the average entrepreneurial venture: Tobias J. Moskowitz and Annette Vissing-Jørgensen, "The Returns to Entrepreneurial Investment: A Private Equity Premium Puzzle?," *American Economic Review* 92, no. 4 (2002): 745–78.

103   the BATNA: R. Fisher, W. Ury, and B. Patton, *Getting to Yes* (Boston: Houghton Mifflin, 1981).

105   Chinese pollution study: Valerie J. Karplus, Shuang Zhang, and Douglas Almond, "Quantifying Coal Power Plant Responses to Tighter SO_2 Emissions Standards in China," *Proceedings of the National Academy of Sciences* 115, no. 27 (June 18, 2018): 7004–9, https://doi.org/10.1073/pnas.1800605115.

105   Samuelson's bet: Paul A. Samuelson, "Risk and Uncertainty: A Fallacy of Large Numbers," *Scientia* 98 (1963): 108–13.

106   The logic behind the sentiment: Kahneman and Tversky, "Prospect Theory."

107 6 percent of all people: Jamie Ducharme, "Why Some People Have Avio-phobia, or Fear of Flying," *Time*, July 6, 2018, http://time.com/5330978/fear-of-flying-aviophobia/.

109 score probability estimates: The solution here is to employ a quadratic scor-ing rule like the Brier score. Published in 1950 in a meteorology journal, the Brier score was devised as a tool for assessing weather forecasters' esti-mates on the probability of rain. Glenn W. Brier, "Verification of Forecasts Expressed in Terms of Probability," *Monthly Weather Review* 78, no. 1 (1950): 1–3. They provide a probability, but we observe only whether it rained or not. The way to score them to reward accuracy is to square the distance between their prediction and the truth. So, if p is the probability the fore-caster assigns to rain, and it rains, then the score is $(1-p)^2$. Lower scores indicate better performance: If the forecaster predicts 100 percent chance of rain and it rains, the score is 0 (since $p=1$ and $(1-1)^2=0$). Forecasting a 0 per-cent chance of rain when it rains yields a score of 1 (since $p=0$ and $(1-0)^2=1$). Traditionally, the Brier score sums scores for all possible outcomes; in this case, that means adding in the score for the prediction on it not raining, in this case $(0-(1-p))^2$. Computed this way, the Brier score is an error score: the worst score is a 2 and the best is a 0. Those who find error scores confusing can either think of this like the game of golf (in which higher scores are bad) or simply reverse score the Brier score by subtracting it from 2.

109 Apple's bet on the Newton: Harry McCracken, "Newton, Reconsidered," *Time*, June 1, 2012, http://techland.time.com/2012/06/01/newton-reconsidered/.

110 Apple had sold something like 1.4 billion: "Global Apple iPhone Sales from 3rd Quarter 2007 to 2nd Quarter 2018 (in Million Units)," Statista.com, 2018, https://www.statista.com/statistics/263401/global-apple-iphone-sales-since-3rd-quarter-2007/.

110 Profits per iPhone: "Apple Earned $151 Profit Per iPhone in Q3 2017: Counter-point," Press Trust of India, December 28, 2017, https://gadgets.ndtv.com/mobiles/news/apple-earned-151-profit-per-iphone-in-q3-2017-counterpoint-1793083.

CHAPTER 5: CLARIFY

117 Koby's given name: "Koby," IMDb, accessed April 19, 2019, http://www.imdb.com/name/nm9697725/.

117 "longest, loudest, and oddest": Shawn Patrick, "Colorado 'American Idol' Contestant Makes Judges Cringe," iHeartRadio, March 12, 2018, https://www.iheart.com/content/2018-03-12-colorado-american-idol-contestant-makes-judges-cringe/.

118   "I thought I sang": "Koby Auditions for American Idol with Original Song You Have to Hear—American Idol 2018 on ABC," YouTube video, posted by "American Idol," March 11, 2018, https://www.youtube.com/watch?v=Zmj6sNmv-yQ.

118   A large literature: Mark D. Alicke and Olesya Govorun, "The Better-than-Average Effect," in *The Self in Social Judgment*, ed. Mark D. Alicke, David Dunning, and Joachim Krueger (New York: Psychology Press, 2005), 85–106.

118   The most frequently cited: Ola Svenson, "Are We Less Risky and More Skill-ful than Our Fellow Drivers?," *Acta Psychologica* 47 (1981): 143–51.

119   pay people for being accurate: That's not because rewarding accuracy elim-inates the motive to impress others, but increasing the incentives for ac-curacy enhances its relative importance. For instance, if I expected to get $1 million prize for an accurately estimating my performance, I would try hard to be accurate. I will still care about impressing others or feeling good about myself, but these motives would shrink in importance relative to the motivation to earn the reward for being accurate.

119   monetary incentives for accuracy: Elanor F. Williams and Thomas Gi-lovich, "Do People Really Believe They Are Above Average?," *Journal of Ex-perimental Social Psychology* 44, no. 4 (2008): 1121–28; Erik Hoelzl and Aldo Rustichini, "Overconfident: Do You Put Your Money on It?," *Economic Jour-nal* 115, no. 503 (2005): 305–18.

119   clarifying the standards: Jennifer M. Logg, Uriel Haran, and Don A. Moore, "Is Overconfidence a Motivated Bias? Experimental Evidence," *Journal of Experimental Psychology: General* 147, no. 10 (2018): 1445–65, http://dx.doi.org/10.1037/xge0000500.

119   overplacement reduced substantially: Michael M. Roy and Michael J. Liersch, "I Am a Better Driver than You Think: Examining Self-Enhancement for Driving Ability," *Journal of Applied Social Psychology* 43, no. 8 (2013): 1648–59.

119   inaccurate claims of superiority disappear: Jean-Pierre Benoît, Juan Dubra, and Don A. Moore, "Does the Better-than-Average Effect Show That People Are Overconfident? Two Experiments," *Journal of the European Economic As-sociation* 13, no. 2 (2015): 293–329.

120   Clarifying what it means: Logg, Haran, and Moore, "Is Overconfidence a Motivated Bias?"

121   Online resources offer advice: Steve Piazzale, "How to Demonstrate You Are Results-Oriented to Get Hired," *techfetch*, June 16, 2013, http://blog.techfetch.com/demonstrate-results-oriented-hired/.

121   how to make their organization's culture: Lou Adler, "How to Create a Re-sults-Oriented Culture," *Inc.*, November 25, 2014, https://www.inc.com/lou-adler/how-to-create-a-results-oriented-culture.html.

121   Some see a choice: Matthew Lieberman, "Should Leaders Focus on Results,

or on People?," *Harvard Business Review*, December 27, 2013, https://hbr.org
/2013/12/should-leaders-focus-on-results-or-on-people.

122 luck plays a role: Robert H. Frank, *Success and Luck: Good Fortune and the Myth of Meritocracy* (Princeton, NJ: Princeton University Press, 2016).

123 more difficult component to quantify: I enthusiastically recommend a few books I have found useful for helping me think about uncertainties, probabilities, and probability distributions: Philip E. Tetlock and Dan Gardner, *Superforecasting: The Art and Science of Prediction* (New York: Crown, 2015), Annie Duke; *Thinking in Bets: Making Smarter Decisions When You Don't Have All the Facts* (New York: Portfolio, 2018); and Nate Silver's *The Signal and the Noise: Why So Many Predictions Fail—but Some Don't* (New York: Penguin Press, 2012).

124 Lake Wobegon: Garrison Keillor, *Lake Wobegon Days* (New York: Viking, 1985).

125 NCLB relied on standardized testing: James Traub, "NO CHILD LEFT BEHIND; Does It Work," *New York Times*, November 10, 2002, https://www.nytimes.com/2002/11/10/education/no-child-left-behind-does-it-work.html.

125 "None of these companies": John Jacob Cannell, "Nationally Normed Elementary Achievement Testing in America's Public Schools: How All 50 States Are above the National Average," *Educational Measurement: Issues and Practice* 7, no. 2 (1988): 5–9.

125 "Publishers are more interested": John Jacob Cannell, "The Lake Wobegon Effect Revisited," *Educational Measurement: Issues and Practice* 7, no. 4 (1988): 12–15.

125 Ditto's study: Peter H. Ditto et al., "Spontaneous Skepticism: The Interplay of Motivation and Expectation in Responses to Favorable and Unfavorable Medical Diagnoses," *Personality and Social Psychology Bulletin* 29, no. 9 (2003): 1120–32.

126 people naturally apply different standards: Ziva Kunda "The Case for Motivated Reasoning." *Psychological Bulletin* 108, no. 3 (1990): 480–98.

127 Trump found the PDB too dense and boring: Ben Brimelow, "Trump Reportedly Isn't Reading the Fabled President's Daily Briefing—Breaking a Tradition Followed by the Last 7 Presidents," *Business Insider*, 2018, https://www.businessinsider.com/trump-doesnt-read-daily-briefings-oral-listens-2018-2.

127 Trump asked for a daily briefing of positive press reports: Leah DePiero, "Trump Received Folder of Positive News Twice a Day under Sean Spicer and Reince Priebus: Report," *Washington Examiner*, 2017, https://www.washingtonexaminer.com/trump-received-folder-of-positive-news-twice-a-day-under-sean-spicer-and-reince-priebus-report.

127   Celebrity CEOs: Ulrike Malmendier and Geoffrey Tate, "Superstar CEOs,"
      Quarterly Journal of Economics 124, no. 4 (2009): 1593–1638.

127   Many Tesla shareholders shuddered: "Elon Musk Smokes Weed with Joe
      Rogan," YouTube video, posted by "Jay Nail," September 7, 2018, https://
      www.youtube.com/watch?v=19WWHzQsHrI.

128   he might have been on LSD: Chris Woodyard, "Elon Musk's Tweet on
      Taking Tesla Private Now Dogged by Drugs Claim from Rapper Azealia
      Banks," *USA Today*, August 22, 2018, https://www.usatoday.com/story
      /tech/talkingtech/2018/08/22/elon-musks-tweet-taking-tesla-private-now
      -dogged-drugs-claims-rapper-azealia-banks/1057815002/.

128   $20 million fine: Matthew Goldstein, "Elon Musk Steps Down as Chairman
      in Deal with S.E.C. over Tweet about Tesla," *New York Times*, November 6,
      2018, https://www.nytimes.com/2018/09/29/business/tesla-musk-sec-settle
      ment.html.

128   On average, corporate acquisitions: Gregor Andrade, Mark Mitchell, and
      Erik Stafford, "New Evidence and Perspectives on Mergers," *Journal of Eco-
      nomic Perspectives* 15, no. 2 (2001): 103–20.

128   "the poster child": Lizzy Gurdus, "Cramer: GE Has Become 'the Poster
      Child for Bad Acquisitions,'" CNBC, November 13, 2017, https://www.cnbc
      .com/2017/11/13/cramer-ge-has-become-the-poster-child-for-bad-acquisitions
      .html.

128   "I didn't know a diddly": "Learn as You Churn," *Economist*, April 6, 2006,
      https://www.economist.com/finance-and-economics/2006/04/06/learn-as
      -you-churn.

128   Joe Cassano story: Michael Lewis, "The Man Who Crashed the World,"
      Vanity Fair, August 2009.

129   AIG-FP became liable for something like $25 billion in losses: Gregory Geth-
      ard, "Falling Giant: A Case Study of AIG," Investopedia, accessed April 11,
      2019, https://www.investopedia.com/articles/economics/09/american
      -investment-group-aig-bailout.asp.

129   The story of Enron's demise: Bethany McLean and Peter Elkind, *The Smart-
      est Guys in the Room: The Amazing Rise and Scandalous Fall of Enron* (New York:
      Portfolio, 2003).

129   McLean's insightful investigation: Bethany McLean, "Is Enron Overpriced?
      It's in a Bunch of Complex Businesses. Its Financial Statements Are Nearly
      Impenetrable. So Why Is Enron Trading at Such a Huge Multiple?," *Fortune*,
      March 5, 2001, http://archive.fortune.com/magazines/fortune/fortune
      _archive/2001/03/05/297833/index.htm.

130   Ray Dalio attempted to make his company: Ray Dalio, *Principles: Life and
      Work* (New York: Simon & Schuster, 2017).

130   "When you're critized": Prachi Bhardwaj, "The Jeff Bezos Approach to Han-

dling Criticism Is a Good Rule Everyone Should Follow," *Business Insider*, April 30, 2018, https://www.businessinsider.com/how-amazon-ceo-jeff-bezos-handles-criticism-2018-4.

130 confronting our imperfections: Dolly Chugh, *The Person You Mean to Be: How Good People Fight Bias* (New York: HarperBusiness, 2018).

131 grit—the tendency to persist: Angela L. Duckworth, *Grit: The Power of Passion and Perseverance* (New York: Scribner, 2016).

132 costs for escalating our commitment: Barry M. Staw, "Knee-Deep in the Big Muddy: A Study of Escalating Commitment to a Chosen Course of Action," *Organizational Behavior and Human Decision Processes* 16, no. 1 (1976): 27–44; Jeffrey Z. Rubin et al., "Factors Affecting Entry into Psychological Traps," *Journal of Conflict Resolution* 24, no. 3 (1980): 405–26.

132 reluctant to sell losing stocks: Terrance Odean, "Are Investors Reluctant to Realize Their Losses?," *Journal of Finance* 53, no. 5 (1998): 1775–98.

132 People have trouble ending abusive relationships: Michael J. Strube, "The Decision to Leave an Abusive Relationship: Empirical Evidence and Theoretical Issues," *Psychological Bulletin* 104, no. 2 (1988): 236–50.

133 "auction fever": Gillian Ku, Deepak Malhotra, and J. Keith Murnighan, "Towards a Competitive Arousal Model of Decision Making: A Study of Auction Fever in Live and Internet Auctions," *Organizational Behavior and Human Decision Processes* 96, no. 2 (2005): 89–103, https://doi.org/10.1016/j.obhdp.2004.10.001.

133 how companies make decisions: Paul Nutt, *Why Decisions Fail: Avoiding the Blunders and Traps That Lead to Debacles* (San Francisco: Berrett-Koehler, 2002).

134 Shane Frederick highlights: Shane Frederick et al., "Opportunity Cost Neglect," *Journal of Consumer Research* 36, no. 4 (2009): 553–61.

138 It is easy to lie: Andrew Gelman and Eric Loken, "The Statistical Crisis in Science," *American Scientist* 102, no. 6 (November–December 2014): 460, https://doi.org/10.1511/2014.111.460.

CHAPTER 6: FORECAST

139 Lion Air flight 610: "Timeline: Boeing 737 Max Jetliner Crashes and Aftermath," *Chicago Tribune*, August 7, 2019, https://www.chicagotribune.com/business/ct-biz-viz-boeing-737-max-crash-timeline-04022019-story.html.

140 over one hundred thousand: "How Many Airplanes Fly Each Day in the World?," Quora, question answered by "Snehal Kumar," accessed May 8, 2019, https://www.quora.com/How-many-airplanes-fly-each-day-in-the-world.

140 about four hundred people: "Accidents Statistics : Fatalities by Year," airfleets

.net, accessed May 7, 2019, https://www.airfleets.net/crash/fatalities_year.htm.

140 less than 0.05 deaths: Laurie F. Beck, Ann M. Dellinger, and Mary E. O'Neil. "Motor Vehicle Crash Injury Rates by Mode of Travel, United States: Using Exposure-Based Methods to Quantify Differences." *American Journal of Epidemiology* 166, no. 2 (July 15, 2007): 212–18. https://doi.org/10.1093/aje/kwm064.

141 The ASRS: "Program Briefing," Aviation Safety Reporting System, https://asrs.arc.nasa.gov/overview/summary.html.

141 Google's use of postmortems: John Lunney, Sue Lueder, and Gary O'Connor, "Postmortem Culture: How You Can Learn from Failure," *re:Work* (blog), April 24, 2018, https://rework.withgoogle.com/blog/postmortem-culture-how-you-can-learn-from-failure/.

141 postmortem form: "Google's Postmortem Exercise," http://perfectlyconfident.com/postmortem/.

142 Google spent over $585 million: Bruce Upbin, "Google+ Cost $585 Million to Build (Or What Rupert Paid for MySpace)," *Forbes*, June 30, 2011, https://www.forbes.com/sites/bruceupbin/2011/06/30/google-cost-585-million-to-build-or-what-rupert-paid-for-myspace/.

142 Google Glass: "The Google Glass Epic Fail: What Happened?," *BGR* (blog), June 27, 2015, https://bgr.com/2015/06/27/google-glass-epic-fail-what-happened/.

142 some companies help their employees accept failure: John Danner and Mark Coopersmith, *The Other "F" Word: How Smart Leaders, Teams, and Entrepreneurs Put Failure to Work* (Hoboken, NJ: John Wiley & Sons, 2015).

143 "Students? A new search engine?": "The Anti-Portfolio," website of Bessemer Venture Partners, accessed June 2, 2019, https://www.bvp.com/anti-portfolio/.

143 Muilenburg boast: Chris Isidore, "Boeing Boasted about Streamlined Approval for the 737 Max. Now It's Cleaning up the Mess," CNN, April 4, 2019, https://www.cnn.com/2019/04/03/business/boeing-737-max-crisis/index.html.

144 Boeing's safety assessment included errors: Dominic Gates, "Flawed Analysis, Failed Oversight: How Boeing, FAA Certified the Suspect 737 MAX Flight Control System," *Seattle Times*, March 17, 2019, https://www.seattletimes.com/business/boeing-aerospace/failed-certification-faa-missed-safety-issues-in-the-737-max-system-implicated-in-the-lion-air-crash/.

144 Orders for new 737 Max: Jackie Wattles, "Boeing CEO Says New Software Update Has Been Tested by Most 737 Max Customers," CNN, April 11, 2019, https://www.cnn.com/2019/04/11/business/boeing-software-dennis-muilenburg/index.html.

144 ultimate cost to Boeing's bottom line: David Gelles, "Boeing 737 Max Troubles Add Up: $8 Billion and Counting," *New York Times*, July 18, 2019, https://www.nytimes.com/2019/07/18/business/boeing-737-charge.html.

144 "premortem analysis": Gary Klein's work on premortems built on the ideas of Mitchell, Russo, and Pennington, who showed that what they called "prospective hindsight" can help people identify possible reasons for future successes and failures. Deborah J. Mitchell, J. Edward Russo, and Nancy Pennington, "Back to the Future: Temporal Perspective in the Explanation of Events," *Journal of Behavioral Decision Making* 2, no. 1 (1989): 25–38, https://doi.org/10.1002/bdm.3960020103.

144 Klein's premortem instructions: Gary Klein, "Performing a Project Premortem," *Harvard Business Review* 85, no. 9 (2007): 18–19.

145 "The time to take counsel": "George S. Patton," Great Thoughts Treasury, accessed June 21, 2019, http://www.greatthoughtstreasury.com/author/george-s-patton-fully-george-smith-patton-jr.

145 Kahneman's premortem instructions: Daniel Kahneman, *Thinking, Fast and Slow* (New York: Farrar, Straus and Giroux, 2011), 264.

146 "If we're going to die": Jack McCaffery, "McCaffery: Sixers Finding That NBA Has Plenty of 'Danger,'" *Delaware County Daily Times*, December 5, 2017, https://www.delcotimes.com/sports/mccaffery-sixers-finding-that-nba-has-plenty-of-danger/article_a5ec2d61-3e73-5f53-ae4b-3d6173084d3a.html.

146 Julie Norem calls it defensive pessimism: Julie K. Norem, *The Positive Power of Negative Thinking* (Cambridge, MA: Basic Books, 2001).

146 the hardest workers are motivated by the potential guilt they envision: Francis J. Flynn and Rebecca L. Schaumberg, "When Feeling Bad Leads to Feeling Good: Guilt-Proneness and Affective Organizational Commitment," *Journal of Applied Psychology* 97, no. 1 (2012): 124.

147 "Invert, always invert": Michael Simmons, "What Self-Made Billionaire Charlie Munger Does Differently," *Inc.*, November 2015, https://www.inc.com/michael-simmons/what-self-made-billionaire-charlie-munger-does-differently.html.

147 on disaster preparedness: Ian I. Mitroff and Gus Anagnos, *Managing Crises Before They Happen: What Every Executive and Manager Needs to Know about Crisis Management* (New York: AMACOM, 2000).

147 Perrow on normal accidents: Charles Perrow, *Normal Accidents: Living with High-Risk Technologies* (New York: Basic Books, 1984).

148 Facebook's storm drills: Robert Hof, "Interview: How Facebook's Project Storm Heads Off Data Center Disasters," *Forbes*, September 11, 2016, https://www.forbes.com/sites/roberthof/2016/09/11/interview-how-facebooks-project-storm-heads-off-data-center-disasters/.

149 "This was not only": Marion Lloyd, "Soviets Close to Using A-Bomb in 1962 Crisis, Forum Is Told," *Boston Globe*, October 13, 2002, available at http://www.latinamericanstudies.org/cold-war/sovietsbomb.htm.

149 Arkhipov story: Rachel Souerbry, "This Man Singlehandedly Prevented World War III—And You've Probably Never Heard of Him," All That's Interesting, June 7, 2018, https://allthatsinteresting.com/vasili-arkhipov.

149 "didn't like talking about it": *Secrets of the Dead*, season 12, episode 6, "The Man Who Saved the World," directed by Eamon Fitzpatrick, aired October 23, 2012, on PBS, https://www.pbs.org/video/secrets-deadman-who-saved-world-full-episode/.

150 Backcasting: John Bridger Robinson, "Energy Backcasting: A Proposed Method of Policy Analysis," *Energy Policy* 10, no. 4 (1982): 337–44.

152 research by Armor, Massey, and Sackett: David A. Armor, Cade Massey, and Aaron M. Sackett, "Prescribed Optimism: Is It Right to Be Wrong about the Future?," *Psychological Science* 19 (2008): 329–31.

152 Unpleasant Truths vs. Comforting Lies: "Cartoon—Comforting Lies vs. Unpleasant Truths," *Henry Kotula* (blog), February 17, 2017, https://henrykotula.com/2017/02/17/cartoon-comforting-lies-vs-unpleasant-truths/.

152 *The Secret* has sold: https://www.thesecret.tv/about/rhonda-byrnes-biography/.

153 Delusional optimism just makes reality: A. Peter McGraw, Barbara A. Mellers, and Ilana Ritov, "The Affective Costs of Overconfidence," *Journal of Behavioral Decision Making* 17, no. 4 (2004): 281–95.

153 people experience the pain of losses: Daniel Kahneman and Amos Tversky, "Prospect Theory: An Analysis of Decision under Risk," *Econometrica* 47, no. 2 (March 1979): 263–92.

153 excessively optimistic beliefs: Botond Kőszegi and Matthew Rabin, "Reference-Dependent Consumption Plans," *American Economic Review* 99, no. 3 (2009): 909–36.

153 students are more optimistic at the beginning of the semester: James A. Shepperd, Judith A. Ouellette, and Julie K. Fernandez, "Abandoning Unrealistic Optimism: Performance Estimates and the Temporal Proximity of Self-Relevant Feedback," *Journal of Personality and Social Psychology* 70, no. 4 (1996): 844–55.

153 As the moment of truth: Scott Richardson, Siew Hong Teoh, and Peter D. Wysocki, "The Walk-Down to Beatable Analyst Forecasts: The Role of Equity Issuance and Insider Trading Incentives," *Contemporary Accounting Research* 21, no. 4 (2004): 885–924.

153 Savoring anticipated pleasures: George Loewenstein and Drazen Prelec, "Negative Time Preference," *American Economic Review* 81, no. 2 (1991): 347–52.

154 fooling yourself: William von Hippel and Robert L. Trivers, "The Evolution and Psychology of Self-Deception," *Behavioral and Brain Sciences* 34 (2011): 1–56.

155 "I demand that the world": Helen Keller, *Optimism: An Essay* (New York: Thomas Y. Crowell, 1903).

155 Definition of optimism: *Merriam-Webster Dictionary*, s.v. "Optimism," http://www.merriam-webster.com/dictionary/optimism.

156 Nate Silver was derided: Ryan Grim, "Nate Silver Is Unskewing Polls—All of Them. Here's How," Huffington Post, November 5, 2016, https://www.huffpost.com/entry/nate-silver-election-forecast_n_581e1c33e4b0d9ce6fbc6f7f.

156 Clinton lost: Matt Flegenheimer and Michael Barbaro, "Donald Trump Is Elected President in Stunning Repudiation of the Establishment," *New York Times*, November 9, 2016, accessed September 22, 2019, https://www.nytimes.com/2016/11/09/us/politics/hillary-clinton-donald-trump-president.html.

156 When forecasts of the economy: Paul Beaudry and Tim Willems, "On the Macroeconomic Consequences of Over-Optimism," SSRN, 2018, https://papers.ssrn.com/sol3/papers.cfm?abstract_id=3194836; David Leonhardt, "The Experts Keep Getting the Economy Wrong," *New York Times*, March 15, 2019, https://www.nytimes.com/2019/03/10/opinion/us-economy-stagnation-growth.html.

157 terminally ill cancer patients: Haider Javed Warraich, "The Cancer of Optimism," *New York Times*, May 4, 2013, https://www.nytimes.com/2013/05/05/opinion/sunday/the-cancer-of-optimism.html.

157 hope for a cure despite its minuscule probability: David Schultz, "Many Terminal Cancer Patients Mistakenly Believe a Cure Is Possible," National Public Radio, October 25, 2012.

157 half of all health-care expenses: Daniel Callahan, "Costs of Medical Care at the End of Life," *New York Times*, January 10, 2013.

157 Deciding to delude yourself about the future: Richard W. Robins and Jennifer S. Beer, "Positive Illusions about the Self: Short-Term Benefits and Long-Term Costs," *Journal of Personality and Social Psychology* 80, no. 2 (2001): 340–52.

157 insanity quote: There is controversy about whether credit for this quote really belongs to Einstein. But someone did say it. See Christina Sterbenz, "12 Famous Quotes That Always Get Misattributed," *Business Insider*, October 7, 2013, https://www.businessinsider.com/misattributed-quotes-2013-10.

158 Original plan for California high-speed rail: "Building a High-Speed Train Network," California High-Speed Rail Authority, 2000, http://www.hsr.ca.gov/docs/about/business_plans/BPlan_2000_FactSheet.pdf.

158   1 percent of passenger-miles: "U.S. Passenger Miles," Bureau of Transportation Statistics, accessed September 29, 2019, https://www.bts.gov/content/us-passenger-miles.

158   China alone: "High Speed Trains Worldwide: A Ranking," Omio, June 2019, accessed September 29, 2019, https://www.omio.com/trains/high-speed.

158   High-Speed Rail Authority aspired: Ralph Vartabedian, "On California High-Speed Rail Project, Newsom to Scale Back Consultants but Push Ahead," *Los Angeles Times*, May 1, 2019, https://www.latimes.com/local/california/la-me-bullet-train-project-update-20190501-story.html.

159   Boston's "Big Dig": Sean P. Murphy, "Big Dig's Red Ink Engulfs State," *Boston Globe*, July 17, 2008, http://archive.boston.com/news/local/articles/2008/07/17/big_digs_red_ink_engulfs_state/.

159   the planning fallacy: Daniel Kahneman and Amos Tversky, "Intuitive Prediction: Biases and Corrective Procedures," in *TIMS Studies in Management Science*, vol. 12 (Mclean, VA: Decisions and Designs, 1977), 313–27; Roger Buehler, Dale W. Griffin, and Michael Ross, "Exploring the 'Planning Fallacy': Why People Underestimate Their Task Completion Times," *Journal of Personality and Social Psychology* 67, no. 3 (1994): 366–81.

161   If you don't want to be late, enumerate: Justin Kruger and Matt Evans, "If You Don't Want to Be Late, Enumerate: Unpacking Reduces the Planning Fallacy," *Journal of Experimental Social Psychology* 40, no. 5 (2004): 586–98.

162   People are less likely: Christopher D. B. Burt and Simon Kemp, "Construction of Activity Duration and Time Management Potential," *Applied Cognitive Psychology* 8, no. 2 (1994): 155–68.

162   auctions like this: Technically, these are "reverse auctions." In regular auctions, buyers bid against each other, raising the price. In reverse auctions, sellers compete by lowering their bids.

163   time and materials pricing: Naturally, more complex compromises are possible. For instance, the buyer could pay a low fixed cost but agree to pay some portion of time and materials costs past a certain point. Again, such an arrangement works best when the buyer can trust the seller's cost accounting.

CHAPTER 7: CONSIDER OTHER PERSPECTIVES

165   Quotes from Ray Dalio and stories about Bridgewater: Ray Dalio, *Principles: Life and Work* (New York: Simon & Schuster, 2017).

166   Bridgewater assets under management: Tom Huddleston Jr., "Billionaire Ray Dalio Says This Is How to Be 'Truly Successful,'" CNBC, August 22 2019, https://www.cnbc.com/2019/08/22/bridgewater-associates-ray-dalio-how-to-be-truly-successful.html.

167 poker players asking her, "Wanna bet?": Annie Duke, *Thinking in Bets* (New York: Penguin, 2018).

167 losing sixty pounds: The one who ate one hundred burgers is not the same person who took the weight-loss bet, in case you were wondering. Michael Kaplan, "Pro Poker Players Bet Away from the Table, Too," *New York Times*, June 29, 2008, https://www.nytimes.com/2008/06/29/fashion/29bets.html.

168 "This led to some good-natured ribbing": Duke, *Thinking in Bets*.

168 Warren Buffett's bet with Protégé Partners: Carol Loomis, "Buffett's Bet: Hedge Funds Can't Beat the Market," *Fortune*, June 9, 2008, http://archive.fortune.com/2008/06/04/news/newsmakers/buffett_bet.fortune/index.htm.

169 Protégé's hedge funds could manage was a 2.2 percent annual gain: Emily Price, "Warren Buffett Won a $1 Million Bet, but the Real Winner Is Charity," *Fortune*, December 30, 2017, http://fortune.com/2017/12/30/warren-buffett-million-dollar-bet/.

170 "naive realism": Lee Ross and Andrew Ward, "Naive Realism in Everyday Life: Implications for Social Conflict and Misunderstanding," in *Values and Knowledge*, ed. E. Reed, E. Turiel, and T. Brown (Hillsdale, NJ: Lawrence Erlbaum Associates, 1996), 103–35; K. Dobson and R. L. Franche, "A Conceptual and Empirical Review of the Depressive Realism Hypothesis," *Canadian Journal of Behavioral Science* 21 (1989): 419–33.

170 "It is only by the collision": John Stuart Mill, *On Liberty* (New Haven, CT: Yale University Press, 1859).

170 Outcome of Hennigan's Des Moines bet: Kaplan, "Pro Poker Players."

172 Day traders lose money: Brad M. Barber et al., "Learning, Fast or Slow," *Review of Asset Pricing Studies* (forthcoming), https://doi.org/10.2139/ssrn.2535636.

173 Rational people will agree: Robert J. Aumann, "Agreeing to Disagree," *Annals of Statistics* 4 (1976): 1236–39.

173 Overconfidence as an explanation for market trading: Kent D. Daniel, David A. Hirshleifer, and Avanidhar Sabrahmanyam, "Overconfidence, Arbitrage, and Equilibrium Asset Pricing," *Journal of Finance* 56, no. 3 (2001): 921–65.

173 the more investors trade: Brad M. Barber and Terrance Odean, "Trading Is Hazardous to Your Wealth: The Common Stock Investment Performance of Individual Investors," *Journal of Finance* 55, no. 2 (2000): 773–806.

174 Buffett quote: Warren Buffett, "Chairman's Letter—1987," 1987, available at http://www.berkshirehathaway.com/letters/1987.html.

174 an annualized 23 percent loss: Brad M. Barber, Yi-Tsung Lee, Yu-Jane Liu, Terrance Odean, and Ke Zhang, "Learning Fast or Slow?," *Review of Asset Pricing Studies* (forthcoming).

175 put your money in index funds: Burton Gordon Malkiel, *A Random Walk down Wall Street* (New York: Norton, 1973).

175   Galton's article: Francis Galton, "Vox Populi (The Wisdom of Crowds)," *Nature* 75, no. 7 (1907): 450–51.

175   Sir Francis Galton: Yes, this is the same Francis Galton who made an appearance in chapter 3. There, we credited him for the Galton Board, also known as the Quincunx, so useful for illustrating the binomial distribution. He was also, as it happens, Charles Darwin's cousin. He got around.

175   These lessons have been reprised: James Surowiecki, *The Wisdom of Crowds* (New York: Random House, 2005).

176   The average poll includes: "FAQs," National Council on Public Polls, accessed June 5, 2019, http://www.ncpp.org/?q=node/6.

176   A poll of that size: Andrew Gelman, "How Can a Poll of Only 1,004 Americans Represent 260 Million People with Only a 3 Percent Margin of Error?," *Scientific American*, March 15, 2004, https://www.scientificamerican.com/article/howcan-a-poll-of-only-100/.

176   the crowd within: Stefan M Herzog and Ralph Hertwig, "The Wisdom of Many in One Mind," *Psychological Science* 108 (2009): 9020–25.

177   "Song of Myself": Walt Whitman, "Song of Myself," accessed September 22, 2019, https://www.poetryfoundation.org/poems/45477/song-of-myself-1892-version.

177   General Motors went from: Alfred P. Sloan, *My Years With General Motors* (New York: Anchor Books, 1963).

178   "Gentlemen, I take it": "Alfred Sloan," *Economist*, January 3, 2009, https://www.economist.com/news/2009/01/30/alfred-sloan.

178   US president Abraham Lincoln: Doris Kearns Goodwin, *Team of Rivals: The Political Genius of Abraham Lincoln* (New York: Simon & Schuster, 2005).

178   When everyone shares the same bias: Surowiecki, *Wisdom of Crowds*.

178   "group polarization": Helmut Lamm and David G. Myers, "Group Induced Polarization of Attitudes and Behavior," in *Advances in Experimental Social Psychology*, ed. Leonard Berkowitz, vol. 2 (San Diego: Academic Press, 1978), 147–95.

178   Study of group polarization in residents of Boulder and Colorado Springs: David Schkade, Cass R. Sunstein, and Reid Hastie, "What Happened on Deliberation Day?," *California Law Review* 95 (2007): 915–40.

179   Studies of grant funding committees: Warren Thorngate, Robyn M. Dawes, and Margaret Foddy, *Judging Merit* (New York: Psychology Press, 2008).

180   the evidence supporting these claims is weak and inconsistent: Don A. Moore and Amelia S. Dev, "Individual Differences in Overconfidence," in *Encyclopedia of Personality and Individual Differences*, ed. Virgil Zeigler-Hill and Todd Shackelford (New York: Springer, 2017).

180   no systematic evidence: And even some anecdotal evidence suggesting the opposite. In the days before our phones' turn-by-turn directions saved us,

it was always my wife who refused to stop to ask for directions. We only sometimes got lost. Getting directions from the phone has done wonders for our marriage.

180   restricted to particular stereotypically male domains: Pedro Bordalo et al., "Beliefs about Gender," *American Economic Review* 109, no. 3 (March 2019): 739–73, https://doi.org/10.1257/aer.20170007.

181   Failure to replicate male overplacement: Don A. Moore and Samuel A. Swift, "The Three Faces of Overconfidence in Organizations," in *Social Psychology of Organizations*, ed. Rolf Van Dick and J. Keith Murnighan (Oxford, UK: Taylor & Francis, 2010), 147–84.

181   women show more overplacement: Bordalo et al., "Beliefs about Gender."

181   Some books that discuss gender differences: Sheryl Sandberg, *Lean In: Women, Work, and the Will to Lead* (New York: Alfred A. Knopf, 2013).

181   women might make better investment decisions: Brad M. Barber and Terrance Odean, "Boys Will Be Boys: Gender, Overconfidence, and Common Stock Investment," *Quarterly Journal of Economics* 116, no. 1 (2001): 261–93.

181   If being too sure: Samantha C. Paustian-Underdahl, Lisa Slattery Walker, and David J. Woehr, "Gender and Perceptions of Leadership Effectiveness: A Meta-Analysis of Contextual Moderators," *Journal of Applied Psychology* 99, no. 6 (2014): 1129; Ashleigh Shelby Rosette, Leigh Plunkett Tost, and Katherine W. Phillips, "Agentic Women and Communal Leadership: How Role Prescriptions Confer Advantage to Top Women Leaders," *Journal of Applied Psychology* 95, no. 2 (2010): 221–35.

181   "believe, irrationally, that they": Randy Komisar and Jantoon Reigersman, *Straight Talk for Startups: 100 Insider Rules for Beating the Odds—From Mastering the Fundamentals to Selecting Investors, Fundraising, Managing Boards, and Achieving Liquidity* (New York: HarperCollins, 2018).

181   "discover something new": "'The Dropout' Part 1: Where Ex-Theranos CEO Elizabeth Holmes Got Her Start," YouTube video, posted by "ABC News," March 16, 2019, https://www.youtube.com/watch?v=kG_F118ruOM.

181   The story of Holmes and Theranos: John Carreyrou, *Bad Blood: Secrets and Lies in a Silicon Valley Startup* (New York: Alfred A. Knopf, 2018).

182   "I want to create": Roger Parloff, "This CEO Is Out for Blood," *Fortune*, June 12, 2014, http://fortune.com/2014/06/12/theranos-blood-holmes/.

183   "that our little girls": Carreyrou, *Bad Blood*.

183   "God wants his people": Art Harris and Michael Isikoff, "The Good Life at PTL: A Litany of Excess," *Washington Post*, May 22, 1987, https://www.washingtonpost.com/archive/politics/1987/05/22/the-good-life-at-ptl-a-litany-of-excess/b694ac2f-516c-42ad-ba52-9998763670b0/.

183   The Bakkers justified: J. Bakker and K. Abraham, *I Was Wrong* (Nashville: Thomas Nelson, 1996).

183 Most people think of themselves: Scott T. Allison, David M. Messick, and George R. Goethals, "On Being Better but Not Smarter than Others: The Muhammad Ali Effect," *Social Cognition* 7, no. 3 (1989): 275–95.

184 We are most prone: Jonathon D. Brown, "Understanding the Better than Average Effect: Motives (Still) Matter," *Personality & Social Psychology Bulletin* 38, no. 2 (December 28, 2011): 209–19, https://doi.org/10.1177/0146167211432763.

184 many people feel that they suffer: Joe Langford and Pauline Rose Clance, "The Imposter Phenomenon: Recent Research Findings Regarding Dynamics, Personality and Family Patterns and Their Implications for Treatment," *Psychotherapy: Theory, Research, Practice, Training* 30, no. 3 (1993): 495.

184 ads featured workers clad in their "bunny suits": "Intel Pentium MMX (1997) TV Ad—'Play That Funky Music' (TV Spot 1)," YouTube video, posted by "CheesyTV," March 7, 2013, https://www.youtube.com/watch?v=5zyjSBSvqPc.

185 Gordon Moore: Gordon Moore (no relation) gets the credit for Moore's law, which describes the rate of increase in the processing speed of computers.

185 Grove and Moore story: Andrew S. Grove, *Only the Paranoid Survive: How to Exploit the Crisis Points That Challenge Every Company* (New York: Crown, 2010).

185 Kahneman's committee: Daniel Kahneman, *Thinking, Fast and Slow* (New York: Farrar, Straus and Giroux, 2011).

187 "If there is any one secret": "Henry Ford 150," website of MotorCities National Heritage Area and the Henry Ford Heritage Association, accessed June 7, 2019, https://www.henryford150.com/.

CHAPTER 8: FIND THE MIDDLE WAY

190 Honnold is different: Honnold does poop, just like other climbers. One can only assume he held it for the hours he was climbing El Cap. Even at the scary parts. What makes Honnold different from most climbers is that they rightly regard free climbing as somewhere between reckless and insane.

190 "The best strategy": Matt Ray, "Free Solo: Alex Honnold on What It Takes to Free Climb," RedBull.com, May 8, 2019, https://www.redbull.com/us-en/alex-honnold-interview-free-solo.

192 absence of underprecision: Don A. Moore, Elizabeth R. Tenney, and Uriel Haran, "Overprecision in Judgment," in *Handbook of Judgment and Decision Making*, ed. George Wu and Gideon Keren (New York: Wiley, 2015), 182–212.

193 "I have not failed": J. L. Elkhorne, "Edison—The Fabulous Drone," *73 Amateur Radio*, March 1967.

193 Edison's failed inventions: Erica R. Hendry, "7 Epic Fails Brought to You by the Genius Mind of Thomas Edison," Smithsonian.com, November 30, 2013, https://www.smithsonianmag.com/innovation/7-epic-fails-brought -to-you-by-the-genius-mind-of-thomas-edison-180947786/.

194 "I think there's a seventy percent": Joshua Quittner, "Person of the Year 1999: Jeff Bezos," *Time Asia*, December 1999, http://edition.cnn.com/ASIA NOW/time/magazine/99/1227/cover3.html.

194 "I predict that one day": Dominic Rushe, "Jeff Bezos Tells Employees 'One Day Amazon Will Fail,'" *Guardian*, November 16, 2018, https://www.the guardian.com/technology/2018/nov/16/jeff-bezos-amazon-will-fail-record ing-report.

195 confidence is the fundamental basis: Francisco Dao, "Without Confidence, There Is No Leadership," *Inc.*, March 1, 2008, https://www.inc.com/re sources/leadership/articles/20080301/dao.html.

195 confidence increases people's influence: Cameron Anderson et al., "A Status-Enhancement Account of Overconfidence," *Journal of Personality and Social Psychology* 103, no. 4 (2012): 718–35, https://doi.org/10.1037/a0029395.

196 "Top con artists": Frank Abagnale, *Catch Me If You Can* (New York: Broadway Books, 2000).

196 specific, factual claims: Elizabeth R. Tenney et al., "Is Overconfidence a Social Liability? The Effect of Verbal versus Nonverbal Expressions of Confidence," *Journal of Personality and Social Psychology* 116, no. 3 (2019): 396–415.

197 it can be hard to discredit them: Jessica A. Kennedy, Cameron Anderson, and Don A. Moore, "When Overconfidence Is Revealed to Others: Testing the Status-Enhancement Theory of Overconfidence," *Organizational Behavior and Human Decision Processes* 122, no. 2 (2013): 266–79.

198 "Experts who acknowledge": Daniel Kahneman, *Thinking, Fast and Slow* (New York: Farrar, Straus and Giroux, 2011).

198 "First and foremost": *The Decriminalization of Illegal Drugs: Hearing before the Subcommittee on Criminal Justice, Drug Policy, and Human Resources of the Committee on Government Reform*, 106th Cong. (1999), https://www.govinfo.gov /content/pkg/CHRG-106hhrg64343/html/CHRG-106hhrg64343.htm.

199 Gaertig and Simmons research: Celia Gaertig and Joseph P. Simmons, "Do People Inherently Dislike Uncertain Advice?," *Psychological Science* 29, no. 4 (2018): 504–20, https://doi.org/10.1177%2F0956797617739369.

199 the expression of confidence: Anderson et al., "A Status-Enhancement Account of Overconfidence."

199 Voltaire quote: "Letter to Frederick William, Prince of Prussia (28 November 1770)," in *Voltaire in His Letters: Being a Selection from His Correspondence*, trans. S. G. Tallentyre (New York: Putnam, 1919), 232.

200 Piccinino's story: "Italy Bridge: The Lives Lost to the Genoa Bridge

Collapse," BBC, August 19, 2018, https://www.bbc.com/news/world-europe -45193882.

201 An article heralding: Guglielmo Mattioli, "What Caused the Genoa Bridge Collapse—and the End of an Italian National Myth?," *Guardian*, February 26, 2019, https://www.theguardian.com/cities/2019/feb/26/what-caused-the -genoa-morandi-bridge-collapse-and-the-end-of-an-italian-national-myth.

201 "Fifty years ago": "Genoa's Morandi Bridge Disaster 'A Tragedy Waiting to Happen,'" France 24, August 15, 2018, https://www.france24.com/en/2018 0815-italy-genoa-morandi-bridge-disaster-structural-problems.

201 recommended new measures to maintain and reinforce the bridge: Mattioli, "What Caused the Genoa Bridge Collapse."

201 Bridge maintenance fell: Gaia Pianigiani, Elisabetta Povoledo, and Richard Pérez-Peña, "Italy Bridge Was Known to Be in Trouble Long Before Collapse," *New York Times*, August 15, 2018, https://www.nytimes.com/2018 /08/15/world/europe/italy-genoa-bridge-collapse.html.

201 "The capacity to develop": Shelley E. Taylor and Jonathon D. Brown, "Illusion and Well-Being: A Social Psychological Perspective on Mental Health," *Psychological Bulletin* 103, no. 2 (1988): 193–210, http://dx.doi.org/10 .1037/0033-2909.103.2.193.

201 Confidence associated with longevity among cancer victims: Joanne V. Wood, Shelley E. Taylor, and Rosemary R. Lichtman, "Social Comparison in Adjustment to Breast Cancer," *Journal of Personality and Social Psychology* 49, no. 5 (1985): 1169–83.

202 Taylor and Brown favor positive illusions: Shelley E. Taylor and Jonathon D. Brown, "Positive Illusions and Well-Being Revisited: Separating Fact from Fiction," *American Psychologist* 49, no. 11 (1994): 972–73.

202 believing that everybody worships: Cameron Anderson et al., "Knowing Your Place: Self-Perceptions of Status in Face-to-Face Groups," *Journal of Personality and Social Psychology* 91, no. 6 (2006): 1094–110.

203 false positives or false negatives: This formulation classifies the decision not to reinforce the bridge as your positive (optimistic) action and the decision to shore it up as your negative (pessimistic) action. Rhetorically, it works. Go with it.

205 we live in the best of all possible worlds: Gottfried W. Leibniz, *Theodicy: Essays on the Goodness of God, the Freedom of Man and the Origin of Evil*, trans. E. M. Huggard, ed. Austin Farrer (London: Routledge and Kegan Paul, 1952 [1710]).

205 The world is richer: Steven Pinker, *Enlightenment Now: The Case for Reason, Science, Humanism, and Progress* (New York: Penguin, 2018).

206 The Madoff story: Diana B. Henriques, *The Wizard of Lies: Bernie Madoff and the Death of Trust* (New York: Macmillan, 2011).

206 La Villehuchet's suicide note: Alex Berenson and Matthew Saltmarsh, "Madoff Investor's Suicide Leaves Questions," *New York Times*, January 1, 2009, https://www.nytimes.com/2009/01/02/business/02madoff.html.

208 Rates of death: Steven Pinker, *The Better Angels of Our Nature: Why Violence Has Declined* (New York: Penguin, 2012).

208 This path of self-acceptance: Tara Brach, *Radical Acceptance* (New York: Bantam, 2003).

208 "choose the mean": Plato, *Republic*, trans. George M. A. Grube and C. D. C. Reeve (Indianapolis, IN: Hackett, 1974).

209 Maimonides advised balance: Moses Maimonides, Joseph Isaac Gorfinkle, and Shmuel Ibn Tibbon, *The Eight Chapters of Maimonides on Ethics* (Sacramento Creative Media Partners, 2018).

209 Ecclesiastes 7:16–18 (Good News Translation).

209 "Every praiseworthy characteristic": Abu Amina Elias, "Moderation and Balance in Islam," *Faith in Allah* (blog), January 2, 2016, https://abuaminae lias.com/moderation-and-balance-in-islam/.

211 supported by accurate self-knowledge: Elizabeth R. Tenney, Simine Vazire, and Matthias R. Mehl, "This Examined Life: The Upside of Self-Knowledge for Interpersonal Relationships," *PLoS ONE* 8, no. 7 (2013): e69605, https://doi.org/10.1371/journal.pone.0069605.

211 "Learn about yourself": Sean Illing, "Why Do Marriages Succeed or Fail?," *Vox*, 2018, https://www.vox.com/science-and-health/2017/10/5/16379910/marriage-love-relationships-eli-finkel.

211 "Modern history has demonstrated": Yuval Noah Harari, *21 Lessons for the 21st Century* (New York: Random House, 2019).

212 Democracies have thrived: Pinker, *Enlightenment Now.*

Index

Entries in *italics* refer to figures and tables.

Abagnale, Frank, 94, 196, 197
Academy Awards, 29
Access International, 206
accidental falls, *43*
accuracy, 10, *56*, 119, 192, 201
    benefits of, 203–6
    confidence intervals and, 20, 47
    feedback and, 108–9
    flashbulb memories and, 20
    histogram and, 83–85, *84, 85*
    hypothesis testing, 47
    individual estimates and, 176–77
    optimism and, 94–95, 152
    probabilities and, 76
    relationships and, 211
    wisdom of crowds and, 175–78
advisers, 194
affirmative action, 178
affirmative answers, 45–46
Afghanistan War, 54
AIDS, 71–72, 82
AIG, 128–30

Airbus, 144
airplanes, 147, 202
    confidence vs. competence and, 94
    fear of flying and, 107–8
    first flight, 65–66
    forecasting and, 78, 87
    postmortems and, 140–41
    safety and, 99, 140, 148
air pollution, 105
Ali, Muhammad, 94
al-Qaeda, 54
alternatives
    hypothesis testing and, 51
    negotiation and, 103–4, 134
    "whiches" vs. "whethers" and, 133–36.
        See also BATNA
Amazon, 44, *47*, 56, 61, 110, 130, 194
American Idol, 117–18, 123
Anderson, Cameron, 195–96
Anderson, Tim, 80
Angelou, Maya, *19, 21,* 29
apocalypse, 42–43, 54, 57, 60, 62

Apple
    mouse and, *19*
    Newton and, 109–10, 122–23
    stock prices and, 172–73
architects, 21–22
Ariely, Dan, 23
Aristotle, 10, 208
Arizona, 156
Arkhipov, Vasily, 148–49
Armor, David, 92, 95, 152
artificial intelligence, 148
Assad, Bashar al-, 76–77
atheists, 154
athletes, 17, 93, 154, 186, 189
auction fever, 133
Augenblick, Ned, 42
auto industry, 177
averaging, 60–61, 109, 175–76
Aviation Safety Reporting System
    (ASRS), 141

backcasting, 115, 150–52
Bacon, Sir Francis, 52
bad news, 126–27, 131
Bakker, Jim, 183
Bakker, Tammy Faye, 183
balloon payments, 25–26
banks, 24, 26–27, 156, 174, 202
Bargh, John, 50–51
BASF, 67, 70
basketball, 17, 48, 146
BATNA (Best Alternative to a
    Negotiated Agreement), 103–4, 134
batting averages, 80
Bazerman, Max, 23, 89–91, 97, 99–100,
    108, 111, 171–72
behavioral economics, 173
Being Wrong (Schulz), 54–55
beliefs
    calibrating confidence in, 54
    finding false, 55
    learning other side, 57
    positive outcomes and, 34
    William James on, 33–36
Belz, Ryan, 80–82
Bennett, Sandra, 198–99
Berkeley, California, 148
Bessemer Venture Partners, 142–43
best-guess estimates, 68–69, 85

better-than-average effects, *192*
betting. *See* gambling
Bezos, Jeff, *44*, *47*, 56, 101, 130, 194
bias, 7
    collective, 24, 178–80
    debiasing strategies, 51, 169
    individual, 24
    men vs. women and, 181
    noble cause and, 183
    overconfidence and, 22–23
    overplacement and, 24
Bible, 41, 209
bidding, 162–64
Bin Laden, Osama, 54
binning, 84–85, *84*, *85*
Boeing 737 Max 8, 139–40, 143–44
Boston Big Dig project, 159
Boulder, Colorado, 78–79
bridge design and maintenance, 21, 200–203
Bridgewater Associates, *44*, *47*, 130,
    165–67, 169
Brin, Sergey, 142–43
Brion, Sebastien, 195
Brogan, Kevin, 16
Brown, Jonathon, 201–2
Buddhism, 208–9
Buffett, Warren, 147, 168–69, 174–75
building design, 22
bungee jumpers, 37
Burrows, Lara, 50
Byrne, Rhonda, 93

Cabell, James Branch, 204
calibration, 6–7, 9–10, 43, 76, 115–16,
    191–92, 194
    probabilities and, 80–87, *84–86*
    testing, 46–47
California High-Speed Rail Authority,
    158–59
Campbell, Keith, 55
Camping, Harold, 41–43, 50, 54, 57, 60
cancer, 49
    positive illusions and, 93, 157, 201
    probability of getting, 72, 98–99
"Cancer of Optimism, The" (op-ed), 157
"can-do" attitude, 145
Cannell, John Jacob, 124, 125
Carnegie Mellon University, 71, 74
Cassano, Joe, 128–29

Catholic Church, 58, 183
causes, correlations vs., 93–94, 96
caution, 122
Census Bureau, 67
Centers for Disease Control and
    Prevention, 71–72
CEOs, 91, 127–30
Challenger space shuttle, 22
Channel Tunnel, 159
Charles I, king of England, 44, 47, 52
Charles II, king of England, 52
cheating, 105
chemotherapy, 157
Chen, Mark, 50
Chen, Steve, 74–75
Chernobyl disaster, 22
Chicago Cubs, 199
children
    deciding to have, 135–36
    sexual abuse of, 183
China, 75–76, 105, 158
Christian Family Radio, 41–42, 44, 47, 50
Chugh, Dolly, 130
Church of Scotland, 52
CIA, 127
Citibank, 27
civil wars, 77–78
climate change, 73, 178
Clinton, Hillary, 156
coal miners, 99
cognitive biases, 22
coin flipping, 68, 77–78, 90, 105, 123
Cold War, 149
colleges and universities
    athletes and, 132
    choosing majors, 138
    low-income students and, 31
Colorado Springs 178–79
Columbia space shuttle, 22
comforting lies, 152–54
commitment(s)
    escalation of, 131–33
    too many, 160
competence, 2, 9, 94
con artists, 30, 94, 100, 119, 196–97, 206–7
confidence. *See also* overconfidence;
    underconfidence
    assumptions about, 13
    benefits of, 211–12

calibrating, 6–7, 9–10, 115–16, 191–92
calibrating, and probability
    distributions, 80–87, *84–86*
competence vs., 9, 94
decision making and, 2
defining, 15–39
displays of, 7–8, 10, 118–19, 195–200
entrepreneurs and, 100–103
failure and, 4, 17
false expressions of, 196–97, 199
forms of, 7–8, 191, *192* (*see* estimation;
    placement; precision)
hypothesis testing and, 45–56
middle way and, 7, 210–12
new view of, 4–5, 13
perfect, 13, 137, 208–9
performance and effort vs., 9, 37
as practice to master, 210–12
self-help books on, 4–5
self-negating, 155–56
success and, 17, 37, 93–96, 154–55,
    194–95, 201–2
survival and, 99
well-calibrated, 32–33, 137, 193, 200
wishful thinking and, 93–96
Confidence Code, The (Kay and Shipman), 29
confidence intervals, 18–22, *19*, 47–48,
    192
confirmation bias, 51–53
considering the opposite, 51, 56, 169, 172
construction projects, 83, 162–64
Cornell University, 28
corporate mergers and acquisitions,
    74–75, 128, 186
correlations, causes vs., 93–94, 96
counterterrorism, 148–50
Cowan, David, 142–43
credibility, 30
credit cards, 26
credit default swaps (CDSs), 129
Crédit Lyonnais, 206
crisis management, 147
critical reflection, 166, 206–7
critics, 62, 116, 130–31, 136. *See also*
    disagreement
Cromwell, Oliver, 44, 47, 52
crowds
    shared bias and, 178–79
    wisdom of, 175–77

Cuba
   Bay of Pigs debacle, 126
   missile crisis, 148–49
cumulative probability distribution, *85*,
   86, *86*
Cunha, Jesse, 42
curriculum committees, 185–86
Currie, Monique, 29
customer demand, 67, 69–70

Daedalus and Icarus, 208–9
Dal Bó, Ernesto, 42
Dalio, Ray, 130, 165–67, 187
day trading, 172–75
death, causes of, 43–44, *43*, *47*, *48*, *49*, 208
De Bondt, Werner, 22
deception, 105
decision making, 2, 6–7
   accuracy and, *192*
   biases and, 22
   calibrating certitude and, 10
   informed, 178–79
   positive expected value and, 122–24
   "whether" vs. "which" decisions and,
      133–36
   wisdom of crowds and, 175–79
Declaration of Independence, 29
Deepwater Horizon oil spill, 22
defensive pessimism, 146–47
delusion, 7, 9, *33*, 152–53, 211
democracy, 211–12
Des Moines, bet on living in, 168–71
devil's advocate, 58–59, *63*
diabetes, 98
dice rolling, 77, 78, 123
difficult tasks, *192*
   underplacement and, 28
disagreement, 58–61, 116, 167–70
disappointment, 153, 157
disaster preparedness, 115, 146–50
disease, 98–99
Ditto, Peter, 125–26
diversity, 59–60, 177–79
divine providence, 78
Dominican Republic, 42
Downes, Doris, 16
downside risk, 136–38
downward counterfactuals, 204
Doyen, Stéphane, 50–51

driving skill, 118–20, 191, 202
drug decriminalization, 198–99
Duckworth, Angela, 131
Duke, Annie, 78, 167
Dunn, Kathleen Colby (Koby), 117–18, 123
Dweck, Carol, 38

earnings forecasts, 153
earthquakes, 99
easy tasks, *192*
eBay, 15
Ebola virus, 98
economic growth, 156, 165, 208
Edison, Thomas, 193, 194
effort, 37, 156–57
Einstein, Albert, 157
El Capitan, 189–90, 194
elections, 156, 176
energy consumption, 150
English Civil War, 52
Enron, 129–30
Entrepreneur magazine, 100
entrepreneurs, 17, 87
   accuracy vs. persuasion and, 195
   failure rate and, 23, 101
   investors and, 93, 123
   over- vs. underconfidence, 100–103
   persistence and, 193–94
environment, 144–45, 148
epidemiology, 71
equity trading, *192*
estimation, 7–8, 191, *192*
Ethiopian Airlines flight 302 crash, 143
European Aviation Safety Agency, 140
European Union, 75–76
exams, 37, 95, 153
expectations, 50, 84–87, 115
expected return, 98
expected utility, 105
expected value, 194
   alternatives and, 135
   asking colleagues to help calculate,
      123–24
   benefits of well-calibrated, 97, 100
   betting on disagreements and, 122, 167
   calculating, 83, 90–91, 107–9, 115, 122,
      138
   coin flip and, 105
   entrepreneurs and, 101–3

Hennigan's Des Moines bet and, 171
imperfect, 108
logic of, 97
lottery and, 137
negative, 73–74, 137
small daily bets and, 106–7
specifying, and probability, 108–11
stock market and, 137, 173
tracking and scoring, 108–11, 123
utility vs., 105–8
well-intentioned failure and, 110
wishful thinking and, 91–96
experts, 76
extroversion, 45–46

Facebook, 148
"fail fast, fail often" mantra, 142
failure, 17
celebrating, 110
defensive pessimism and, 146–50
Edison and, 193, 194
Ford and, 142
learning from, 142, 166, 207
overconfident optimism and, 157
postmortems and, 139–44
premortems and, 144–46
results orientation and, 121–22, 142
rewarding, 122–23
standards and, 151
talking self into, 34–35
well-intentioned, 110, 122–23
faith, 34, 42–44, 93
Falcon 1 launch failures, 18
false claims, 118–20, 199. *See also* con artists
fear of failure, 34, 145
disaster preparedness and, 146–47
subjective probability and, 97–100
fear of flying, 107–8
Federal Aviation Administration (FAA),
141, 144
Filo, David, 91–92
financial crisis of 2008, 22, 24–27, 169
Finkel, Eli, 211
firefighters, 99
fire walk, 3–4, 9
fixed-price bidding, 163
flashbulb memories, 20
Forbes magazine, 44, 47
Ford, Henry, 142, 187

forecasting, 67–78
averaging outcomes, 109
backcasting vs., 150
geopolitical events and, 75
good judgment and, 75–78
histogram and, 83–85, *84, 85*
optimism and, 115, 153
planning fallacy and, 158–64
point prediction and, 67–68
probability distribution and, 69–70
time requirements, 83–84, 161–65
tracking and scoring, 109–10, 123–24
uncertainty and, 70–75
fossil fuels, 73, 150
Foster, Jodie, 29
Fox, Craig, 48
Francis, Pope, 59
Franken, Al, 62
Frederick, Shane, 134
Free Solo (film), 190
Freud, Sigmund, 33

Gaertig, Celia, 199
Galton, Sir Francis, 81, 175–76
gambling
daily small bets and, 106
expected values and, 171–72
negative expected-value bets, 73–74
probability and, 78–79
proposition betting, 167–71, 197–98
subjective probability weighting
function and, 73–74
structuring bets and, 197
Gates, Bill, 101
GE, 128
gender differences, 29–30, 180–82
General Motors (GM), 15, 157
genocides, *43*
geopolitical forecasting, 176
Gillibrand, Kirsten, 29
Girls, Inc., 169
Glamour magazine, 183
goals
impossible, 36, 39
realistic, 103–5
setting right, 55
"stretch," 104–5
Golden Mean, 208, 210
gold prices, 165

Gombaud, Antoine, 78
Good Judgment Project (GJP), 75–76,
    108–9
Google, *19, 21*, 49, 142–43
    Google+, 142
    Google Glass, 142
    Google Video, 142
    postmortems and, 141–42
    venture capital and, 142–43
    Yahoo! and, 92
    YouTube and, 74–75, 142
grades, *35*, 120–21
Grammy Awards, 29
grant funding committees, 179–80
Great California ShakeOut, 148
Greek myths, 208
grit, 131–32. *See also* persistence
group polarization, 178–80
Grove, Andy, 184–85
Grow Rich While You Sleep, 1
guilt, 146–47

Harari, Yuval Noah, 211
Harvard University, 33–34
heart disease, 49, 98
heaven, 154
hedge funds, 165–66, 168–69, 174, 206
Heilman, Jeff, 16
Hennessey, John, 92
Hennigan, John, 167–71
Heritage USA, 183
Highland High School, 2
high-speed rail, 158–59
hindsight bias, 109, 111
histogram distribution, 70, 83–84, *84*,
    151, *192*
histogram response scale, *69*
HIV transmission risk, 71–72
Holmes, Elizabeth, 181–83
honesty, 30–31, 184, 197–200
Honnold, Alex, 189–91, 194
housing bubble, 26, 129
Hovey, Dean, *19, 21*
Howey, Hugh, 32
hucksterism, 100
Hunsaker, David, 196
hypothesis
    focusing on single, 68
    testing, 45–56

Ibn Manzūr, 209
ibuprofen sales, 67–70, 78
ideological certainty, *192*, 211
illusion of knowing, 20
imposter syndrome, 28–30, 186, 192, *192*
independent thinkers, 166–67
index funds, 175
individual differences, 180–82
Indonesia, 42
inflation, 156
information gathering, 56–57
initial public stock offerings, 186
injuries, *43*, 49
innovation, 109–10, 157
insurance, 73–74
Intel, 184–85
intelligence, false claims of superior, 119–20
Intelligence Advanced Research Projects
    Activity (IARPA), 75–76
interest rates, 25–26, 156
International Monetary Fund, 29
intertemporal inconsistency, 157
introversion, 45–46
intuition, 23
investing, 107, 191, 194. *See also* venture
    capital
    considering the opposite and, 147
    day trading and, 171–75
    mortgage-backed securities and, 24
    passive vs. active, 168–70, 175
    pessimism and, 136–37
    selling decisions and, 132, 134
iPhone, 110
Iraq War, 54, 98
ISIS, 97–98

James, LeBron, 17, *19, 21*
James, William, *19, 21*, 33–36, 38–39
Jefferson, Thomas, 28–29
Jerusalem, fall of, *53*
job
    chances of getting, 89–91, 97, 99–100,
        108, 111, 171–72
    expected values and, 138
job applicants, 17, 79, 179
job interviews, 79–80, 119
job performance, 120–21, 123
Jobs, Steve, *19, 21*, 182
John Paul II, *44, 47*, 56, 58–59

Jordan, 42
judgment, 22–23
Judgment Day, 41–42
Judgment in Managerial Decision Making (Bazerman), 23
juggling, 28
Jung, Carl, 33

Kahneman, Daniel, *19*, *21*, 22–23, 73, 105–6, 145–47, 159, 185–86, 198
Katahdin, Mount, 132, 134
Kay, Katty, 29–30
Keillor, Garrison, 124
Keller, Helen, 155
Kennedy, Jessica, 195
Kennedy, John F., 126, 149
Kidder Peabody, 128
Kissinger, Henry, 182
kitchen remodeling, 163–64
Klein, Gary, 144, 147
Koby (Kathleen Colby Dunn), 117–18, 123
Kodak, 157
Komisar, Randy, 181
Kruger, Justin, 28
Ku, Gillian, 133

Lagarde, Christine, 29
Lake Wobegon effect, 124–25
Laplace, Pierre-Simon de, 77–78
La Villehuchet, Thierry Magon de, 206–7
leadership, 195–200
Lego-building exercise, 159–61
Leibniz, Gottfried, 205
Lepper, Mark R., 51–52
liar loans, 25–27
Lickle, Brett, 99
Lieberfeld, Daniel, 132
lightbulb, 193
Lincoln, Abraham, 178
LinkedIn, 143
Lion Air flight 610 crash, 139–40, 143
Logg, Jennifer, *95*, *96*
Lord, Charles G., 51–51
Los Angeles Fire Department, 3
losses, 106–7, 153
lotteries, 74, 78, 102, 108, 137
luck, 122
Lyons, Rich, 62

MacCoun, Rob, 198
Madoff, Bernard, 206
Maimonides, 209
Major League Baseball, 80
Malhotra, Deepak, 133
malnutrition, 49
managers. *See also* CEOs; leadership
    criticism and, 62
    passive vs. active, 168–69
    philosophy and, 56
Maneuvering Characteristics Augmentation System (MCAS), 143–44
Mariana Trench, *19*, *21*
marijuana decriminalization, 198–99
marriage, 211
Mars, 15
Masada, *44*, *47*, 53
Massey, Cade, 92, 152
Mastermind, 37
Mattis, James, 182
McLean, Bethany, 129
meetings, 179–80
Mellers, Barbara, 75, 76
Michigan, 156
Microsoft, 92
middle way, 13, 189–92, 200–12
Miekle, Nate, 196
Mill, John Stuart, 171
Minson, Julia, 85
Mitroff, Ian, 147, 148
mobs, 177–78
Monday-morning quarterback, 109
Moore, Gordon, 185
Moore, Sarah, 82–83, 135
moral superiority, 182–84, *192*
Morandi, Riccardo, 200–201
Morandi Bridge collapse, 200–201
mortgage-backed securities, 22, 24–27, 129
Mosteller, Frederick, 138
motor vehicle accidents, *43* 44, *47*, 49
Motorola, 157
mountain climbers, 34, 36–37
    rock climbing, 99, 189–91, 202
    summit fever and, 131–32
Muilenburg, Dennis, 143–44
Munger, Charlie, 147
murders, *43*
Murnighan, Keith, 133

Musk, Elon, 15–18, 38–39, 105, 127–28
Musk, Kimbal, 15–16

naive realism, 171
naked body, 30–31
Narcissism Epidemic, the (Twenge and
    Campbell), 55
National Medal of Arts, 29
National Science Foundation (NSF),
    179–80
National Transportation and Safety
    Board, 140
NBA, 17, *19*, 21
NCAA quarterfinals, 48
negotiation, 103–4, 134–35
Newsom, Gavin, 158
news vendors, 70
New York Times, 157
NFL, 186
NINA (no income, no asset) loans, 25–26
NINJA (no income, no job, no assets)
    loans, 25–26
Nobel Prize, 29
noble cause, 182–84
No Child Left Behind (NCLB), 124–25
noise, 175–76
Norem, Julie, 146
North Carolina, 156
Northern California, 99
nuclear-armed submarines, 148–49
nuclear power plants, 147
Nutt, Paul, 133–34

Odysseus, 209
Oettingen, Gabriele, 37
O'Neil, Shaquille, 10
opportunity costs, 134
optimism, 10
    accuracy vs., 152
    calibrating, 131
    disappointment and, 153
    downers about, 204–5
    entrepreneurship and, 101–3
    forecasting and, 115
    influence of, on outcomes, 95–96, 152,
        154–56
    overconfidence and, 155
    persistence and, 96
    premortems and, 145
    short- vs. long-term and, 152–57

underconfidence and, 155
    well-calculated confidence vs., 193
    wishful thinking and, 92–93, 95
organizational culture
    premortems and, 145
    transparency, 166
    wisdom of crowds and, 176
outside view, 116, 184–87, 194
overcommitment, 160–64
overconfidence, 55
    biases and errors and, 22–27
    cheating and, 105
    collective, 24–25
    common, 191
    confidence vs., 10
    drivers of, 118–21
    men vs. women and, 180–82
    middle way and, 201–3
    optimism and, 155
    pitfalls of, 4–6, 21–22, 202
    premortems and, 145–46
    risks of, 36–39, 101, 202
    self-delusion and, 9
    stock market and, 173
    underconfidence vs., 191–92, *192*
overconfident optimism, 155–60. *See also*
    optimism
overestimation, 8, 74, 92, 190–91
overplacement, 8, 24, 27, 30–31, 118–21, 181
overprecision, 8, 20, 25, 26–27, 56, 68,
    173, 180–82

Page, Larry, 142–43
Pascal, Blaise, 78
Patton, George, 145
PayPal, 15, 18
Pennsylvania, 156
percentile scale, 23
performance
    defining, 115, 121–24
    overconfident optimism vs., 155–57
    quantifying, 6–7
Perrow, Charles, 147
Perry, Katy, 117–18
Perry, William, 182
persistence, 38, 55, 96, 193–95
    escalation of commitment and, 131–33
Person You Mean to Be, The (Chugh), 130
pessimism, 10, 95, 204
    confidence and, 155

downside risk of, 136–38
exaggerated, 97–100
reasons for cultivating, 99–100
Philadelphia 76ers, 146
Philippines, 75–76
physical therapy, 93
Piccinino, Ersilia, 200
Pinterest, 143
placement, 7–8, 191, *192*
planning fallacy, 158–64, *192*
taking outside view and, 185–86
Plinko, 80–82, *81*, 87
Plous, Scott, 22
point prediction, 67–68
histogram distribution vs., 84, 85–86,
85, 86
single best-guess, 68
poker players, 79, 167–68, 171, 174
polarization, 23, 178–79
police officers, 99
political polls, 91, 176, 178
political uprisings, 76
politicians, 17, 154, 156, 208
Popper, Karl, 51, *53*
population, *19, 21*
posers, 30
positive illusions theory, 201–3
positive thinking, 1
positive visualization, 34–38
postmortems, 115, 140–44, 207
poverty, 208
Powerball, 108
power posing, 5
praise, 130–31
prayer, 52
precision, 7–8, 191, *192*
Predictably Irrational (Ariely), 23
premortems, 115, 144–47
backcasting and, 151
defensive pessimism as, 147
"Prescribed Optimism" (Armor, Massey,
and Sackett), 92–93
present value, 90
Presidential Medal of Freedom, 29
President's Daily Brief (PBD),
126–27
Preston, Elizabeth, 51–52
Price is Right, The (TV show), 81
Prince, Chuck, 27
Principles of Psychology, The (James), 33

probability distributions, 67–87, *69, 81,
85,* 123, 151, 163
probability estimates, 48–49, 56, 101
averaging, 60
backcasting and premortems and, 151
continuous, 109
data and, 137–38
displays of confidence and, 199–200
potential disasters and, 99
utility and, 107–8
for various outcomes, 123
tracking, 109
probability scale, 70–72
probability theory, 70–72, 78–87
probability weighting function, 72–73, *72*
product launches, 67, 69–70, 151
Project Storm, 148
promotions, 83, 120–21
proposition betting, 167–71, 197–98
prospect theory, 105–6
Protégé Partners, 168–69
public opinion polls, 207–8

Quincunx, 81–82, *81*

railroad construction, 162
Rakoff, David, 32
Rao, Justin, 42
rare behaviors and events, 28, *192*
Raynor, Michael, 38
recessions, 156
regrets, 206–7
Relations Between Physiology and
Psychology (James), 34
relationships, 191, 202–3, 211
religious leaders, 41–43, 183
renewable energy, 150
results orientation, 121–22
risk-aversion, 73
risks and risk-taking
of being wrong, 53–55
daily bets and, 106–7
gambling and, 73
intuition and, 23
subprime mortgage crisis and, 25–27
taking right, 105–8
underconfidence and, 27–30
when to take seriously, 99
well-intentioned failure and, 110, 122
Robbins, Tony, 2–4, 103

Robinson, John, 150
rock climbing, 99, 189–91, 202
romantic relationships, 37, 132, 138
Roosevelt, Franklin, 98
Roosevelt, Theodore, 10
roulette, 68
Rubin, Jeffrey, 131–32, 134
rumination and worry, 8, 99, 136, *192*
Russell, Bertrand, 54

Sackett, Aaron, 92, 152
safety procedures, 99, 132
saints, canonization of, 44, 47, 56, 58–59
same-sex marriage, 178
Samuelson, Paul, 105–7
Savage, Tom, 129
Savitsky, Ken, 28
Schlesinger, Arthur, Jr., 149
school achievement tests, 124–25
Schulz, Kathryn, 54–55
scientific research, 50, 73
Sears, 157
Secret, The (Byrne), 93, 152
Securities and Exchange Commission, 128
Seides, Ted, 168
self-acceptance, 208
self-affirmations, 5, 36
self-aggrandizement, 118
self-assessment, 55, 131
self-criticism, 118
self-delusion, 9, 100–102, 119, 154, 157, 201–2
self-diversity, 177
self-doubts, 27, 29, 30, 34, 184
self-efficacy, 37
self-esteem, 38, 55
Self-Esteem Trap, The (Young-Eisendrath), 38
self-reliance, 55
self-selection, 100
self-serving bias, 24, 28
September 11, 2001 attacks, 20, *44, 47*, 54, 97–98, 149
shelf life, 70
Shipman, Claire, 29–30
shoehorn, 28
Shultz, George, 182
Siddhartha Gautama, 209
Silicon Valley, 142, 182
Silver, Nate, 156
Simmons, Joe, 199
single point prediction, 68

Sixtus V, Pope, 58
Sloan, Alfred P., 177–78
Smartest Guys in the Room, The (McLean), 129–30
Snyder, Mark, 45
social benefits, 211–12
social norms, 210
social priming, 50–51
Socrates, 208
software, 83
soldiers, 99
"Song of Myself" (Whitman), 177
South China Sea, 75
sovereign wealth funds, 24
Soviet Union, 148–49
SpaceX, 15–16, 18, 39, 151
sports, 17, 91, 109, 199
Standard & Poor's 500, 168–69
standards
    clarification of, 119–20
    positive vs. negative results and, 125–26
    probabilities and, 151
Stanford University, 91, 92, 181
statistics, lying with, 138
status quo, 61–63
Steinbeck, John, 29
stereotypes, 50
stock market, 23, 107, 165, 172–75, 181, 187
strategy, 17, 145
Strategy Paradox, The (Raynor or Baynor), 38
stress interview, 79
subjective assessment, 115
subjective probability weighting function, 72–74, *72*, 76, 108
subjective utilities, 124
suicide, *43*, 53, 204, 206
summit fever, 131–33
surfing, 99
Surowiecki, James, 100, 178
Svenson, Ola, 118–19, 120
Swann, William B., Jr., 45
Sydney Opera House, 159
Syria, 76–77, 123

TAA saliva reaction test, 125–26
Tanzania, 42
Taylor, Shelly, 201–2
Tenney, Elizabeth, 95–96, 196, 211
tenure decisions, 58
terrorism, 73, 97–98, 149–50

Tesla, 15, 18, *19*, *21*, 39, 127–28
Tetlock, Phil, 75, 76
Thaler, Richard, 22
Theranos, 181–83
Thessalonians, 41
Thinking, Fast and Slow (Kahneman), 23
3M, 110
time commitment, 83–84, 161–65
Titanic (ship), 22
tobacco companies, 73
Tony Awards, 29
tortoise and the hare, 156–57
transparency, 166
trivia tests, 95–96
Trump, Donald, 127, 156
truth, 18–19, 192, 203–6, 210
unpleasant, 152
Tufts University, 131
Tversky, Amos, 48, 73, 105–6, 159
Twenge, Jean, 55

UC Berkely, 58, 61, 62, 100
uncertainty
    calibrating, 76
    certainty vs., 199
    forecasting and, 70–75
    improving hitting percentage, 80
    knowledge vs., 77
    middle range of, 74
    probability distributions and, 48,
        68–70, 82–86
underconfidence, 6, 9, 27–33
    avoiding, 207–8
    common, 191
    optimism and, 155
    outside view and, 186
    overconfidence vs., 99–100, *192*
underestimation, 8, 161–64, 190–91
underplacement, 8, 28, 30, 192
underprecision, 191–92
University of Toronto, 150
"Unleash the Power Within" (Robbins), 2–3
unrealistic expectations, 55
US Congress, 198–99
US Constitution, 29
US government bonds, 26
US government contractors, 16
US intelligence, 75, 126–27
US Senate, 62
utility, 105–8

value, 108–11, 122–23. *See also* expected
    value
Vancouver, Jeffrey, 36–37, 156
Vazire, Simine, 211
venture capitalists, 123, 142, 194
Verizon, Yahoo! bought by, 92
virtue, belief in our own, 183–84
Voltaire, 199

waffle irons, 28
war, *23*, *43*
wedding invitations, 82–83
weight guessing, 68–69, *69*, 175–76
weight loss, 37
Welch, Jack, 128
West of England Fat Stock and Poultry
    Exhibition, 175
"whether" decisions, 133–34
"which" decisions, 134–36
Whitman, Walt, 176–77
Winfrey, Oprah, 3, 4
Wisconsin, 156
wisdom, 13, 208–9
    of crowds, 175–78
    to see truth, 22
wishful thinking, 8, 13, 91–97, 104, 147,
    150, 152, *192*
Wix, 143
World health Organization, 49
Wright brothers, *19*, *21*, 65, 67,
    186–87
wrong
    asking why you might be, 177, 192
    being less, 56–59
    considering ways you might
        be, 13
    estimating probability of being, 56
    realizing you've been, 55

Yahoo!, 91–92
Yang, Jerry, 91–92
Yelp, 143
Yosemite National Park, 189–90
Young-Eisendrath, Polly, 38
YouTube, *19*, *21*, 127
    Google purchase of, 74–75, 142

Zealots, 44, *47*, 53–54, *192*
Zip2, 16, 17
Zoppi, Diego, 201

About the Author

———

Don A. Moore, PhD, is a professor of management of organizations at the University of California–Berkeley's Haas School of Business. He is the coauthor of *Judgment in Managerial Decision Making*, one of the bestselling textbooks in the field, and has penned columns for sources such as the *New Yorker*, the *Wall Street Journal*, *BusinessWeek*, *Fortune*, *USA Today*, *San Francisco Chronicle*, and *Harvard Business Review*. His work has been covered in the the *New York Times*, *Money*, the *Economist*, the *Financial Times*, *Forbes*, the *Washington Post*, the *Christian Science Monitor*; on PBS's *Nightly Business Report*, CNN, NPR, KCBS; as well as at Freakonomics.com and numerous other media outlets and websites. He is only occasionally overconfident.